Teaching College in an Age of Accountability

Related Titles

Successful College Teaching: Problem Solving Strategies of Distinguished Professors
Sharon A. Baiocco and Jamie N. DeWaters
ISBN: 0-205-26654-1

Faculty Work and Public Trust: Restoring the Value of Teaching and Public Service in American Academic Life
James S. Fairweather
ISBN: 0-205-17948-7

Emblems of Quality in Higher Education: Developing and Sustaining High-Quality Programs
Jennifer Grant Haworth and Clifton F. Conrad
ISBN: 0-205-19546-6

Writing for Professional Publication: Keys to Academic and Business Success
Kenneth T. Henson
ISBN: 0-205-28313-6

Learner-Centered Assessment on College Campuses: Shifting the Focus from Teaching to Learning
Mary E. Huba and Jann E. Freed
ISBN: 0-205-28738-7

Revitalizing General Education in a Time of Scarcity: A Navigational Chart for Administrators and Faculty
Sandra L. Kanter, Zelda F. Gamson, and Howard B. London
ISBN: 0-205-26257-0

The Adjunct Professor's Guide to Success: Surviving and Thriving in the College Classroom
Richard E. Lyons, Marcella L. Kysilka, and George E. Pawlas
ISBN: 0-205-28774-3

An Introduction to Interactive Multimedia
Stephen J. Misovich, Jerome Katrichis, David Demers, and William B. Sanders
ISBN: 0-205-34373-2

Teaching Tips for College and University Instructors: A Practical Guide
David Royse
ISBN: 0-205-29839-7

Creating Learning-Centered Courses for the World Wide Web
William B. Sanders
ISBN: 0-205-31513-5

Designing and Teaching an On-Line Course: Spinning Your Web Classroom
Heidi Schweizer
ISBN: 0-205-30321-8

Leadership in Continuing and Distance Education in Higher Education
Cynthia C. Jones Shoemaker
ISBN: 0-205-26823-4

Shaping the College Curriculum: Academic Plans in Action
Joan S. Stark and Lisa R. Lattuca
ISBN: 0-205-16706-3

The Effective, Efficient Professor: Teaching, Scholarship and Service
Phillip C. Wankat
ISBN: 0-205-33711-2

For further information on these and other related titles, contact:

College Division
ALLYN AND BACON
75 Arlington Street, Suite 300
Boston, MA 02116
www.ablongman.com

Teaching College in an Age of Accountability

Richard E. Lyons
Indian River Community College

Meggin McIntosh
University of Nevada, Reno

Marcella L. Kysilka
University of Central Florida

Boston   New York   San Francisco

Mexico City   Montreal   Toronto   London   Madrid   Munich   Paris

Hong Kong   Singapore   Tokyo   Cape Town   Sydney

*To Marcy Kysilka, my adviser, mentor, and friend, who helped me
discover my voice and challenged me to share it with others—REL*

*To Bill Cathey, a mentor, a confidant, and a "boss"
who will never be surpassed—MM*

*To my students for helping me to continue the quest for excellence in teaching
and learning, for which I will always be eternally grateful—MLK*

Executive editor and publisher: *Stephen D. Dragin*
Series editorial assistant: *Barbara Strickland*
Manufacturing buyer: *Andrew Turso*
Marketing manager: *Tara Whorf*
Cover designer: *Suzanne Harbison*
Production coordinator: *Pat Torelli Publishing Services*
Editorial-production service: *Argosy*
Electronic composition: *Argosy*

For related titles and support materials, visit our online catalog at www.ablongman.com.

Between the time Website information is gathered and then published, it is not unusual for
some sites to have closed. Also, the transcription of URLs can result in unintended typographical
errors. The publisher would appreciate notification where these errors occur so that they may
be corrected in subsequent editions.

Library of Congress Cataloging-in-Publication Data

Lyons, Richard E.
    Teaching college in an age of accountability / Richard E. Lyons, Meggin McIntosh,
Marcella L. Kysilka.
        p. cm.
    Includes bibliographical references and index.
    ISBN 0-205-35315-0
    1. College teaching—Handbooks, manuals, etc. 2. Educational
accountability—Handbooks, manuals, etc. I. McIntosh, Meggin II. Kysilka,
Marcella L. III. Title.

LB2331 .L96 2003
378.1'3--dc21

                                                                    2002074385

Printed in Canada

1 2 3 DPC 11 10 09

CONTENTS

7 **Instructor-Directed Learning Methods   121**

8 **Student-Driven Learning Methods   141**

12 Bringing Your Course to an Effective Conclusion 226

13 Evaluating the Effectiveness of Your Teaching 238

PREFACE

In recent years, many colleges and universities have experienced unprecedented intrusion into their domain by a variety of external stakeholders. Increasingly consumer-minded parents and students are demanding more accountability for rising tuition and related costs. Taxpayers—perhaps especially those not invested in the success of higher education—pressure their legislators to limit what they perceive to be its skyrocketing costs. Business leaders call for, and expect, graduates who are better prepared to staff positions that have become more exacting. Regional and programmatic accrediting associations impose more stringent academic standards. Trustees of private and public institutions alike mandate quality enhancements to ensure that the effectiveness and prestige of their institutions satisfy applicants, parents, and alumni—who each have escalating expectations. In short, a tidal wave of accountability demands is engulfing the academy, and many feel powerless to stem its impact.

Until now, institutional administrators have borne the brunt of these mandates that included an increasing array of performance-based budgeting and institutional effectiveness initiatives. Since the terrorist attacks on the United States, these initiatives have more urgency in the allocation of scarce public and private resources. Many in higher education have concluded that instructional practices must adapt in order to make their institutions appropriately accountable to bona fide stakeholders. With its traditions of academic freedom and faculty collegiality, the academy has been slow to address an issue that on the surface seems to threaten its culture and future.

Seeking to provide a balanced, comprehensive view, *Teaching College in an Age of Accountability* has been developed by three professors from diverse institutional backgrounds who have held varied administrative positions. The book has been developed to provide faculty members—new and veteran, full-time and part-time—with the insights and skills required to implement sound accountability principles into their teaching practices.

Organization

Chapter 1 provides an analysis of the various dimensions of the accountability movement—the political, marketing, and financial pressures increasingly active in today's higher education environment.

Chapter 2 examines strategies for integrating accountability practices into teaching. It introduces proven techniques for improving student recruitment, retention, graduation, and placement, and examines the thorny issue of treating students as customers.

Chapter 3 provides a thorough look at why today's students are different from those in the past. It examines the societal factors that have fostered the changes. It also highlights the personal rewards that can accrue to professors who adapt to those changes.

Chapter 4 focuses on adapting strategic practices for addressing accountability issues into course planning. It helps the professor to develop learning strategies that emphasize evaluation throughout and to design an effective course syllabus—a document viewed by many today as a contract between the student and professor.

Chapter 5 focuses on the first retention milepost within the course—the initial class meeting and its follow-up. It details proven strategies for ensuring that professors and students can begin the course on the same page.

Chapter 6 outlines strategies for organizing your materials and yourself to achieve the objectives of your course plan. It includes proven techniques for managing large classes and discusses the term's second retention milepost—the first exam or submission of the first major assignment—as well as other critical but often overlooked issues.

Chapters 7 and 8 focus on the array of teaching and learning methods available to today's professor, with the former focusing on instructor-directed strategies and the latter on student-driven methods. Tips for achieving more accountable results are provided for each method.

Chapter 9 highlights a variety of ways to integrate the use of technology into teaching and course management, in order to achieve more accountable student outcomes.

Chapters 10 and 11 focus on the nuts and bolts of evaluating student learning, with the former focusing on examinations and the latter on alternative forms of assessment. These two chapters provide especially useful exercises in their appendixes for ensuring mastery of the overall evaluation process.

Chapter 12 is designed to help you master strategies that enable the successful completion of each course by the overwhelming majority of students enrolled. It highlights strategies for energizing the classroom and helping students more effectively manage their time and project completion.

Chapter 13 provides strategies for more effectively managing the evaluation of your teaching. It emphasizes informal methods of evaluation prior to the administration of formal course evaluations and observations by instructional administrators.

Chapter 14 provides suggestions for helping you maintain your edge in the increasingly accountability-minded environment of the future. Among its highlights are strategies for building strong mentoring relationships—both as a protégé and mentor.

At the close of each chapter are four recurring components designed to help ground the reader's understanding of the chapter content. Following the most basic, a Summary of Key Points, appears perhaps the richest, Through the Professors' Eyes. The latter provides insight into the material from the perspectives of three professors: a veteran nearing retirement, a midcareer professor seeking to enhance his promotion potential, and a new professor just launching her career. Each of these characters are composites of different professors the writers have known over their careers. The next section is Tips for Thriving, geared to help the reader achieve maximum success with the accountability dimensions of the material in the chapter. The fourth recurring element is a list of Suggested Readings, most of relatively short length, useful for exploring further the issues raised within the chapter. A majority of the chapters also include an appendix—a teaching-style self-assessment exercise, a student profile form, an exam construction exercise, and so on—for implementing the strategies included therein.

Teaching College in an Age of Accountability is designed to be the kind of book you will carry in your briefcase and refer to often, as well as one in which you will highlight content that is critical to your needs. To ensure that it maintains its currency for your situation, we are providing an array of resources—teaching tips posted weekly, additional forms and other tools, and links to online resources—at www.developfaculty.com. Please let us know through that site how we might further support your success.

Acknowledgments

Besides the resources listed throughout, this book would not have been possible without the input of a number of special people. We want to thank Violeta Mutafova-Yamboli of the University of Nevada, Reno; Rui Wang of Indian River Community College; Eileen Atkisson of the University of Central Florida; and Tara Gray of New Mexico State University for their review of key sections of the manuscript. We also want to thank Pat Profeta of Indian River Community College and Syna Erb of the University of Nevada, Reno, for their research assistance and Mary Huba of Iowa State University for her helpful comments on the manuscript. Lastly, we want to thank the subscribers to the Professional and Organization Development Network in Higher Education (POD) listserv (http://listserv.nd.edu/archives/pod.html), whose thought-provoking postings have provided rich insights and perspective critical to the mission of this book.

Teaching College in an Age of Accountability

1 The Rise of Accountability in Higher Education

FOCUS QUESTIONS

- What factors have contributed to the increased call for accountability?
- How have stakeholders' perceptions and needs impacted the movement?
- Where is the accountability movement headed?
- How should those in academe respond?

"Take a look at the student on your left. Now look at the person on your right. One of you probably won't be here next term."

Many of us were introduced to our first college classes with some robustly spoken rendition of this challenge. While professors no doubt intended their words to communicate their high academic standards, the primary feelings such pronouncements triggered among their students—many of whom were the first from their families to attend college—were often intimidation and self-doubt. For a minority of the students, the challenge helped them focus their energies away from around-the-clock partying and other distractions, and toward studying. For many others, especially those ill equipped for the rigors of higher education, the threatening words were unfortunately prophetic.

All of us have had bright friends with tremendous potential who did not survive their initial exposure to the academic environment. Although they returned home to disappointed family members, some blossomed a little later and eventually completed their degrees at another, albeit less prestigious institution. Others, however, never got past their initial failure; they saw their careers and personal lives stagnate, and their goals, ambitions, and dreams go unfulfilled for a lifetime. At a time when our society needs fully developed minds and strength of character to solve the array of challenges facing us, we have paid dearly for these students' failures to succeed. Parents, employers, and other concerned citizens who finance what they perceive to be an ineffective higher education system have paid a price as well. Many have now become frustrated, even angry, with a system that permits this waste of human potential to occur, and they are demanding change.

Rising Expectations of Stakeholders in Higher Education

Not so long ago, institutions of higher education were perceived from both inside and outside as isolated from the rest of society. Influenced first by the British and then the German models, colleges and universities embraced the traditions of "academic freedom," which empowered professors to pursue their research interests freely, and the tenure system, which protected professors' ability to work long term in what many regarded as an ivory tower—immune from external checks and balances. Decision making (or "governance," as it is called in academe) was driven by collegiality and was achieved slowly through extensive deliberation among faculty committees and administrators. Institutions established high standards for admission that focused on standardized test scores, high school class rankings, and other "objective" predictors of success.

Regular internal reviews and assessments by regional accrediting bodies affirmed the integrity of traditional institutions of higher education and their faculties. But many outside academe misunderstood or did not fully appreciate its value to society. Beginning nearly a century ago with John Dewey (1916), a small but slowly growing number of stakeholders, both internal and external, claimed that we should do better for a larger number within our society. They lobbied methodically to change the goal of admissions "gatekeeping" from exclusion to inclusion, arguing that colleges should employ a wider range of admissions criteria that did not penalize late bloomers or those from working-class families. World War II veterans used the GI Bill to kick open the college and university doors, which were then left ajar while the civil rights movement pushed in many others who had been blocked, de facto or de jure, from passing through the esteemed gateway to increased life opportunities.

In the past few decades, the perceived divide between academe and the rest of society has eroded markedly. Esteemed professors appear on television news and talk shows to discuss matters of concern to an increasingly informed populace—and, in the process, to promote their latest books, private consulting practices, or research projects in need of public support. Not only do colleges and universities market their sports teams to the masses, but they also try to attract niche groups to such specialized resources as theaters, accompanied tours of foreign countries, and Elderhostel programs, in hopes of increasing their enrollments, prestige, and financial support. Interviewing committees evaluate potential college presidents for their fund-raising and crisis management experience, as much as for their academic leadership skills (Bowen, 2001).

Since a college degree has become universally accepted as a ticket to upward mobility, enrollments have increased significantly, and much of the mystique of the ivory tower has evaporated. To meet the demand for courses by those in the workplace, for example, institutions expanded their course schedules into evenings, and then weekends, and the number of part-time students grew to match that of full-time students. Unlike a relatively short time ago, most citizens can now proudly boast of at least one bright relative who has gone to college. Graduates and other former students shared their experiences—both positive and negative—through the family and neighborhood grapevines.

Very much to the chagrin of many traditionalists, but not without significant reasons, the public has widely imposed a paradigm of higher-education-as-business-enterprise on academe. Although there will always remain significant differences between higher education and business enterprises (Birnbaum, 2000), this perception has been reinforced by several factors, such as colleges' increased use of adjunct faculty and distance education, and more widespread discussion of higher education budgeting issues. The establishment of the business paradigm has invited the ubiquitous consumer mind-set into higher education and fostered dissatisfaction among an ever-widening circle of stakeholders. The process provided support to the grassroots call for increased accountability from all who work in higher education.

Market Pressures

Along with the rise in the consumer mind-set, students, parents, and employers began to demand increased value from their investments in education. Nearly all institutions installed student ratings of faculty and courses. While once reserved for instructional decision makers, the findings of student ratings have been ever more widely disseminated—most recently online to increasingly technology-savvy student-consumers. *U.S. News and World Report* annually publishes a highly popular special edition that ranks institutions on such critical student satisfaction factors as percentages of classes with fewer than 20 students and freshmen retention rates. Although publications like the Peterson's college guides have long existed, they along with a number of online ratings services are now providing rankings based on a widening array of factors (Carlson, 2001).

Many highly rated institutions, and their faculty members, initially resisted consumer-driven incursions into their cultures but have now come to embrace such evaluations for their own benefit. One need not look far to see *U.S. News* and other ratings featured in institutions' print and online marketing efforts, with the marketing objective of differentiating their "product" from that of others in the increasingly competitive higher education marketplace. Some of the leading institutions recruit the "best" students as aggressively as the best athletes, in hopes of also making themselves more attractive to second-echelon students, and to potential donors interested in winning more than football bowl games or NCAA Final Four basketball tournament appearances.

Over the past few years, for-profit institutions, most notably the rapidly expanding University of Phoenix, have begun to have a dramatic impact on the delivery of higher education. Employing a "skimming" strategy, they typically target the most lucrative market segment—the increasing numbers of bright working professionals who are older than the traditional student and who are willing to juggle an array of responsibilities as they pursue degrees in highly popular disciplines such as business, technology, and health care. Regionally accredited "for-profits" have developed "campuses" in urban and suburban office parks and typically offer classes in an accelerated format that students interested in rapid achievement perceive as more convenient and manageable. Their classes are typically highly standardized—in contrast to those at traditional institutions that emphasize academic freedom—with few gaps or overlaps in content from one course in each curriculum to the next.

The courses at the for-profits are usually facilitated by adjunct professors employed full-time in their areas of specialization—which most of their students see as a benefit. The for-profits typically invest heavily in the training and development of their part-time instructors, minimizing many of the problems encountered by traditional institutions that view the employment of part-time faculty as a cost-saving but necessary evil. Students at for-profits typically expect their courses to mirror the fields in which they work or aspire to work more closely than courses at traditional institutions do. The success of the highly competitive for-profits—especially measured by student enrollment in the most popular degree programs—has been nothing short of phenomenal (Borrego, 2001).

In need of employees with cutting-edge skills, team-oriented attitudes, and a vision of the future (Senge, 1990), and less than satisfied with the return of the millions of dollars they have invested in higher education, over two thousand businesses have established their own "corporate universities." Such initiatives represent a very significant, long-term commitment for the corporations and their hundreds of thousands of employees. In their efforts, administrators of corporate universities have become increasingly mindful of the array of benefits—including portability and integrity of coursework—from accreditation of their educational programs. Many have aligned themselves with established colleges or universities or have sought accreditation in their own right. While the full impact of corporate universities on traditional institutions has yet to be played out, their active presence in the culture of higher education is certain to affect accountability standards (Meister, 2001).

Forward-looking traditional institutions have responded to the increasingly competitive threat from the for-profits and corporate universities by targeting a similarly upscale, fully employed, older market, while maintaining a portion of the traditional academic culture. Because such programming has proved highly popular and financially rewarding, institutions have redirected resources toward its expansion, while also closely assessing degree programs whose productivity is problematic in comparison. Not surprisingly, friction has developed between departments that generate significant income and those that do not.

As other products and services in the economy have become available 24/7/365, demand for quality college instruction that can be delivered to time- and place-bound students has also increased. Many institutions—led by the for-profits—have responded with a variety of distance education initiatives. In some cases, they have formed creative consortia to reduce costs and enhance their marketing clout through offering "branded products." While early distance-learning efforts were of relatively poor quality, and thus easy targets for criticism by educational traditionalists, such programs have greatly improved in the past few years. The highly competitive, financially rewarding instructional software industry has invested large sums in research and development and is now providing interactive products that are far more student friendly than courses delivered in many regular classrooms, especially those presented in lecture halls seating hundreds of disengaged students.

Along the way, both business leaders, who were grounded in the principles of total quality management and mindful of the importance of a well-educated workforce and parents, who were suffering from "sticker shock," began to assert that they had a stake in the colleges and universities they supported through taxes, tuition payments, and gifts. Armed with data on such wasteful practices as high dropout rates in expensive programs (Lovitts and Nelson, 2000) and excessive credit hours accumulated by students, these powerful stakeholder groups began calling on their state legislators and institutional boards of trustees to justify tuition increases and to provide more effectively taught classes, more student-friendly practices and processes, more efficient articulation between institutions, and more comprehensive support services. Mindful of the growing number of term-limit initiatives, governors, legislators, and other elected officials have responded to these demands more immediately than predecessors ever did (Ewell and Jones, 1994).

External Political Pressures

The legislatures of California, Texas, Florida, and Pennsylvania—all highly populated states with growing college-age populations and a strong constituency favoring tax containment—as well as those of over thirty other states have implemented significant accountability measures into their public higher education systems (Schmidt, 2002). More recently the federal government has criticized higher education for failing to retain and graduate students in a timely fashion and is considering interceding where it has historically remained distanced (Burd, 2002). While varied in their approaches, these measures tend to focus on the following objectives:

1. Making higher education more accessible for all citizens who can benefit from it, as a strategy for expanding the tax base and reducing the costs of other social services (Waller et al., 2000).
2. Increasing productivity by limiting credit hours within degree programs, limiting students' accumulation of excessive credits through more effective student advising and "seamless" articulation between institutions, and improving student retention, graduation, and placement rates (Selingo, 2001).
3. Integrating higher education funding and review processes with state economic development objectives, especially workforce development (Schmidt, 2001).
4. Deregulating public higher education by strengthening consumer information about institutional performance (Wellman, 2001).

State legislatures typically promote the achievement of these goals by implementing "performance-based budgeting" measures that are not unlike zero-based budgeting, continuous quality improvement, and related initiatives that have been used in the private and public sectors over the past several decades (Ruppert, 1995). While typically having a small initial impact on institutional budgets, performance-based budgeting has riveted the attention of faculty and administration alike (Burke, 1998). Opinion leaders increasingly concerned about the potential impact of such initiatives on institutional funding, especially during lean budget times, have reacted with an array of measures to deal with "the threat" (Lovett, 2001). In spite of problematic evidence of the impact of performance-based budgeting in public higher education, as well as widespread skepticism among many faculty and administrators, increased accountability measures are expected to evolve well into the future (Schmidt, 2002).

Meanwhile, at many private colleges and universities, the trustees, who are often drawn from the business community, have become more active in the decision making. In response to their alumni, benefactors, parents, and other stakeholders, private colleges and universities are scrutinizing investments of institutional resources that were once rubber-stamped. In their increasingly visible roles, trustees seek to ensure the achievement of their institutions' widely communicated missions and to reinforce their institutions' image among their especially demanding stakeholders (Ehrenberg, 2000).

Accreditation Pressures

With so much riding on the results—students' ability to obtain financial aid, the institution's ability to transfer credits to and from other institutions, and institutional prestige, among others—accreditation, or reaccreditation, is arguably the most pressure-packed activity within the higher education environment. Whether it is granted by one of the eight regional accrediting commissions or by one of the many specialized disciplinary groups, accreditation epitomizes accountability. Within the context of our discussion, the accreditation process can be viewed as a vehicle that mitigates the pressures between higher education's external stakeholders and its member colleges and universities with their myriad missions.

In recent years, the regional accrediting commissions have instituted an array of changes in their approaches, criteria, and procedures to foster institutional effectiveness and accountability. One significant development has been the formation of an umbrella group, the Council for Higher Education Accreditation, to provide institutions a united voice, especially with the federal government and overseas institutions seeking accreditation within the United States. Another significant change among accrediting commissions that will more directly influence institutions has been a shift in primary focus from "inputs" and "must statements" relative to educational processes—such as the academic preparation of professors and the number of resources in campus libraries—and toward a focus on "student outcomes." Said another way, rather than maintaining a "one standard fits all" approach, the regional accrediting commissions are increasingly focusing on individual institutions' results in achieving their unique missions. Influenced by the quality movement in business—which is exemplified by the Malcolm Baldridge National Quality Award program—the accrediting associations are seeking to focus on, and hold institutions accountable for, legitimate indicators of quality within their specific environments (Eaton, 1999).

Synthesizing the various stakeholder perspectives, accrediting organizations are reemphasizing the obligation of member institutions to offer their students a sound education, and thus they are playing a leading role in defining "institutional effectiveness." As evidence, one of the nation's eight regional accrediting commissions, the Southern Association of Colleges and Schools (SACS), which serves nearly eight hundred institutions in eleven states (including the populous Texas and Florida), is instituting a massive overhaul of its accrediting approach. One of its goals in doing so was to increase its members' focus on institutional mission and effectiveness (Hoey, 2001). Such diverse discipline-specific associations as the Accrediting Board for Engineering and Technology (ABET) and the AACSB—the International Association for Management Education—have made dramatic changes in their standards to include significantly greater emphasis on student learning outcomes (Eaton, 2001). These accrediting associations, and no doubt others likely to follow, have thus put institutions and programs on notice to comprehensively examine their core operations and make a greater commitment to high quality student learning (Wellman, 2000).

Institutional Effectiveness

Rather than decrying the motives and strategies of accountability—a strategy employed by many defenders of traditional paradigms (Ohmann, 2000)—those within higher education will need to understand what the regional accrediting commissions are saying. More fundamentally, they must come to understand the perspective of those paying the bills. The day has arrived for most, and soon will for the rest, to explain their practices in a context that stakeholders will be likely to support; the alternative is to face an increasingly unwinnable challenge. The truth be told, there is much about our culture of higher education that is simply not supportable in today's inclusive, global, technology-enhanced society, in spite of that culture's relative strength vis-à-vis higher education systems in other parts of the world.

Institutional effectiveness is a valid expectation for the stakeholders in any of our major, evolving societal organizations. Most institutions of higher education currently define effectiveness in terms of student recruitment and retention, program/degree completion, and placement of graduates. The phrase has become the mantra both of accrediting commissions and of a growing number of institutional administrators throughout the nation. The focus on institutional effectiveness is evident not only in the actions of state legislatures but also in those of individual institutions, as exemplified by the Ohio State University initiative to "tax" all its instructional programs in order to reward those, recognized by faculty, as leading the university toward its goal of achieving a higher standard among the full range of its stakeholders (Wilson, 2001).

The institutional effectiveness initiative will no doubt foster an increasingly closer examination of programs with low enrollments, high dropout rates, or other deficiencies to which stakeholders are sensitive. The wisdom of continuing to fund programs with such deficiencies is becoming increasingly questionable. Some academic traditionalists will delay responding to this emerging fact of life as long as possible. Others will see it as an opportunity to improve the quality of their institutions and thereby enhance the lives of students worldwide who might otherwise see their dreams go unfulfilled.

As has already occurred in business, a massive shakeout of duplication and inefficiency is occurring in higher education, as evidenced by institutional mergers, an improved system of interinstitutional articulation leading to "seamless" degree programs, and the "just-in-time" delivery of education (D'Souza, 2001). In government, in publicly funded K–12 school systems, and in nearly every other arena of public life, stakeholder expectations have steadily risen and changes have been widely implemented. As Baby Boomers who grew up with values rooted in both social consciousness and consumerism mature, calls for increased accountability and demands for increased institutional effectiveness will no doubt continue. Colleges and universities will be required not only to do more with less financial support from outside but also to establish creative partnerships to fulfill their missions. One need only look at a current issue of the *Chronicle of Higher Education* to read about some new collaborative effort one institution has begun with another, either close by or on the other side of the globe, with a noneducational institution, or with a vendor of products. Leveraging such synergistic opportunities will increasingly drive success for institutions of higher education (Ruben, 2001).

Impact on Institutional Practices

Calls for increased institutional effectiveness invariably used to come from powerful institutional stakeholders, and responding was the exclusive domain of administrators. Their responses included such initiatives as establishing "first-year experience" programs that address the long-standing freshman class retention problem and creating more inviting space in student unions to foster bonds between diverse students. Other creative, "intrapreneurial" practices are no doubt on the way.

Yet administrators ultimately can do little to directly foster program reputation—which is what most influences the attraction of new students. And administrators have even less control over the thornier issues of student retention, program/degree completion, and graduate placement. Further complicating the issue of institutional effectiveness is the rather widespread faculty perception that improving retention requires the lowering of academic standards. Yet, although the research in this area is limited, studies that have been done indicate that "dumbing down" the curriculum is an ineffective practice. Both the research that has been done and collective personal experiences have led us to believe that the overwhelming majority of students and faculty members can meet higher achievement standards by employing the strategies we outline in this book.

Entrenched in their research and teaching, regular faculty members have often steered clear of institutional effectiveness dialogue. They see such talk as meddling similar to earlier intrusions that failed for lack of grounded integrity or widespread support. More insightful observers, however, are acknowledging that the long-held belief that the richness of a liberal collegiate experience is largely sufficient to produce a truly educated person is legitimately being challenged. Numerous factors have coalesced to convince a critical mass of academicians that the delivery of higher education has been changed fundamentally forever. With that change is coming not only heightened accountability for educational outcomes but also an increased scrutiny of such traditional values and practices as academic freedom, tenure, and shared governance. The widening circle of stakeholders in higher education appear fully committed to win out over traditionalists who seek to hold on to arcane practices that appear to benefit only those within academe.

Becoming a leader in bringing about the instructional changes needed to improve institutional effectiveness requires a "paradigm shift" of the kind identified by Thomas Kuhn in the third edition of his landmark work *The Structure of Scientific Revolutions* (1996):

> [Those] who embrace a new paradigm at an early stage must often do so in defiance of the evidence provided, having faith that the new paradigm will succeed with the many large problems that confront it. . . . A decision of that kind can only be made on faith. (p. 158)

Someone once said there are three kinds of people—those who make things happen, those who watch things happen, and those who ask "What happened?" Institutions of higher education, about to be engulfed by a tide of accountability mandates, include members at all levels that fit each of the three categories. As in business, government, health care, and other societal institutions, the achievement of greater accountability within higher education depends on the willingness of its frontline representatives to embrace its tenets. Faculty will either transform their practices to focus on student learning or see themselves and their institutions increasingly marginalized by those who achieve such transformation. The following chapter discusses the implications of accountability on teaching today, while the remaining chapters equip you with the insights and skills you will need to survive and thrive in this rapidly changing environment.

Summary of Key Points

- Allegiance to British and German traditions and practices fostered an exemplary system of higher education in North America.
- For decades, higher education practiced a de facto policy of exclusion in its admissions policies.
- As students from the middle class increasingly came to participate in higher education, the divide between educational institutions and the rest of society closed.
- The public increasingly perceives higher education as a form of business enterprise.
- As "consumers" of higher education, stakeholders want their expectations to be met or surpassed.
- Marketing and financial pressures play an increasingly significant role in the way higher education is administered.
- Over the past few decades, private businesspeople and public officials have adopted accountability measures in their arenas to improve attainment of desired objectives.
- Legislatures in a growing number of states have mandated accountability measures for public institutions of higher education and have tied those measures to continued funding through "performance-based budgeting."
- Legislative mandates tend to focus on improved access to higher education, student retention, program completion, and placement of graduates.
- Private colleges and universities have adopted parallel accountability measures.
- If it is to meet the expectations of increasingly influential external stakeholders, the institutional effectiveness movement must be led together by administrators, faculty, and staff.

Through the Professors' Eyes

At the conclusion of each chapter, the section headed "Through the Professors' Eyes" shares the views of three professors at different stages in their careers. Each is a composite of professors whom the authors have personally known or learned of in countless other ways. In the following section, the professors will introduce themselves and share their ideas related to the content in Chapter 1. They will continue their dialogue at the conclusion of each succeeding chapter.

PAT: My name is Pat, and I have been a successful university professor for over thirty years. Two years away from retirement, I still very much enjoy my position at my university, where the enrollment exceeds thirty thousand students. Active in my professional organizations, I make presentations at national and international meetings annually, write and publish in my field, and edit a major journal. On my campus, I conduct workshops for new faculty, adjunct instructors, and graduate teaching assistants—a group that provides as many rewards as working with my own students. I encourage the young faculty and graduate students to give presentations at professional meetings, and I regularly help them with their proposals and research. Working with the new faculty reminds me of the excitement I felt when first entering the academy. Although I have received awards for my teaching, research, service, and leadership to my university and profession, I was only doing what was expected of me as a professor. At present, we are seeing many changes triggered by the accountability mandates of our state legislature. Some of my colleagues are up in arms over what they perceive as a threat to academic freedom, tenure, and the academic culture, but I realize that we have seen other developments over the years that, while initially feeling like threats, have turned out to be positive contributors to the evolution of higher education. I believe that we are overdue for some changes that will help us fulfill the potential of education that John Dewey spoke of and wrote so much about a century ago. Although my career has been very rewarding, I am anxious to move on to other challenges and adventures; however, before doing so, I will do my utmost to ensure that there is a cluster of young professors who will carry on the tradition of quality education so many of us have helped build at this university.

DALE: I'm Dale, an associate professor at a medium-size private college. I have devoted the last five years of my twelve-year career to obtaining promotion to full professor, working diligently on my research and publishing agenda. My research has been highly recognized and has given me several opportunities to leave my institution. But I like the freedom I have to establish my own class schedule, which allows me ample time to pursue my research agenda. Although I do a good job of teaching, my students do not always appreciate my efforts. I believe that my college coddles the students too much, and that they could learn more if they put forth greater effort and gave up some of their extracurricular activities. Faculty members here are often turned into scapegoats for poor performance of students. Since my research provides additional funding for the department, my chair says little about my teaching. Active in two professional groups, I present my research exclusively at their annual conferences. Although my college offers a variety of workshops to improve teaching, the only ones I am interested in are related to technology, because of its ability to save me time that I can invest in my research. Many of my colleagues approach their responsibilities as I do, but some of the newer faculty seem to think we veteran faculty are out of touch with contemporary society. Perhaps they just don't understand what is important in the life of a professor: research and publications are primary, while teaching is secondary. I have a good rapport with the students who are majors in my field of study, so I prefer to teach only the advanced classes. Unfortunately, I don't always get to do that and have to take my turn at teaching the introductory courses, which I find less than challenging.

KIM: My name is Kim. I received the equivalent of my bachelor's and master's degrees at institutions in Asia before coming to North America to study for my doctorate. I just graduated, and I have accepted my first position as an assistant professor. During my doctoral program I was a teaching assistant in classes, but I have not had a chance to teach my own classes. I am excited about my new position and want to be certain that I do a very good job to make those who have supported my education proud of me. My parents are especially proud that I have been successful in getting this professorship! I hope to return home soon to share my good fortune with them and with the rest of my family. My major concerns at this time are improving my ability to make my speaking understood by my students, and mastering the high level of vocabulary necessary to establish my credibility with my students and colleagues. Although I read, write, and converse in English fairly well, I find formal speaking difficult. My English skills have improved a lot since arriving here, but I know some of my professors did not always understand me. Because I am concerned about communicating effectively with my students, I have been attending the various workshops the institution is offering on improving college teaching, using technology, making the curriculum more responsive to today's needs, and working with challenged students. My institution is growing rapidly, and we are adding new faculty every year. These workshops help us get to know one another. I have met some wonderful colleagues whose concerns are similar to mine, and we frequently go to lunch and talk about our successes and failures. I also want to get involved in a professional organization so that I can meet those at other universities who might help me grow. I know I can be a good professor, and I want very much for my students to accept and respect me.

Tips for Thriving

Although many of us chose to enter academe partly to insulate ourselves from what we perceived as a politicized society, it is critical for us to attend to the decision making of external stakeholders. The *Chronicle of Higher Education*, *Change*, and *University Business*, available in nearly all campus libraries as well as online, are especially effective resources to review on a regular basis. The *Chronicle's* Web site (http://chronicle.com) is especially current and comprehensive, permitting convenient access to information on student recruitment and retention practices at diverse institutions throughout the world and providing a host of other information relative to accountability.

Replete with their own multiple grapevines, individual campuses typically have at least one especially reliable person who can serve as a resource for assessing the impact of such issues as external calls for increased accountability. As you begin this book, it might be wise to identify and build a dialogue with one such wise resource in your institution. Pertinent articles and documents that cross that person's desk might be directed your way for review, and you can reciprocate when your increasingly keen eye happens on material that they might not otherwise see.

SUGGESTED READINGS

D'Souza, D. (2001). "Rich Men, Poor Men, Businessmen, and Scholars." *Chronicle of Higher Education* 47, no. 47 (August 3), pp. B14–B15.

Eaton, J. (1999). "Advancing Quality through Additional Attention to Results." *CHEA Chronicle* 1, no. 11, www.chea.org/Chronicle/vol1/no11/index.cfm.

Johnson, S. (1999). *Who Moved My Cheese?* New York: Putnam.

"Making Quality Work." (2001). *University Business* 4, no. 6 (July/August), pp. 44–50, 78, 80, 85.

Ruben, B. (2001). "We Need Excellence Beyond the Classroom." *Chronicle of Higher Education*, 47, no. 44 (July 13), pp. B15–B16.

CHAPTER

2

Implications of Accountability on Your Teaching

FOCUS QUESTIONS

- How does accountability affect course planning and classroom activities?
- How can you assess your readiness to infuse accountability into your teaching?
- What are some proven guidelines for facilitating increased accountability?
- How can you effectively manage the key accountability objectives?

> *Whenever a significant opportunity to improve teaching and learning comes along, you ought to spend the time and effort and resources needed to take advantage of it.*
>
> —William Massy

While administrators scramble to implement efficiency-oriented processes to demonstrate their institutional effectiveness to disparate stakeholders, the front-line learning leaders—faculty members—will ultimately decide whether the accountability movement will take hold within their institutions. In the new environment, effectiveness will be defined in terms of authentic student learning outcomes and students' mastery of well-defined learning objectives. This chapter explains the underlying principles of accountability and discusses how these will affect your teaching. It is designed to help you assess your effectiveness from several perspectives, and to provide a foundation upon which to build accountability strategies into your teaching and classroom management practices.

In their initial reaction to accountability mandates, some professors stated that higher education was unique among societal institutions and that what professors do cannot be measured (Ohmann, 2000). Many argue that retention and graduation rates can be improved only by relaxing student performance standards—for example, by giving unwarranted higher grades or "dumbing down" content. Upon deeper reflection, however, faculty opinion leaders seem to be realizing that such practices are the antithesis of accountability and that they serve to postpone a genuine solution to the problems accountability proponents have identified. True accountability, they realize, can be achieved only by holding students to consistently higher standards and employing enlightened strategies to help them achieve those standards. When it hits the "critical mass" stage, systemic accountability will effectively help prepare students for their long-term futures within their formal educations, their careers, and their lives as citizens. Professors are now realizing that they must transform their courses to engage students' minds more efficiently and effectively and that they must proactively eliminate as many barriers to student success as possible.

Colleges and universities are reevaluating their standard operating procedures—including their promotion and tenure practices—in order to reward effective teaching and the achievement of student learning outcomes. Early adopters of sound strategies to achieve accountability in their teaching will undoubtedly discover (or rediscover) the satisfaction that comes from meeting students' complex needs. In the process, their contributions to their institutions will be magnified.

To achieve accountability, professors must challenge existing paradigms by:

- Acknowledging the legitimacy of diverse stakeholder voices and regularly adapting their course plans, instructional methods, and evaluation strategies to respond to those voices.
- Recognizing that, as much as being experts in their disciplines, they are facilitators of learning within those disciplines, as well as conduits to a larger body of knowledge.
- Accepting the fact that while students come to them with vast differences in their pre-existing knowledge, individual learning styles, and objectives for completing the course, each student should benefit regularly from participating in the learning environment.
- Accepting an active management role in the recruitment and retention of students.
- Employing teaching methods that fit well with students' existing knowlege, interests, and learning styles.
- Making a concerted and genuine effort to foster a learning relationship with each student enrolled in their courses.
- Regularly, and more authentically, assessing student success in learning critical concepts.
- Employing technology appropriately to manage learning efficiency and effectiveness.
- Continuously developing skills that foster not only their own disciplinary knowledge but their pedagogical skills as well.

- Collaborating actively with colleagues to eliminate gaps, reduce redundancy, and otherwise improve the instructional effectiveness of the entire curriculum.

Achieving these objectives will require keen ongoing analysis and sober wisdom. It will also require a large degree of the "emotional intelligence" about which so much has been written in recent years. In his book *Emotional Intelligence* (1995), Daniel Goleman reminded us: "Our passions, when well exercised, have wisdom; they guide our thinking, our values, our survival. But they can easily go awry, and do so all too often" (p. xiv). Just as enlightened physicians have improved their bedside manners and office practices by creating "healing partnerships" with their patients, so must professors actively develop "learning partnerships" with their students. This means reaching past the few outward overachievers to develop relationships with a wide range of those who come into their classrooms. In an age of accountability, it is critical that professors employ their emotional intelligence to foster positive perceptions among students and other stakeholders. Such long-term changes in approach and technique require diligent, consistent effort, grounded in contemporary core values and current research.

Sound accountability strategies will focus on the achievement of the four major goals identified in Chapter 1: student recruitment, student retention, student completion of instructional programs, and placement of graduates. Traditionally, faculty members thought their exclusive task was to teach those who registered for their classes and that student recruitment was the exclusive task of the institution's marketing arm. The accountability paradigm recognizes that a market for higher education has developed that is not unlike the market for other professional services. All faculty members have a responsibility to become more committed to students' long-term academic and career success. This translates into accepting more active roles in recruitment and retention.

Before the idea of accountability took hold in health care and higher education, physicians stayed abreast of research and treated ailments, while professors conducted research and taught classes. Now following the recognition of accountability, physicians are expected to anticipate problems with, maintain, and restore their patients' health, while professors are expected to facilitate grounded learning in students that undergirds effective lifelong learning. This fundamental paradigm shift requires both types of professionals to invest in the long-term well-being of those they serve and to intercede proactively to ensure the prescribed outcomes. Just as patients who vacate suggested treatment regimens may fail to recover fully, students who fail to embrace sound learning strategies may not reach their intellectual potential. Both may eventually dictate extraordinary interventions, which require extensive additional resources. Just as an accountable physician must monitor patient progress, and perhaps refer patients to specialists for fully successful outcomes, the accountable professor must manage student progress and work with colleagues of varied specialties to ensure a continuity of learning.

Professors who understand higher education's connections to a larger arena have long played a role in mentoring their highest-achieving graduates, assuring their intellectual development and their successful employment or continued education. The accountability paradigm will likely have little effect on them, other than to increase the degree of their activity. Professors who have not played this role will need to develop a network of new contacts—a resource that can add considerable richness to the academic experience.

Some readers might ask at this point, "Doesn't accountability serve to trump academic freedom and thus to discount the role of the professor?" Although we have frequently heard such questions, we believe there is a larger context that must be considered. As our system of higher education has evolved from its rather cloistered traditions, its practices must respond to significant changes. Rather than being viewed as a threat, the accountability movement can also be seen as an opportunity to expand the influence of ongoing learning into a wider sphere. Academics can extend opportunities for more fulfilling lives to all citizens while retaining the freedom they have always valued.

Grounding Your Teaching and Learning Effectiveness

As professors contemplate their expanded role as facilitators of learning, it would be wise of them to develop a more grounded understanding of their existing attitudes and skills. Although research skills and publication record are accepted indicators of success among college professors, the correlation of those skills with teaching effectiveness is not as strong as the common perception assumes (Feldman, 1987). One major study found that "teacher's knowledge of subject" was the ninth most important dimension both in student achievement and in student satisfaction ratings. Among more significant factors were teacher's clarity, stimulation of interest, openness to opinions, and sensitivity to class progress—each largely functions of emotional intelligence (Feldman, 1998).

At this important juncture, you may well find it useful to engage in several forms of self-assessment to help you better understand the dimensions of your own teaching and learning practices. Three we would recommend are (1) an analysis of your personal strengths, weaknesses, opportunities, and threats (SWOT) that affect your teaching; (2) the development of a personal philosophy of teaching and learning; and (3) an assessment of your personal learning and teaching styles.

To conduct a personal SWOT analysis, focus first on your own natural talents, learned skills, and educational experiences to identify your personal teaching strengths and weaknesses. A form is provided in Appendix 2.1 to facilitate your work. We emphasize that strengths and weaknesses are both internal factors that include your values, beliefs, knowledge of teaching and learning theory, and communications skills. Next focus on the environment affecting your teaching—your institutional culture, the students about to arrive in your class-room, the current political climate in which education operates, and other such factors—to identify the external opportunities and threats imposed on your teaching. Although they influence your teaching, these environmental factors are generally beyond your control. We suggest you complete the SWOT analysis in these two steps, allowing at least several hours between identifying your strengths and weaknesses and identifying your opportunities and threats. Analyzing the results of this exercise is very likely to provide you with some insights that would otherwise have gone unnoticed—insights that could have a powerful influence on your teaching as you contemplate an effectiveness paradigm.

A second form of self-assessment is to develop a personal philosophy of teaching and learning. If you may have already crafted such a philosophy, revisit and refine it. As you do so, you might want to review the example in Appendix 2.2. Conducting this exercise will enable you to ground your approach to teaching in your beliefs about students, learning, and other essential factors and will likely help you determine potential new directions and strategies that you might consider for your teaching (Haugen, 2000).

A final tool—and one that has proved useful to a number of analytically minded users—is the assessment of your personal teaching and learning style (see Appendix 2.3). It engenders a deeper understanding of your course planning, instructional delivery, classroom management, and student evaluation practices. The self-reflection that this exercise fosters can lead to potentially extensive gains in your teaching effectiveness.

Together these three exercises, conducted over a period of several days, should provide you with a comprehensive picture of your unique qualities as a facilitator of learning and help you identify barriers and set objectives to direct your own self-improvement. You cannot attain a complete understanding of your potential, however, until you examine the unique learning styles of your students—the focus of our next section.

Understanding Individual Learning Styles

Over the past several decades, imaging technology that enables researchers to monitor the brain's functioning has generated some truly breakthrough findings. A number of researchers have theorized that students vary significantly in how they process new and difficult information, and that each student has a distinct, definable learning style. Although much of the research into learning styles has focused on children, several models are applicable to college students. Some academicians consider learning-styles research to be controversial, but for others it seems to hold genuine potential for empowering students to manage their own learning and for increasing the quality of their mental engagement with difficult material. From an accountability perspective, implementing learning-styles strategies into course delivery methods offers potential for reducing the impact of learning bottlenecks—that is, situations in which students have difficulty mastering critical concepts—thus improving course completion and graduation rates.

We will discuss three of the more distinctive models of learning styles in this section. The first, developed by David A. Kolb (1983), identifies four learning dimensions—concrete experience, reflective observation, abstract conceptualization, and active experimentation—and yields four types of learning behavior. Type I learners prefer to engage in "hands-on" learning, rely on intuition rather than logic, and enjoy applying learning to real-life situations. Type II learners prefer to look at issues from many points of view, create categories for information, and use imagination and personal sensitivity when learning. Type III learners enjoy solving problems, completing technical tasks, and finding practical solutions—but they shy away from interpersonal issues. Type IV learners are concise and logical; they thrive on abstract ideas and rational explanations. In recent years, Kolb's research has been supplemented by that of Anthony F. Gregorc (1986), who has modified the model into one that focuses on random (top-down, look at the whole task) and sequential (bottom-up, one step at a time) processing of information to yield four style types: concrete sequential, abstract sequential, abstract random, and concrete random (Kelly, 1997).

Second, Richard Felder's model (Felder and Silverman, 1988) of individual learning styles focuses on five factors:

1. How students prefer to perceive information (i.e., by sensory or intuitive means).
2. Through which channel individuals perceive information most effectively (i.e., visual or auditory).
3. How students organize information most comfortably, i.e. inductively or deductively.
4. How students prefer to process information (i.e., actively or reflectively).
5. How students progress toward understanding of concepts (i.e., sequentially or holistically).

The third, and arguably the most comprehensive, model of learning styles was promulgated initially in 1971 by Rita Dunn and Kenneth Dunn, who have since continued to research and refine it. The Dunn and Dunn (1999) model postulates that a student's ability to learn and retain difficult information is a function of twenty factors, which are grouped into five categories. Physiological factors include light, background sound, temperature, and the degree of formality in the design of the learning environment. Emotional factors include motivation to learn, persistence, responsibility, and structure. Sociological factors include learning by oneself, in a pair, with peers, as a member of a team, under the direction of an authority figure, or through varied methods. Physiological factors include perceptual modality (i.e., visual, auditory, kinesthetic, or tactile), intake of food and drink during learning, time of day, and mobility while learning. Psychological factors are global versus analytic processors (similar to the random versus sequential Gregorc factors), and impulsive/reflective. The Dunn and Dunn model employs an assessment instrument that yields a continuum score on each factor for each learner. For any given learner, only six to twelve of the factors affect learning style significantly. The model states that by informing students of their individual strengths and providing them adequate sensitive support, professors can manage the learning environment to maximize each student's mental engagement and retention of material that is new and difficult to students (Dunn and Griggs, 2000).

The common elements of these and other learning-styles models include the impact of perceptual modalities (e.g., visual, auditory, tactile, and kinesthetic learning preferences), and the role of mental processing styles (e.g., inductive versus deductive). Research indicates that professors who teach at levels through law school (Boyle and Dunn, 1998) and employ strategies grounded in these factors not only reduce the impact of learning bottlenecks within their courses, they may also achieve higher levels of student success.

Links to additional information and assessment tools for each of the three learning-styles models discussed above are available at www.developfaculty.com. We suggest you delve a bit further, become comfortable with at least one of the models, and complete at least one of the assessments. (There also may be resources on your campus through which you might complete one or more or find detailed information on another model.) Our premise is that once you have revealed to yourself how you approach the learning of new, difficult material, it will sensitize you to the fact that all of your students have their own discrete ways of accomplishing the same objective. Since their learning styles are likely different from your own—and you, more than they, influence how material is introduced in your courses—you should give consideration to modifying your instructional delivery methods as needed to better achieve accountability objectives.

Developing a Teaching Style That Fits Students' Learning Styles

You have likely heard throughout your entire teaching career that people teach as they have been taught. While we are not aware of specific research on this issue relative to professors, we do not doubt the basic veracity of the statement. Digging a bit deeper, however, we are convinced that people derive much of their individual teaching styles from their individual learning styles—that is, people teach as they learn. You may think that what worked for you as a student would likely work for most students, but that may or may not be true (Wankat, 2002). Your completion of the SWOT analysis, the personal philosophy of teaching and learning, and the teaching-styles self-assessment has helped you understand the impact of your primary talents, learned skills, abilities to respond to external forces, and core values on what has become your unique teaching style.

Within our popular culture during the last few years, *insanity* has been defined whimsically as "doing the same thing, while expecting different results." To avoid such insanity, the enlightened instructor can ask which of two logical strategies is most likely to enhance students' learning effectiveness. That is, should the professor initially adapt to the preferred learning styles of students, or instead, should the professor expect students to adapt to his or her preferred teaching methods? It is a complex issue with no instant answers, and each situation requires some study and individualized decisions to arrive at the "best" approach. Some professors can adapt quite effectively to the learning styles of students, whereas others would lose so much self-confidence they might become less effective in the classroom. As in most any endeavor, the key is getting started.

In an age of accountability, you identify gaps between desired and achieved student retention rates, or if the graduation rates from your program are not what you and other stakeholders, expect, perhaps it is time to modify your teaching styles. We are convinced that the rather magical interchange that occurs between the professor and the student is the very heart of the accountability issue. When the interchange works well, retention, program completion, placement after graduation, and other desired outcomes often take care of themselves.

Richard Felder (1998) concludes that to address the issue of mismatches between the learning styles of students and their own dominant teaching styles, professors initially should:

- Balance between concrete and abstract information.
- Make extensive use of visuals before, during, and after presenting verbal material.
- Conduct small group exercises in class regularly.
- Have students cooperate on homework assignments.
- Encourage creative solutions to problems, even "wrong" ones.

Research conducted by Rita and Kenneth Dunn (1999) indicates that the following tactics can improve learning outcomes of college students with diverse learning styles:

- Conduct a personal conference with each student to inform them of the critical dimensions of their individual learning style.
- Introduce new concepts with both "global" (deductive) and "analytical" (inductive) phrasing.
- Adapt classrooms with areas of varying light and both hard and soft seating.
- Attend to students' need for structure by employing agendas and other guides.

- Employ tactile and auditory materials as well as kinesthetic activities that introduce students with those dominant perceptual modalities that are new and difficult to them.

As evidence mounts on the benefits of employing learning-styles strategies, institutions with an accountability paradigm are likely to fare well with them. Judging by what is known, we believe the approach holds significant potential for enhancing students' ability to manage their own learning more effectively and for contributing to the attainment of retention and program-completion objectives.

Fostering Student Responsibility

While accepting the mantle of accountability requires professors to commit to the continuous improvement of teaching, learning, and classroom management practices, it also engenders a concomitant obligation among learners. Giving students knowledge of their own individual learning styles has proved to be an effective way of developing their sense of responsibility—that is, it empowers them to take control of their learning. Naysayers often tell us that students have become "slackers," yet exemplary teachers say that the majority of those who populate our classrooms are willing to produce at higher levels than those at which they are currently working. Our developing teaching styles and instructional strategies must energize these individuals and shift the paradigm toward learning rather than teaching.

Think about it. Today's students are teaching themselves far more than we likely taught ourselves when we were their age. Many have taught themselves an array of technological skills on their home computers or in labs at their schools. Many were emotionally isolated by the significant adults in their lives yet taught themselves social skills—albeit sometimes ineffective ones—to survive in the resulting vacuum. Many have taught themselves occupational skills by working at fairly sophisticated part-time jobs (Howe and Strauss, 2000). An individual student's skill list can be quite extensive. Our challenge is to understand them for who they are, leverage their existing skills, and become a partner in moving them toward where they really want, and need, to be. Sometimes it requires "tough love"; at other times quiet, nonjudgmental listening is the major requirement. For their long-term good, as well as to meet externally generated accountability mandates, we must rise to the challenge if we are to call ourselves educators.

Developing a philosophy and style that improve students' learning requires a significant change in mind-set for many professors. Finding proven resources that facilitate the change is critical. One guide that has been especially successful for us—and for millions of other professionals in higher education, as well as in other arenas embracing the accountability movement—was published in 1989 by longtime professor Stephen R. Covey. We will leverage it to make direct applications to college teaching and learning, which will facilitate the assimilation of accountability principles into your regular practices.

The Seven Habits of Highly Effective Professors

Written especially for an accountability-minded reader, *The 7 Habits of Highly Effective People* (Covey, 1989) provides a practical foundation on which to build successful recruiting, retention, completion, and placement strategies. We will leave some of Covey's concepts—such as the "circle of concern, circle of influence" and the "emotional bank account"—for you to explore (which you can do by reading the book or by listening to one of the many audiotapes related to it), but we will look closely at the seven habits themselves.

Habit 1: Be Proactive

Traditionally, professors have built relationships with students slowly—often not until the students' senior year or entry into graduate school. One could logically surmise that in the meantime, many other students had left school because of poor academic performance, family or other personal reasons, or the need or desire to accept full-time employment. Our experience is that many of these challenges can be overcome when a professor provides wise counsel during the student's crisis. Proponents of the accountability movement believe that the retention of students through graduation is in the best interests of students, the employment market, and our larger society. Therefore, it is incumbent on professors to play a more active role in students' success.

To be proactive, professors should:

- Anticipate challenges students are likely to face and plan for their solution.
- Initiate a dialogue with as many students as possible, early in the term.
- Gather sufficient information from students in order to meet their needs.
- Orchestrate a rich initial class meeting that achieves multiple objectives.
- Follow up promptly on student inquiries for information and on absenteeism.

Habit 2: Begin with the End in Mind

Many in higher education have long believed that the richness of a liberal arts classroom combined with a comprehensive campus experience was sufficient in and of itself to produce an educated person. While there is unquestionably much to value in that paradigm, the student population has changed significantly since that belief was formulated. As we will discuss in more detail in Chapter 3, today's college and university students are far more likely than yesterday's to attend classes part-time while working full-time. They are also more likely to be older and to have family responsibilities (whether in child-rearing or caring for aging parents). These factors, along with the expectations of the stakeholders enumerated in Chapter 1, have heralded a call for more measurable educational outcomes than were common during the height of traditional liberal arts education.

To begin with the end in mind, professors should integrate the following tactics into their teaching:

- Identify specific, up-to-date learning objectives for each course that reflect the consideration of multiple stakeholders.
- Develop richer assignments that lead to the achievement of these objectives that are relevant to students' lives.
- Provide detailed, eye-appealing syllabi that clearly explain course objectives, strategies, and guidelines.
- Develop exams and other assessment tools before course material is addressed.
- Clarify throughout the term the objectives communicated in the course syllabus.

Habit 3: Put First Things First

When students were housed in dormitories, sorority and fraternity houses, and other on-campus housing, and when they focused their energies entirely on their college experience, management of class time was not as major an issue as it has now become. Both commuting students and on-campus residents with wide access to support resources (e.g., computer access at home or in the dorm rooms) expect a highly focused and rich course experience. Effective professors manage their class meeting time not only to address the most critical concepts when students are physiologically receptive but also to regularly connect activities and assignments to the core content of the course.

To put first things first, the most successful professors will learn to employ the following tactics:

- Develop a detailed agenda for each class meeting that includes time parameters.
- Address critical learning objectives early in the class meeting while students are most fresh and receptive.
- Develop assignments and exams that foster students' mastery of the most critical content of the course.
- Dedicate class time to content on which students will be evaluated.
- Provide an overview of the following class meeting that enables students to organize their thinking in advance of new instruction.
- Communicate regularly with students via e-mail to provide reinforcement and clarification of upcoming classroom events.

Habit 4: Think Win/Win

In his book, Covey presents "six paradigms of human interactions"—(I) lose/(you) win, lose/lose, win, win/lose, win/win, and win/win or no deal—and states that most highly effective people employ the latter two regularly. Often professors are perceived by students to employ win and win/lose strategies in their interactions. Such interactions commonly lead to outcomes that are increasingly undesirable in today's higher education environment. For example, has any professor ever really won an argument with a student? Using a win/win approach will allow professors and students to achieve shared instructional success. Students who see the professor as a caring human being truly invested in their well-being will not only extend themselves to meet higher expectations but also internalize high standards for subsequent performance.

Sensitized professors who think win/win will regularly employ the following tactics:

- Provide positive feedback to students in front of their peers.
- Encourage flexibility on assignments to enhance students' mastery of course learning objectives.
- Prepare students thoroughly for exams—especially the first one in the course.
- Foster students' performance by providing and reviewing the scoring rubric for each assignment as it is being made.
- Provide prompt, individualized feedback on scored exams and assignments.
- Talk regularly with students—before and after class meetings and via e-mail between classes—about their progress toward their personal learning goals.

Habit 5: Seek First to Understand, Then to Be Understood

The mind that articulated the instructional phrase "Look to your left, now look to your right . . ." seemed to expect listeners to understand the subject material instantly. Being the exploring, experimenting beings they are, however, students seldom grasp complex ideas by hearing a professor talk at them. In *The 7 Habits of Highly Effective People*, Covey eloquently explains the folly of such an approach to achieve effectiveness within any relationship. When we reflect on it, most of us would admit that those who have had the greatest impact on our lives first listened to us unconditionally or, to use Covey's word, *empathically*. They took the initiative to truly understand us, before expecting us to embrace their view of the world. Effective professors have learned that they do not "teach a discipline" so much as they teach students—students who have the potential to grow well beyond the multiple challenges they bring with them to the classroom. Such professors will say that the most rewarding aspect of their profession is to see the lights come on in the eyes of their students. It will always be so.

Seeking first to understand and then to be understood is facilitated by employing the following tactics:

- Use a student profile form, such as the one in Appendix 5.1 of Chapter 5, to gather useful information on each student.
- Employ the form throughout the term to note key points that surface in conferences with students and related critical events.
- View students' various characteristics, experiences, and attitudes as potential enriching elements of the classroom environment.
- Use vocabulary and examples to which your students can relate.
- Solicit "informal" feedback from students throughout the term.

Habit 6: Synergize

Synergy is typically defined as "an interaction or situation in which the whole is more than the sum of its individual parts." Covey refers to synergy as "creative cooperation." A professor who works toward synergy believes that a particular course should be more than the sum of its assignments, exam results, and classroom dynamics. Each course should truly enrich the lives of students by giving them a foundation on which to build an understanding of subsequent classes, life experiences, and personal insights. As former (and current) students ourselves, we have taken many courses, some of which achieved great synergy and others that did not. Achieving synergy requires embracing the first five habits to draw students in and to make the course an individualized learning event.

To synergize, professors can employ the following tactics:

- Draw out students' experiences that relate to classroom topics.
- Link assignments and discussions to students' real-world lives.
- Employ small groups of students to focus on learning goals.
- Encourage out-of-class study groups.
- Create a community that celebrates the unique nature of learning.

Habit 7: Sharpen the Saw

Covey relays a number of parables, including one about watching a man working to saw down a tree. The man admits to being at the task for more than five hours. When asked why he didn't stop to sharpen the saw, he exhaustedly exclaims, "I don't have time. I'm too busy sawing." Many professors become frustrated when their once-successful techniques fail with a particular group of students or, even worse, with all of their students. But, like the sawing man, they do not take the time to sharpen their tools. They do not realize that their results will not change until they change the way they approach the work.

In the last few years, truly fascinating research has been conducted on human learning. As professionals, we should invest the time to become familiar with at least some of this research and assess its ramifications on teaching and learning methodologies.

Continuously developing educators can employ the following tactics to "sharpen the saw":

- Establish mentoring relationships with effective veteran instructors.
- Mentor a novice professor, regularly discussing effective teaching strategies (Zachary, 2000).
- Annually extend beyond a single discipline to read a well-received book on teaching and learning practices.
- Make use of on-campus workshops, discussion groups, and related resources—which are often sponsored by one of the growing number of teaching and learning centers.
- Access online resources (e.g., www.developfaculty.com).

The 7 Habits of Highly Effective People is a comprehensive vehicle for facilitating the integration of accountability principles into your teaching. While we recommend this particular book for its proven track record in our, and others', professional lives, there are unquestionably additional resources available that might help you achieve similar success in yours. Why not invest a small amount of time to develop the foundation that will enable you to achieve greater accountability with your various stakeholders for the remainder of your teaching career?

Managing the Mileposts of the Term

Effective managers in many arenas commonly embrace a concept called the Pareto rule, or sometimes the 20/80 or the 80/20 rule. This rule states that 80 percent of the success (or failure) of any endeavor is derived from 20 percent of its contributing factors. For example, 80 percent of the milk sold is consumed by 20 percent of milk drinkers, and 80 percent of customer complaints flow from 20 percent of the reasons customers complain. In the context of teaching—if the Pareto rule holds true in the milk market and in the area of customer complaints—professors are likely to see that 80 percent of all D's and F's earned by students within a particular degree program are attained in 20 percent of the program's courses—a strong reason to employ an intervention in those courses. Within a single course, we are likely to see that 20 percent of our class meetings correlate with 80 percent of student dropouts. Further analysis would likely tell us that the critical 20 percent of class meetings are the initial meeting, the one at which the first examination is administered or major assignment is submitted, and the midterm meeting. If those 20 percent of meetings are managed effectively, we are likely to solve 80 percent of the course retention problems (Goetsch and Davis, 1999).

While initial class meetings are critical times for professors, Covey's Habit 5—Seek first to understand, then to be understood—should help them remember that it is a challenging time for students as well. Typically confronted by a very brief drop–add period, students must quickly decide whether a given course is a wise investment of their time, money, and self-esteem. Our experience has led us to reject the idea that most students are truly looking for "an easy A" and instead to say that most are in fact searching for an experience that is rewarding and relevant but that also allows them to pursue other critical activities in their lives. To play an active role in attaining sufficient numbers of properly prepared students at the first class meeting, professors can promote courses in advance to previous classes and to individual students outside of class. They must then ensure that students attending the first class meeting perceive that they can be trusted to orchestrate a rewarding, relevant experience throughout the term. Students who encounter such professors will not only be more likely to return for the second meeting of the class but will also recruit their peers during the drop–add period. Chapter 5 will provide a comprehensive plan for launching your courses effectively.

The second, and in most cases even more significant milepost is the first examination or the submission date of the first major assignment, such as a written paper or an oral presentation. Students may stumble if the professor does not clearly set forth the content and approach of the exam or the performance standards of the assignment. To eliminate this obstacle, professors may preview exam content in a manner students can assimilate, whether through a study guide, an oral review, the completion of practice tests, or some other means. Chapter 10 provides details on managing the exam process. For other assignments, the most critical key is the design and thorough explanation of a scoring rubric that will be employed to evaluate it. Chapter 11 addresses this issue comprehensively.

Within the context of a single course, the third key retention milepost is usually the midpoint of the term. While the midterm meeting often coincides with a second exam or the submission of a major assignment, the most significant factor at this juncture seems to be students' weighing of the resources they are required to invest against the outcomes they expect. Energizing the midterm class meetings, talking with individual students, communicating encouragement via e-mail, and other proactive measures will usually help students pass this milepost and complete the course. Chapter 6 provides additional information on managing the context of your course.

When the focus shifts from the completion of a single course to the completion of an entire degree program, the last class meeting typically supplants the midterm meeting as the third most critical retention milepost. Chapter 12 addresses tactics for closing the course effectively to maximize accountable outcomes.

Thinking of Students as Customers

A sure way to get up the ire of many professors is to launch a discussion of some dimension of students being consumers, customers, or clients. Those opposed to that paradigm often cite reasons such as the following:

- Our college (or university) is not a business. We teach, not "train," and therefore we should not "service." We are not a factory that turns out products.
- The legislature (or the trustees) and parents pay the bills; therefore, if we have any clients, it is they.
- Knowledge isn't a product to be sold.
- If I treat students like clients, then I will have to lower my standards, give them grades they do not deserve, entertain them, resist challenging their existing beliefs, or otherwise lower my standards.
- The business/client model is an insult to which I will not even respond (Slaughter, 2001).

At the opposite end of the continuum are those who support the paradigm of students being clients, and who suggest the following:

- A college (or university) has both fixed and variable expenses that must be offset through sufficient tuition revenues. Such revenues can be generated only by meeting most expectations of those who register for our classes.
- Like any revenue-producing organization, colleges and universities have an array of clients, but the most critical are those who register for its classes. When they are not pleased with the quality of the "product" or "service" they receive, they will make that fact known to external stakeholders who will come to their support.
- Physicians, architects, engineers, attorneys, writers, and other professionals market their knowledge to clients with the expectation of receiving prestige and financial rewards in return. Professors today are not significantly different.
- The quality movement in business has demonstrated that retaining customers over the long term requires raising standards rather than lowering them.
- Although, admittedly, there are some unsavory businesses, much of the success of our society is attributable to the entrepreneurial, profit-achieving strategies of businesses, each of which is predicated on the requirement to meet or exceed their clients' expectations.

Leading faculty members is sometimes described as similar to "herding cats." Ours is a fiercely independent profession, and most of us thrive on intellectual challenges (Bowen, 2001). Probably somewhere between the two polarized positions outlined above is one that you can articulate for yourself that will enable you to achieve consistency in your approach to students.

When we have presented the suggestions in this chapter to veteran professors, we have commonly received feedback such as "We haven't had to do this before," or "Do these changes coddle students?" We agree that many professors have never before looked at their students as clients, but perhaps had we been more fully meeting students' needs previously, the approach we are suggesting now would not seem like coddling. Again, the bigger picture is that the environment of higher education, like that of so many other institutions, has fundamentally changed. When leading institutions change the way they teach to more effectively accommodate the needs of students, competition dictates that others must adapt. As Spencer Johnson stated in his best-selling book *Who Moved My Cheese?* (1999), "If you do not change, you could become extinct" (p. 46).

Summary of Key Points

- Achieving accountability in higher education is dependent on the critical mass of faculty members embracing its benefits.
- Fostering accountability requires professors to get outside their discipline areas periodically to view their teaching in a greater context.
- Improving accountability outcomes requires greater focus on students, collectively and individually.
- Conducting a personal SWOT analysis and developing a personal philosophy of teaching and learning will help focus your instructional energy and decision making.
- Knowledge of learning-styles research holds great potential for enabling professors to develop a more effective and consistent teaching style.
- Employ proven ways to get students to accept more responsibility for their own learning.
- Stephen Covey's *The 7 Habits of Highly Effective People* is a valuable tool for guiding professors in the continuous improvement of their teaching effectiveness.
- Student retention and program completion rates will improve markedly as professors work to manage the key mileposts of the term.
- Students are clients, albeit of a special type.

Through the Professors' Eyes

DALE: I find all of this emphasis on accountability very disturbing. It seems that the trustees, politicians, and college administrators believe that faculty members need to be held accountable for student retention and degree completion, with little thought to students' accountability. I think the emphasis on accountability is misdirected—it is the students who should be held accountable for their actions.

I'm not opposed to institutional initiatives, like the "first year experience" our administration installed that helps freshmen shift their focus from "binge drinking" and the like, by engaging them in positive activities designed to help them adapt to campus life. The dean said yesterday that the program has improved the retention of freshmen by 11 percent since it was installed. I know I would have benefited a great deal had such an initiative been in place when I went away to the university at eighteen. But to expect faculty members to play an active role in such programming detracts from our time and thus our ability to stay current in our areas of expertise. The Covey 7 Habits stuff that was the focus of a workshop here today was well presented and logical, but I'm not convinced that I have to make many adjustments to my teaching to achieve more effective results. The college simply needs to do a better job of recruiting and screening applicants! Knowing what my students need after they arrive on campus is my responsibility.

KIM: I am beginning to feel overwhelmed. Before accepting this position, I never thought much about my role as a professor—I was too busy being a student. At my first department meeting today, one agenda item was to improve student retention. I cannot imagine someone holding me responsible for whether or not my students learn! I realize that some of my role models were the older and wiser professors who listened to their students and helped them in many ways. But that role seems so great as I start my career. I do not know if I can do all those things and teach too. I spoke by phone last night to my dissertation adviser, who recommended that I seek out a mentor to help me. She knows a senior faculty member from this university, who is also of Asian background but from another country, and she offered to have him call me. I wanted that opportunity! She also encouraged me to become "proactive" about learning English by borrowing language tapes through the local community college and joining Toastmasters, a club where people meet others from the community and give speeches. She emphasized that I cannot afford to let students "ding me" over my language flaws on the end-of-term evaluations. She also encouraged me to call her every Friday afternoon. There is so much to learn about being a good professor in this culture!

PAT: I really believe that professors need to be held accountable for the success or failure of their students. I've always believed that what I did best was to be a role model, and I've tried consistently to exhibit the kind of learning and behavior I expect from my students. At this stage of my career, I know my personal strengths and limitations. I know how I learn best and I have become conscious of my students' learning styles. I feel obligated to try to accommodate them, even if what I do does not match my particular preferences for learning. Some of my colleagues voice concern about the impact of accountability on academic freedom. I must have sounded really ancient when I said to one of them, "Academic freedom has never been about protecting the rights of professors to be bad teachers." I already practice many of the habits related to treating students as individuals discussed in our meeting today. Maybe that's why I find them helpful, not threatening.

Tips for Thriving

Effective professionals in any field realize they are always—directly or indirectly—recruiting new clients. Although many professors are uneasy with "selling" their classes to prospective students, we would ask that you consider perhaps a new perspective. We are fortunate to work in a profession whose focus is valuable to all who avail themselves of it. If we believe that higher education changes lives in countless positive ways, shouldn't our eye be sensitized to the bright, diverse citizens that we encounter who just might be underemployed and unfulfilled? Are we not being humanitarian when we make those who have seemingly been left out of the good life aware of the resources available on our campuses to help them improve their lot in life? By reaching out and inviting in those who see higher education as an ivory tower surrounded by a moat, aren't we heeding the call of John Dewey and other educators who viewed education as critical to fostering a more democratic society? We think so.

SUGGESTED READINGS

Covey, S. (1989). *The 7 Habits of Highly Effective People*. New York: Simon and Schuster.

Dunn, R., and S. Griggs, eds. (2000). *Practical Approaches to Using Learning Styles in Higher Education*. Westport, CT: Bergin and Garvey.

Felder, R. (1998). "How Students Learn, How Teachers Teach, and What Goes Wrong with the Process." Tomorrow's Professor Listserv, Message 51, Stanford University Learning Laboratory, http://sll.stanford.edu/projects/tomprof/newtomprof/postings/51.html.

Goleman, D. (1995). *Emotional Intelligence*. New York: Bantam.

Haugen, L. (2000). "Writing a Teaching Philosophy Statement." Tomorrow's Professor Listserv, Message 193, Stanford University Learning Laboratory, http://sll.stanford.edu/projects/tomprof/newtomprof/postings/193.html.

Kelly, C. (1997). "David Kolb: The Theory of Experiential Learning and ESL." *Internet TESL Journal* 3, no. 9.

APPENDIX 2.1

Teaching and Learning SWOT Analysis

Strengths	Weaknesses
Opportunities	**Threats**

APPENDIX 2.2

Personal Philosophy of Teaching and Learning (Example)

Beliefs about Students:
- Students should be held accountable for their own learning.
- Students have legitimate differences in their learning styles and other factors that influence their learning effectiveness.
- Students should come to class prepared to learn.
- Students should help others learn when possible and never infringe on anyone else's learning.
- Students should derive an array of rewards from learning.

Beliefs about Professors:
- Professors should be held accountable for facilitating learning in their students.
- Professors should be active participants in a learning community with colleagues.
- Professors should adapt their teaching styles to the learning styles of students.
- Professors should evaluate students' work according to consistently high standards.
- Professors should seek to regularly update and improve their teaching skills.

Beliefs about the Learning Environment:
- Expectations of the environment should be formed with input from students.
- The environment should be interactive and should validate diverse perspectives.
- The environment should protect the dignity of all its participants.
- A nonthreatening environment facilitates learning.

Beliefs about the Subject Matter:
- All disciplines recognized by the institution are worthy of study and, where appropriate, connections should be made between or among them.
- Content should be regularly examined for accuracy, currency, and appropriateness.

- The content of each course should dovetail with that of other courses in the curriculum.
- Course content should be driven by the needs of students and other stakeholders.
- Students' existing base in the subject matter should be assessed before teaching and factored into instructional practices.

Beliefs about Learning:
- Learning goals should be challenging yet achievable.
- Effective learning can occur in a wide variety of environments—in and out of school.
- No method of learning is effective for all students, all of the time.
- Appropriate, frequent feedback is essential to effective learning.
- All students are motivated to learn, but their motivations differ in nature.

APPENDIX 2.3

Teaching Style Self-Assessment

Directions: This instrument is designed to provide insights into your individual teaching style. For each of the following sections, indicate the priority of your decisions or actions relative to each factor, by allocating a total of 100 points among those identified.

My instructional planning is driven by:

____ 1. An accrediting association, department of education, or other external standards.

____ 2. Recommendations of the entire faculty within my department.

____ 3. My perceptions from past experiences of the needs of the class as a whole.

____ 4. My assessment of external stakeholders (e.g., employers or transfer institutions).

____ 5. Content of the course textbook and its ancillary materials.

____ 6. Students' individual characteristics, including their learning styles.

____ 7. My personal strengths, experiences, interests, and time availability.

____ 8. Other: _____.

100   TOTAL

My instructional delivery practices are driven by:

____ 9. Standard procedures agreed on by faculty within my department.

____ 10. My personal strengths and interests, including my learning style.

____ 11. The need to address the course material in the time allocated.

____ 12. The need to keep the class as a whole focused on course objectives.

____ 13. The characteristics of individual students in each section.

____ 14. The need to provide students with an enjoyable experience.

____ 15. How I have been taught as a student.

____ 16. Other: _____.

100   TOTAL

The instructional environment of my courses is driven by:

____ 17. The furniture, equipment, size, and other aspects of classrooms in which I teach.

____ 18. The needs of students to accommodate their abilities and learning styles.

___ **19.** My need to maintain control of the whole class.
___ **20.** My desire to maximize overall class outcomes (e.g., passing rates).
___ **21.** My desire to foster an accepting and enjoyable environment.
___ **22.** My desire to maximize learning for individual students.
___ **23.** Other: _____.
100   TOTAL

The process of evaluating student achievement within my courses is driven by:
___ **24.** Externally mandated standards (e.g., licensing exams, transfer requirements).
___ **25.** Practices agreed on by all faculty within my department.
___ **26.** My own time availability for developing and scoring assessments of student learning.
___ **27.** My own experiences as a student.
___ **28.** The need to defend grades to instructional leaders, students, and others.
___ **29.** My comfort level with alternative methods of assessment.
___ **30.** Other: _____.
100   TOTAL

Follow-Up:
Because of differences within disciplines, institutional missions, and other factors, there are no target scores on the factors within this self-evaluation. The value comes in pondering and writing a private response to each of the following questions—and perhaps others that might enter your own mind—then reviewing your responses with a trusted colleague now or revisiting your responses alone at an appropriate milepost in the future:

1. Does your instructional planning take into account all relevant perspectives?
2. In what ways might your instructional delivery practices become more effective?
3. How can you manage your instructional environment to increase student learning?
4. Do your evaluation methods improve the quality and quantity of student learning?
5. What preexisting perceptions did this exercise confirm?
6. What additional insights did this exercise provide?
7. What other specific changes might you consider making to improve student learning?
8. Who should be consulted in your decision making? Why?
9. How will you test your recommendations?

Today's College Students

FOCUS QUESTIONS

- What are the significant demographic changes among college students?
- How have perceptions toward attending college changed in the last generation?
- How should professors structure their teaching to meet the needs of today's students?
- How might knowledge of multiple intelligences and learning styles improve outcomes?

Most of today's professors attended college full-time shortly after completing high school, with cohorts largely similar to themselves. Sometimes they are baffled by how much students have changed. Over the last several decades, student populations at most colleges and universities have become increasingly diverse—in age, gender, ethnicity, working status, and other significant factors. To be successful, a faculty member must understand this new student population in terms not only of its demographic makeup but also of its social conditioning. This chapter will help you understand the dimensions of the increased diversity of undergraduate students and will suggest ways you can address varying student backgrounds, attitudes, and approaches to learning.

The Big Picture

According to data provided by the National Center for Educational Statistics (2001), enrollment at U.S. colleges and universities increased from 12.2 million in 1985 to 14.6 million in 1998, a 20 percent increase. The projected college enrollment in 2010 is 17.5 million, another increase of 20 percent. Much of this increase has been, and will continue to be, due to growing numbers of part-time students, who now constitute nearly half of the total college enrollment. By the end of the first decade of the new millennium, women are expected to constitute 58 percent of the total college-going population, continuing to be the majority gender, as they have been since the mid-1980s.

Although patterns of the latter part of the twentieth century reflected a huge increase in the number of older students going to college, this trend is expected to reverse somewhat through the early part of the twenty-first century. The number of students aged eighteen to twenty-four is expected to rise to 10.5 million by 2010 (an increase of 25 percent from 1998), and their proportion within the total college population to rise to 60 percent by 2010 (from its 1990 proportion of 50 percent). Even if these predictions prove to be true, there will still be a huge population of older students, especially among the ranks of part-timers. This situation is quite different from that which existed up through the early 1980s, when even the occasional twenty-two-year-old classmate seemed somewhat exotic. While there is a great deal of common ground between students of any age, it is critical for today's professors to understand some of the key differences between younger and older students.

In recent years, much has been written and spoken of a generational gulf—an inability or unwillingness of those in one generation to understand and value how those of markedly different ages perceive and react to the world. An ineffective professor will accept the gulf as a given, and such acceptance may contribute to the development of a fragmented classroom environment in which individuals work at cross-purposes. The enlightened professor will proactively manage the classroom so that, regardless of the course or discipline, students will learn to work cooperatively and, in the process, create a synergy that intensifies the class experience for both students and professor. Throughout the rest of this chapter, we will discuss the different "generations" of students that you are likely to see in your classrooms—usually all at the same time.

"Traditional" and "Nontraditional" Students versus Generations

Before we discuss the different generations you will see in your classrooms, let us define two common terms and explain why they may no longer apply. "Traditional" students are considered to be high school graduates who begin college at eighteen and finish at twenty-two, reside on campus, limit their work to on-campus positions, belong to campus-based social and political groups, and have yet to start families. "Nontraditional" students are those older than twenty-two, who typically reside off campus and work part-time or full-time to support themselves; these students may have already launched their chosen careers, started families, and begun to participate in the full array of adult activities.

Although, as noted above, many students still fall into the "traditional" category, they are not in the majority on many campuses. They are also nearly nonexistent in evening and weekend classes, and some campuses have none at all. Because the terms traditional and nontraditional are no longer as illuminating as they once were, in most of the discussion in this chapter we will speak instead of the generations of students that we are likely to see. We will make some generalizations about these generations, but let it be stated at the outset that these generalizations are just that—general—and are thus not meant to account for every student who fits into the age range of the particular generation being discussed.

The Generational Matrix

So that you can fully understand the critical issue of generations of students, take a moment to complete the exercise in Figure 3.1. You may not be familiar with the labels, but fill in the boxes to the best of your ability. While noting that demographers disagree somewhat on the beginning and ending dates of each generation, focus on the core issues that affected the way each of the three generations described in the figure came to perceive the world. Write as many *major* ideas in each box as you can. Keep in mind that an entry might not fall within the parameters of the birth years provided for the generation. For example, the youngest members of the Baby Boom Generation were born in 1961, but nearly every member was dramatically affected by a historical event that came to a head around 1967 and did not conclude until the mid-1970s.

After you have filled in the matrix, see what ideas a colleague, especially one from a generation other than your own, might contribute beyond what you have identified. After brainstorming as much key information as possible, compare your completed matrix to that in Appendix 3.1. (Note there that a final set of entries has been made on the ramifications for teaching each generation.) Be aware that there are likely to be honest differences of opinion on such issues as whether the women's movement had a greater impact on the Baby Boomers, or on Generation X. When we conducted this activity in a workshop with a group of new faculty (of varying ages), we observed what could only be called a "Grand Aha!" The matrix illuminates so much of why there are differences in ways of perceiving the world among the various generations. As these differences play themselves out in a diverse classroom, they can either inhibit or foster learning among students, depending on how the professor facilitates discussions.

The Baby Boom Generation

Many professors are well acquainted with the Baby Boom Generation—because this is the generation to which they belong. The baby boom began at the end of World War II, when those who had served in the armed forces returned home

	Baby Boom Generation Born between 1943 and 1961 Today's age range:	**Thirteenth Generation (Generation X)** Born between 1962 and 1981 Today's age range:	**Millennial Generation** Born between 1982 and 2000 Today's age range:
What historical events shaped the generation?			
What social dynamics influenced the generation?			
What technology had a bearing on the generation?			
What values are shared by the generation?			

FIGURE 3.1   Generational Matrix

and the United States entered into a period of postwar prosperity. Professors from this generation tended to be college students right after high school (or right after serving time in the armed forces during the Vietnam War). Going to college at age twenty is quite different from going to college at age forty-five or fifty, so even though Baby Boom Generation professors share many values with the students they have from this generation, they may find it challenging to identify with these students' life experiences.

Baby Boom students have seen their ranks grow dramatically in recent years, especially in the evening and weekend classes that faculty members are increasingly expected to teach. Many of these students have lost their jobs to the new economy; that is, they have been displaced by technology and/or have been unable to sustain an income that would enable them to provide adequately for their families. While a disproportionate number of evening students are single mothers, many others are single men, often also with children. A fair number of these students may be grandparents and may have full responsibility for their grandchildren, for one reason or another. Some of these students lack a support system, whereas others have in place a strong system of family and longtime friends. Although their employers might have a policy of supporting their education financially, their co-workers sometimes resent their leaving work early, or arriving late, to pursue their college education.

Older students who are attending college either after a long hiatus or for the very first time frequently doubt their ability to succeed. The other time-consuming challenges in their lives—children and family, aging parents, work, and civic and religious responsibilities—often prevent them from preparing adequately for class or from coming to class regularly. These students commonly display test anxiety, a lack of confidence in their writing and mathematics skills, and hesitancy in utilizing computers and other forms of technology.

On the upside, many older students somehow make it all work. Thirsty for the knowledge they did not get when they should have, they overcome the initial obstacles of attending college, achieve a measure of success, and become quite self-directed. They are motivated first to pass and then to achieve high grades. Older adult learners often become overachievers who will rewrite entire papers to gain an extra point or two. While younger students sometimes demand special privileges as their right, many older students will not ask for the smallest extra consideration (e.g., permission to turn in a project a few days late).

As their successes grow, older students often become highly motivated to serve as role models for their children or even grandchildren, who may be struggling in school. They often speak of posting their successful exams and assignments on the family refrigerator. Younger students often mask their disappointments behind a blank countenance, but older students tend to display their feelings openly on their faces or in their voices. Older students are far more likely to stay after class to share their frustrations with an empathetic instructor and/or to discuss stimulating concepts from the course material. In the process, it is not uncommon for them to develop emotional reliance, or even a crush, on the professor—a situation that requires careful handling.

Many older students learn best by doing—that is, by applying the theory of textbooks to the rich set of experiences they have accumulated over the years and to the reality of tomorrow at work. They have a great deal they want to share, and they will usually do so in a safe, informal environment. In the process, they make connections for themselves with the learning goals of the course—and for other students in the class who may not have anywhere near the experience that these older students do. Baby Boomers tend to be problem-centered, rather than content-centered, and will often lose focus with an instructor who is intent merely on getting through the material. Adult learners, recalling the classrooms of their childhood, tend to respond most effectively when the classroom environment is organized and relatively quiet, and when they perceive they have ready access to the instructor, even though they might not take advantage of that access.

Generation X

Students in the generation following that of the rebellious Boomers are staying close to home to attend college, while working full- or part-time. Many have been at least partially supporting themselves for several years and have accumulated significant debt due to tuition costs that have been rising at rates faster than the inflation rate or to the purchase of items that were once considered luxuries but are now seen as necessities for students (cars, electronic equipment, etc.).

Generation X students are more likely than students of previous generations to come from families that do not conform to the nuclear pattern (two parents, married, and two or more children at home). Their parents may have divorced one or more times, remarried, and/or formed blended families. Other students are the children of parents who have never been married. Such situations may have contributed to the stifling of psychological and academic development during the student's most formative years, residually affecting their college-age performance.

The Baby Boomer parents of students in this age bracket are likely to have been employed under the unsettling circumstances of downsizing and rightsizing and to have changed jobs and residences. As a result, Generation X children changed elementary and secondary schools far more often than was the custom a few decades before. Such students often exhibit socialization problems throughout their college years, isolating themselves, becoming medically depressed and sometimes turning to unhealthy lifestyles. Many Generation X students were "latchkey kids" and may have been entertained frequently by television programs and videos with violent and otherwise negative themes. Their parents, exhausted when they arrived home after working long hours and traveling an extended commute, often did not read to them nor provide coaching for homework assignments during their early years.

Likely to have worked part-time while in high school—often well past what most would consider reasonable hours—today's "twenty-to-thirty something" college students have not been as focused on school success as those of two decades ago. Because of their employment, they are less likely than their predecessors to have played organized sports or been involved in other constructive school activities. When they were barely old enough to drive an automobile, some even maintained their own households, frequently cohabitating with equally unsophisticated peers. They may have engaged in other adult experiences for which they were insufficiently prepared and have developed extensive coping mechanisms for dealing with the challenges of their lives. Without structure and consistently communicated standards, many Generation Xers have not developed the self-discipline typically associated with success in higher education.

From another perspective, Generation X students have grown up in a society largely influenced by consumerism, materialism, increased demands for individual rights, and decreased time horizons for nearly everything. One fast-food chain promised to deliver its products "your way"—a theme that has been replicated in thousands of advertising messages that have inundated the minds of students in this age bracket. Conditioned by Watergate, Three Mile Island, insider trading, and other high-profile business scandals, these students have developed cynicism and lack of respect for all authority figures—including, not surprisingly, college professors. Speaking spontaneously and angrily of the alleged misdeeds of others and lodging complaints—even lawsuits—have become common behaviors. Students of this generation are quick to proclaim their rights. Some perceive professors as service providers, class attendance as a matter of individual choice, and grades as "pay" to which they are entitled for meeting what they perceive to be reasonable standards.

A litany of reasons—including but certainly not limited to depersonalized schools, teacher-turnover rates, and overemphasis on standardized tests—have contributed to a less than effective primary and/or secondary education for many students. A large number of Generation X students began college and required remediation in reading, writing, and mathematics skills (U.S. Department of Education, 2000). Conditioned by the hours they have spent surfing through MTV and dozens of other cable channels, playing computer games, and enjoying instantaneous access to the entire world through the Internet and other widespread technology, these students often exhibit extremely short attention spans and an affinity for color and rapid movement—qualities difficult to re-create in many traditional classrooms. These students have heard themselves identified as members of Generation X and they perceive the outside world as disliking them or, perhaps even worse, being unwilling to invest the time to understand them. The results are boredom, negativity, and lowered academic expectations that exhibit themselves in the classroom.

Many college professors become frustrated when students of Generation X do not appear as responsible and appreciative as they remember students of their generation to be. However, investing quality effort only with those students who display more conservative, traditional values is not a prescription for achieving learning success. All educators have a responsibility to all students—and to the profession—to accept all students where they are and to guide them toward an outcome that our highest standards indicate is appropriate. As you will recall from Chapter 2, Stephen Covey, himself a professor and author of *The 7 Habits of Highly Effective People*, encourages us to "seek first to understand, then to be understood." To achieve success with Generation X students, professors must adopt this habit.

The Millennial Generation

There is a new generation beginning to grace the doors of colleges and universities—the Millennial Generation. Neil Howe and William Strauss, authors of *Millennials Rising: The Next Great Generation* (2000), have defined this generation as follows:

> As a group, Millennials are unlike any other youth generation in living memory. They are more numerous, more affluent, better educated, and more ethnically diverse. More important, they are beginning to manifest a wide array of positive social habits that older Americans no longer associate with youth, including a new focus on teamwork, achievement, modesty, and good conduct. (p. 4)

This generation, born between 1982 and 2000, is beginning to make their presence known in the college classroom. Most do not want to be lumped in with the Generation Xers, whom they find to be negative, cynical, unfocused, rule-breaking slackers. Millennials are very clear on how different they are, and they want to be recognized as such.

The children and young adults of this generation typically feel more wanted than those of any previous generation. Their parents may have gone to great lengths to conceive them, and they have heard the media broadcast the fact that the United States is now a child-centered society. From the chief executive to individual parents, we are seeing an unprecedented focus on children and what is good for them.

Some of this focus has resulted in a generation that has been supervised more closely, has spent more time with parents, and has done more things that are family-oriented than some state-of-the-family critics would have us believe. Compared to previous generations, Millennials are growing up with a better sense of self and of the possibilities for the future. The Millennial Generation is more optimistic, not only about the future of society but also about themselves and what they can achieve. This certainly has potentially positive ramifications for the college classroom.

Millennials entering the college arena have grown up in an era of increased academic standards and high-stakes testing. Many are signing up for advanced placement or other types of more intensive high school classes and are striving for high grades. In addition, students in this generation feel pressured about getting accepted to the college of their choice. We hear constantly about the amazing curriculum vitae that students have already compiled by the time they leave high school—and still are not admitted to their schools of choice because of the intense competition. So, depending on the college or university where you teach, you may have some students from this generation who are thrilled and thankful to be there—and others who feel they had to settle and therefore have a different attitude. (Leaders would be wise to be mindful of acceptance pressures as they admit their new classes—so that all students are given the sense that they are fortunate to have been chosen and that the institution is proud to have them.)

In addition to being the largest generation (potentially 100 million when new immigrants are counted), Millennials are the most ethnically diverse generation. African Americans, who up to now had constituted the largest minority population, have been surpassed in number by Latinos. While professors may see the college classroom as becoming more diverse, Millennials may not see anything unusual or different. Large numbers of students have grown up in schools and neighborhoods that were populated by more than one race, and significantly large numbers of Millennials are the result of unions between parents of more than one race.

As you prepare to teach increasing numbers of diverse students, be aware of the array of benefits that can arise from working in teams—an environment in which your students are likely to be comfortable. Millennials also want to know what the rules are—not so they can break them, but so they can follow them. These students are used to feeling pressure, which does not mean that they enjoy it, but they have experience with the drive that it takes to succeed. And, although it may seem to go without saying, integrating technology into your courses and your expectations for student work will be mandatory. This is the first generation that will use technology from cradle to grave. It is a natural part of their lives and what they do both with their free time and with their work time, so they would notice its absence far sooner than they would remark on its presence.

As with the other generations presented, the information offered here is general and certainly does not apply to every member of the generation. The themes are what we must attend to—and all signs point to some positive themes running through the Millennial Generation (Howe and Strauss, 2000).

Emerging Influences

Proactive faculty members must continuously seek to understand the perspectives of students, not only through research reports and talking with colleagues but also through listening intently and nonjudgmentally to individual students themselves. They need to identify well in advance any differences among students that might become evident in the classroom and influence learning. They also need to incorporate students' knowledge base into the richer environment that is created when more diverse perspectives are represented. Professors may be hired to teach a particular course, but their role may be more appropriately defined as creating an environment and providing appropriate stimuli for students to master a particular set of concepts, skills, and/or attitudes. The ultimate goal is to equip students to become their own lifelong teachers.

Besides the generation to which students belong, other factors have a significant impact on their perceptions of college and the way they prefer to learn. Today 25 percent of all undergraduate students are members of minority groups, a figure that has doubled in the last twenty years. The sharpest percentage growth in minority enrollment in recent years has occurred among Asian Americans, Hispanics, and Native Americans. While we might debate the merit of various initiatives that have fostered this increase, most would agree that our society becomes stronger when those previously left out of higher education now participate in greater numbers. In many metropolitan colleges and universities, recent immigrants are an especially significant student population. Professors must be sensitive to their students' ethnicity, language, religion, culture, and sexual orientation, for each of these factors influences students' learning paradigms. The successful professor views these differences as an opportunity rather than a threat.

Multiple Intelligences

Research of recent years tells us that there is not a single form of intelligence. When professors accept only the traditional definition of the word intelligence, they foster an atmosphere in which too many students are likely to fail. Seeking to broaden the scope of human potential beyond the traditional IQ score, Howard Gardner (1999), renowned for having developed the most well-known theory of multiple intelligences, defines *intelligence* as "a biopsychological potential to process information that can be activated in a cultural setting to solve problems or create products that are of value in a culture" (p. 34).

Gardner has challenged the validity of measuring intelligence by taking people out of their natural learning environments and asking them to complete isolated tasks they have never done before. His position that intelligence has more to do with solving problems and creating products in a context-rich environment has grown from his research, which now yields nine comprehensive categories, or what have come to be called intelligences:

- Verbal/linguistic intelligence—the capacity to use words effectively (think Toni Morrison). Students who possess this intelligence have generally been successful in school because their intelligence lends itself to traditional teaching.
- Logical/mathematical intelligence—the capacity to reason and to employ numbers effectively (think Alan Greenspan). In addition to the students who

possess high verbal/linguistic intelligence, the students in this group also tend to do well in traditional classrooms where teaching is logically sequenced and students are asked to conform.

- Visual/spatial intelligence—the ability to accurately manipulate mental representations of large or small spaces (think Chuck Yeager or Bobby Fischer). These learners like to see what is being talked about in order to understand.
- Bodily/kinesthetic intelligence—expertise in using the entire body to express ideas and feelings (think Ichiro Suzuki or Michelle Kwan). Through their constant movement and expressive body language these students often give the professor every indication of what sort of intelligence they possess.
- Musical intelligence—the capacity to perceive, discriminate, transform, and express musical forms effectively (think Yo-Yo Ma). These learners use patterns, rhythms, instruments, and musical expression to represent their world.
- Interpersonal intelligence—the ability to perceive and make distinctions in the moods, motivations, and feelings of other people (think Dr. Phil McGraw). These learners are noticeably people-oriented and outgoing and do well working in groups or with a partner.
- Intrapersonal—self-knowledge and the ability to act adaptively on the basis of that knowledge (think Meryl Streep). These learners may tend to be more reserved, but they are actually quite intuitive about what they learn and how it relates to them.
- Naturalist—recognizing patterns in the living world (think Charles Darwin). A student possessing the naturalist intelligence demonstrates an ease in identifying and classifying living things.
- Existentialist—a proclivity for asking the fundamental questions about life (think the Dalai Lama). This is Gardner's newest intelligence, and one that is likely to be more extensively explored in the coming decade. Those with the existentialist intelligence ask questions like "Why are we here?" and "What is our role in the world?"

It is likely that as you read through the brief descriptions listed above, you found yourself described by at least one—and it is also likely that you closely identified your academic field with one of the intelligences. For example, if you are an art professor, it would not be surprising if you believe that you possess visual/spatial intelligence and that your students (well, your best students) also possess this intelligence. Likewise, if you are working with graduate students who are preparing to be clinical psychologists, we hope you see evidence of both interpersonal and intrapersonal intelligence in them.

Some educators have taken the concept of multiple intelligences and made it into a cottage industry. A few have even promoted the teaching of every concept in a way that addresses all intelligence types, but Gardner himself has rejected such ideas. Our intention here is not to introduce you to a complex concept in an oversimplified way, but rather to alert you to the fact you will have students whose talents and problem-solving abilities support their learning in a variety of ways. Your students' talents and abilities may or may not be well suited to the content and style of your teaching. If not, then both you and your students must put forth more effort in order for them to learn.

In the traditional paradigm, students either possess intelligence or they lack it. In Gardner's paradigm, students have more of, or less of, a wider variety of intelligences. In the process of helping all students in your class approach their fullest potential, not by imposing preconceived limitations but by proactively soliciting their individual input into learning decisions that have an impact on them, both your job and your perception of the human development process will become far more rewarding.

Understanding generations and diversity of students, multiple intelligences, and individual learning styles will help you view each student as unique. Get to know each one of your students as well as you can: welcome and get to know them at the first class meeting, review their completed student profile, and require them to visit you during office hours. Throughout the term, build an ongoing dialogue with individual students that will enhance your insights and foster students' willingness to approach you. We believe you will usually experience markedly improved motivation and attention levels, which will translate later into improved retention and completion rates. One of the greatest rewards of teaching is allowing yourself to be sufficiently vulnerable so that you empower students to share their thoughts and feelings with you and with their peers. It is critical that you regularly assess your values and predispositions and that you share discussions with both veteran as well as new instructors. Their feedback can help you deepen your own understanding.

Common Problem Situations

Regardless of the demographic makeup of your institution's student body, you can consistently encourage self-direction and responsibility in all students. Our society seems to have instilled a sense of victimization among those who face challenges; such students will judge your standards and procedures accordingly. Be intellectually prepared and consistently willing to push students to turn out their best work. They may resist at first, but most will finish the term thanking you for helping them meet your high expectations.

Some students, especially those with low self-esteem or especially difficult histories, may challenge your best-intended words as discriminatory. Following the suggestions in Chapter 5 for proactively building your understanding of your students early in the course will help with problems that arise later on. It is critical that in preparing each class meeting you think through your words on topics related to sex, race, politics, or any other potentially sensitive area. Doing so can help you prevent challenges or meet any that are raised. Common problems you can expect from students are tardiness, absenteeism, test anxiety, and lack of focus. Rather than becoming upset and taking punitive action, you should plan for these situations and build solutions into the design of your course. You can minimize the disruptions caused by tardy entry into your classroom, for example, by reserving a section of the room for late arrivers. Should you find several weeks into the course that the overwhelming majority of your students come in late, you might enlist the class's help in finding solutions that will allow everyone to experience the class fully and achieve the learning objectives.

We believe that when the professor makes a concerted effort to foster a learning relationship with each student early in the term (see strategies in Chapter 5) and establishes an effective learning environment, absences, motivation problems, inappropriate behavior, and other such problems will largely take care of themselves. Retention will improve incrementally. While there will always be a handful of students whose behavior is inconsistent with your acceptable standards, it is critical not to punish the entire group because of the actions of a few. The key is to uncover the root cause by listening actively. You can then address the problem in an objective, frank manner that preserves the dignity of the student. As in most other arenas of life, ignoring the problem and hoping it will fix itself can only lead to unsatisfactory results. From the first class meeting, it is critical to demonstrate structure, establish your standards, reinforce those standards through consistent behavior, and take action promptly when warranted (McKeachie, 2001).

In an age of accountability, each professor is obligated to adopt a proactive posture toward potential extreme behavior than was previously required. Triggered by some of the factors identified in the discussion of generations earlier in the chapter, a very small minority of students may encounter emotional challenges, abuse substances, commit crimes, or even contemplate suicide. Become familiar with your campus resources so that when a student divulges troubling information during an office visit, you are able to make an informed referral. Use the student profile forms you collected in the beginning to track patterns of behavior in case you need to refer to them later.

What Students Want from College Instructors

Although each student subgroup has particular characteristics that affect the dynamics of a college learning environment, what students need from their college instructors is fairly consistent among all groups and types. Students want instructors to:

- Know them and care about them.
- Give clear, consistent expectations of student performance that are reasonable in quantity and quality.
- Be sensitive to the diverse demands on students and be flexible in accommodating them.
- Use class time effectively.

- Create a classroom environment that values student input into decisions and dialogue and protects their dignity.
- Present a classroom demeanor that includes humor and spontaneity.
- Design assessments that are clearly tied to the information addressed in class, appropriate to the level of the majority of students in the class, punctually graded and returned, and used fairly to determine final class grades.
- Consistently show positive treatment of individual students, which includes being willing to spend extra time prior to or following class meetings to provide additional support as needed.

In *Making the Most of College: Students Speak Their Minds* (2001), Richard Light reports students believe that they:

- Learn through extracurricular activities (participation should be encouraged by professors).
- Learn more in classes that are highly structured, with many and frequent assessment activities.
- Are more successful in their homework when they study with others rather than alone.
- Benefit markedly from mentoring opportunities with faculty.
- Learn much from their diverse peers when activities are effectively orchestrated.
- Benefit most when they are taught to manage their time to include opportunities for interaction focused on academic pursuits.
- Care about becoming better writers.
- Benefit from coaching in study skills.
- Are especially enthusiastic about literature and foreign-language study.

While perhaps surprising in many ways, these findings show that professors can have a rich impact on the lives of today's students—students who not only have high expectations but who are also willing to invest of themselves to receive the fullest possible benefits from their college experiences.

Students with Special Needs

One of the most drastic changes on college and university campuses in recent years has been the influx of those with physical, mental, or psychological disabilities. Like other minority groups, students with disabilities (and their families) have become quite politically active and assertive—expecting the educational community to more fully address their specific needs. Professors would do well to accommodate such reasonable requests. (Note: Generally, there is an office of support for students with disabilities on campus. Those who work in these offices can offer instructors counsel and suggestions.)

New state and federal laws require postsecondary institutions to adopt policies that will guarantee all students who disclose their disabilities full access to educational resources. Since these provisions have the backing of the courts, you must ensure that accomodations are made for any students in your classes who have disclosed special needs.

There are several ways to determine what special needs students might have. Like a growing number of institutions, the University of Nevada, Reno, now requires all course syllabi to contain some version of the following statement:

> Each student who qualifies with a disability is to provide the instructor with a letter from the Disability Resource Center on campus stating the appropriate accommodations for this course. If you have a documented disability and wish to discuss how these academic accommodations will be implemented for this course, please contact the instructor as soon as possible.

Even if you have not been told to use such a statement in your course syllabi, it would be prudent to find out if you are required to include one and, if so, what the proper wording is. Even if there is not a requirement, however, we believe it is incumbent on you as a responsible faculty member to add such a statement to your syllabi and then to make every effort to accommodate students who respond.

Using a student profile form will allow students to share their needs with you privately. Asking the students to talk to you about their challenges during their initial office visit will help you organize learning materials to accommodate their needs. For example, one of the authors of this book had a class in which there were two students with special needs. Lydia was legally blind, having only one functioning eye, which she used to read magnified text. Although she was quite adept at using the computer, she frequently needed extra time to complete in-class examinations and other written work because it took her longer than her classmates to proofread her responses. Lydia used "readers" (peer volunteers) to help her get through the massive amounts of required reading for the class. Several accommodations were made for Lydia, including:

- Reproducing print materials in large-size type and sending them to her as e-mail attachments. Thus, Lydia could enlarge materials further if necessary and was not subject to scrutiny from her peers.
- Making an extra copy of all transparencies used in class lectures so that Lydia could enlarge and review them at home.
- Producing a copy of all examinations in large-size print and allowing Lydia to use her laptop with accompanied magnifier to answer the questions. Following consultation with the professor, Lydia was given additional time to complete examinations.

- Announcing to the class, with Lydia's permission, that Lydia had lost one of her readers and could not locate another. Several students volunteered to help.

Natasha was another special-needs student; she had a neurological problem that affected her muscles. She could not sit in one position for longer than fifteen or twenty minutes, and her hands would get sore if she tried to take notes for too long. At times, she had massive muscular spasms and needed to lie down to relieve the pain. Accommodations for Natasha were relatively simple:

- She brought a lounge chair to class that was set up in the back of the room, away from the main traffic flow. She took a seat on an aisle in the class, but after fifteen to twenty minutes she would move to the lounge chair and stretch out. During the three-hour class sessions, she would rotate between a regular seat, the lounge chair, and standing.
- She recorded the lectures and other classroom activities on audiotape and supplemented these recordings with notes she could take. Other students shared their notes with her.
- Because of her inability to sit for extended periods, Natasha was given additional time to complete in-class examinations. Although she never asked for more time for out-of-class assignments, it was rather common knowledge that she required longer to complete assignments than did other students, except perhaps for Lydia.

Accommodating both Lydia and Natasha was not difficult. Fellow students understood the accommodations and volunteered to help any way they could. They were particularly helpful during group presentations, making sure that these two young women had roles that they could fulfill without undue hardship. Both of these students had excellent verbal communication skills and often were central to the presentations; other students provided visual aids and supplementary resources that fostered the learning of all. Rather than being a hardship, accommodating these students was a rich learning opportunity for the rest of the class.

While we typically think in terms of teaching accounting, world religions, or some other course or of teaching night students, athletes, or some other group, those professors who derive the greatest reward from their teaching careers, and demonstrate the greatest accountability to diverse stakeholders, have adopted a different paradigm. They see their classrooms as mosaics made up of individuals—each with a unique background of academic, occupational, family, social, economic, military, recreational, and other categories of experiences. Such teachers are energized by students who are "in the dark" because they relish the challenge of helping these students "turn on the light." Such professors view differences of opinions as adding depth to the classroom rather than challenging their authority. They view themselves as facilitators of learning rather than "sages on the stage."

Summary of Key Points

- Today's college students are far more likely to be older and part-time than those of previous times.
- For very understandable reasons, many Generation X college students lack self-discipline and academic foundation.
- The newest generation of college students (the Millennials) are more eager to learn, to engage, and to make a difference.
- Students of whatever age or generation have challenges, issues, and constraints that affect their level of involvement in college.
- The concept of multiple intelligences is worth further study because it helps make professors more sensitive to the variety of ways in which students process information.
- More and more students with disabilities are enrolling in college. Professors have a responsibility to support their learning in appropriate ways.
- Professors should anticipate common student success problems prior to the class and design solutions into the course.

Through the Professors' Eyes

KIM: After meeting two of my classes, I am so excited about the term ahead! My students know so much from their employment and other experiences. One had even been a missionary in my home country. Some of my students are several years older than I am, and sometimes they intimidate me. I know that should not be so, and I will work to overcome it. I like the fact that most of my students are technologically astute; that will make it easier for me. I want to integrate technology into my classes, making it possible to shift the focus of the class away from my lack of command of English. The Web makes it so easy for me to find sources to use in my classes, and I think the students I have met so far will respond well. Dr. Zhang called me today, and we are having lunch tomorrow to discuss a possible mentoring relationship.

DALE: This generation of students is a real trip. They expect me to make all of the adjustments because they lead such busy lives! What they really need to do is prioritize their lives. Their education should be their number one priority and everything else should take a backseat. So many of the students put education at the bottom of their list of priorities and then complain when the work gets too heavy or too hard. I don't have much patience with their whining. They need to learn how to work harder and smarter, and then everything would be okay. I see no need to change my expectations or ways of teaching.

PAT: While today's generation of students is very different from the young people I taught early on in my career, I certainly don't believe they're less bright. Students have so many more obligations and pressures than those of three decades ago, many of which, like families spread all over the world, they didn't ask for. In one class, I have a large number of thirty-somethings who are juggling work, parenting, and school. I also have a few older students who are upgrading their careers, and five special-needs students. One is in a wheelchair, three have various learning disabilities, and one is deaf. Wow! When I was in graduate school, we marched for civil rights in our society, but having these students who used to be so marginalized from society is a different kind of civil rights story! I am not always sure how to accommodate these special students' needs without altering my expectations for them. I don't think I should make my classes easy, but I need to think about how to adjust assignments to challenge and provide meaningful learning opportunities for students, without overburdening their time. I really need to think more about the diversity that exists in my classes and use it as a learning resource. I truly want to meet their needs, but I don't want to compromise my standards. There's an old story about what poor students today's young people are that is attributed to Socrates, so it seems that every generation has bemoaned the quality of its students. I'm afraid that when we say we can't teach them, we're creating a self-fulfilling prophecy that blocks us from being as proactive as we should be.

Tips for Thriving

The most effective facilitators of learning discovered long ago the value of feedback to individual students. The qualities of feedback that enable the most marginal students to thrive are FAST—Frequent, Accurate, Specific, and Timely. As will be discussed in Chapter 9, technology can be an especially useful tool to achieve frequency and timeliness, as can more proactive emotional intelligence applied in the classroom. Accuracy and specificity require early progress on Covey's Habit 5—Seek first to understand, then to be understood—which can be developed through extensive review of information provided on individual student profile forms and individual conferences early in the term. Our experience shows that professors who provide FAST feedback—using an array of high tech-and high-touch methods—develop a natural attraction for students that solves most any recruitment problems for subsequent terms and achieves student retention and course completion goals far above the norm for their departments.

SUGGESTED READINGS

Gardner, H. (1999). *Intelligence Reframed: Multiple Intelligences for the 21st Century.* New York: Basic Books.

Howe, N., and W. Strauss. (2000). *Millennials Rising: The Next Great Generation.* New York: Vintage.

Light, R. J. (2001). *Making the Most of College: Students Speak Their Minds.* Cambridge, MA: Harvard University Press.

APPENDIX 3.1

Generational Matrix, Completed

	Baby Boom Generation	Thirteenth Generation (Generation X)	Millennial Generation
	Born between 1943 and 1961	Born between 1962 and 1981	Born between 1982 and 2000
What historical events shaped the generation?	GI Bill Korean and Cold Wars Launch of Sputnik, NDEA Cuban missile crisis Vietnam War Assassinations of JFK, RFK, MLK, Malcolm X, John Lennon Antiwar movement Civil rights movement Woodstock Man landed on moon Women's movement	Fall of Communism AIDS epidemic *Challenger* explosion Wedding of Charles and Diana Stock market downturn (1987) Desert Storm Princess Diana's death	Oklahoma City bombing Columbine massacre Extended economic prosperity War in Kosovo Clinton scandal, impeachment O. J. Simpson trial Rodney King riots Terrorist attack on World Trade Center and Pentagon, and aftermath
What social dynamics influenced the generation?	2–3 children per family Families moved away from small towns and big cities, but revisited often Beginning of suburbia Mom's outside work provided supplemental income Illicit drug use Neighborhood schools School consolidation Interstate highways	1–2 children per family Divorce reached 50 percent Child custody issues Mom's outside work provided essential family income Latchkey children common Blended families Single heads of households Rise of European Union and Pacific Rim economies Downsizing of corporations	1 planned child per family Parents protect, plan children's futures (soccer moms) Grew up with integrated schools, metal detectors Falling divorce, abortion, child abuse, and crime rates Prolonged economic boom

	Baby Boom Generation Born between 1943 and 1961	Thirteenth Generation (Generation X) Born between 1962 and 1981	Millennial Generation Born between 1982 and 2000
What technology had a bearing on the generation?	Automobile The Pill Mainframe computers Black-and-white television in most homes Plastics Shopping malls	Calculators, transistors Computer games Color, cable television in child's room Push-button telephones	Personal computers The Internet Multichannel television Remote control Beepers and cellular phones Nintendo
What values are shared by the generation?	Rebellious Challenge status quo Get on with changes Question authority	Disconnected Fragmented Freelancers Importance of education and training Delayed emotional development	Values-conscious Team-oriented Increasing respect for authority
Ramifications for teaching members of the generation?	Provide latitude in assignments that foster personal benefits Provide well-supported positions during discussions Encourage reworking of assignments for higher grade	Provide lots of structure and support Limit lecture time to twenty-minute segments Increase use of visual aids "Sell" personal benefits of course and assignments	Infuse technology into instruction Use team-based methods of instruction Provide opportunities for "service learning" Reinforce ethics and professional standards

Source: Adapted from Neil Howe and William Strauss, *Millennials Rising* (New York: Vintage, 2000).

4 Strategic Course Planning

FOCUS QUESTIONS

- How do you design quality into the courses you will teach?
- Why is the syllabus critical to the success of your course?
- What elements and characteristics should an effective syllabus possess?
- What resources should you consider incorporating into your course design?

One of the primary themes threaded throughout this book is that accountability requires professors to think more strategically than ever before about their teaching and the learning they intend to foster. Teaching strategically means that there is a plan and a customized design for ensuring that students meet specific, valid learning objectives. It means that each professor's courses coordinate with others within a specific curriculum to eliminate gaps and minimize overlaps. The goal is to design and build quality and accountability into each course and degree program, not to have it "inspected in" after the fact by those with a less grounded understanding of effective education. Within this and subsequent chapters, we will employ the following three definitions:

1. *Strategic teaching*: instruction that is deliberately and intentionally designed to achieve a particular effect or learning goal. Although students can (and do) learn through serendipitous experiences in the classroom, they learn more, and more of what professors want them to learn, when professors have carefully considered the desired learning outcomes and then have deliberately planned instruction so that these learning outcomes are achieved. Strategic teaching will increase student achievement in the classroom.

2. *Strategic learning*: learning that is deliberate and conscious. Students who are strategic learners are mindful of their strengths and weaknesses as learners and of what they must do to be effective and efficient during the learning process. Professors can expedite students' learning by making sure that they know *how to learn* and are *intentional* in their learning. Ensuring that students are strategic learners will serve them while they are in college as well as throughout the rest of their lives.

3. *Strategic course planning*: course planning that is deliberate, intentional, and considered, with the overall objective being to ensure student learning. Strategic course planners focus on their destination and then determine how to get all students there efficiently and effectively.

In this chapter, we will concentrate on ways to design a course so that your students learn what you want them to learn and so that the experience is positive and successful for everyone.

Designing an Effective Course

Your role in actual course design might vary between two extremes. If yours is a standard lower-division course, your department might already have designated an outline, a syllabus, a textbook, and course materials and activities that you are expected to use so that all students are equally prepared for advanced courses. If this is the case, you may be required to do little more than embellish the course material with your personal experiences and insights. More likely, however, as a recognized expert in your field, you will be asked to design and manage all aspects of courses that you are especially qualified to teach. The demands of designing a course from scratch may be daunting, but the rewards can be substantial. Between these extremes is a whole continuum of possibilities. Regardless of your position on this continuum, you must understand the basic processes of course design, since the design you choose may have a long-term impact on students.

The following sections describe items that should go into most course syllabi. As you read each section, we encourage you to apply the suggestions to an upcoming course you must plan. Note, however, that although we have laid out these suggestions as if they occur as a series of steps, strategic course planning is actually quite recursive. One does not move linearly from step to step to step, but rather from one step to another, then back to a previous step, then forward, then back, and so on until all the elements coalesce into a comprehensive whole, driven and supported by sound instructional objectives. The essence of strategic planning is making sure that there is consistency between and among the various components of the course and its syllabus.

At this point, you might want to get a legal pad, a pen or pencil, materials that will enable you to flag key sections, and a copy of your institution's or department's catalog. If you prefer, you might also want to sit at your computer as we review each element of your strategic course planning.

1. Title

First identify the official name of the course, so that you remain focused in your planning. Remember, strategic course planning involves identifying a target and then considering potential tactics for reaching that target.

2. Official Catalog Description

Write out the catalog description of the course. It may be worded exactly as you would have written it (maybe you did write it), or it may no longer match what the course is conceived to be. Either way, you need to know what the catalog says, and you should provide the catalog description in your syllabus. If there is a perfect match between the catalog wording and your concept of the course, fine. If not, then either adjust your plan for what you are going to teach or tell students that there has been a shift in focus, and why.

3. Your Description

Most college or university catalogs wisely limit the number of words that can be used in the official course description. Even if you are planning to teach exactly what the catalog description says, expand that description so that it no longer sounds like a telegram. Use words that your students will easily understand. In a succinct paragraph, identify the nature and overall goals of the course. While primarily for the benefit of students, this tactic also helps you stay focused on your target in planning and teaching the course.

4. Purpose

You may eventually fold the purpose of the course in with its description, but at this point specify (again, for students and for yourself) the purpose on its own. Is the purpose to build writing skills? To enhance critical thinking? To explore career options in the health professions? To learn methods of teaching mathematics? The possibilities are endless, of course, but in a sentence or two, tell why this course is being taught. You may find this easy to do or you may find it difficult, but either way, invest the time to do it.

5. Prerequisites, Co-requisites, and Other Requirements

Often the information on prerequisites and other such requirements is listed in the catalog. If so, find out if it is valid. Were the prerequisites decided years ago and no one has since paid attention? Or are these valid, rigid requirements that you will need to enforce? Also, can you assume that the prerequisites give a particular knowledge base? (Note: This assumption—a dangerous one—will be addressed in Chapter 7.) If this information is not readily available, ask a knowledgeable person within your department. It is better to know ahead of time whether you can count on (and/or must police for) prerequisites.

If your course has official prerequisites, identify their names and call numbers. Avoid adding prerequisites that may frustrate potential students and limit the enrollment in your course. It is unlikely that increasingly cost-conscious administrators or other stakeholders will support such a tactic. Contemporary educators view this section of their course description as a tool for helping students make informed decisions on whether their enrollment is likely to lead to success.

In addition to traditional prerequisites, are there any other requirements or necessary preconditions for this course? For example, must students already be admitted to a particular program? Are they expected to have their graduate committee formed prior to enrollment in this class? Do they need to be enrolled in another course (a co-requisite) while they are in yours? Strategic professors know the answers to these questions, and they make sure their students know the answers too.

6. Description of the Students

Your work on the preceding issues should enable you to identify what kinds of students will likely enroll in your course. If you have taught the course before, you may be right on target with your description. If not, you may or may not be able to predict who your students will be. Either way, you should write a description of students who have enrolled in the course and add it to the syllabus so that prospective students will know whether they "match" the criteria.

7. Goals and Objectives

Identifying course learning objectives is one of the most difficult yet necessary aspects of strategic course planning. Typically, students are not as attentive to the course goals and objectives as you might wish them to be. However, that fact should not diminish your commitment to this core process of strategic teaching.

For the aims of this chapter, we define goals as "the broad purposes toward which your teaching is directed." Objectives are defined as "the more specific learning outcomes you are seeking." Although there are some who use these terms interchangeably, we think there is value in thinking about them separately.

Write down one to five goals you have for your class, remembering to think broadly. Complete this sentence: "As a result of being participating members of my class this semester, students will _____." Examples might be "develop an appreciation for poetry," "realize that accounting is not just about numbers," "develop a sense that they are capable of speaking in public more effectively than they thought they were," or "find out whether they are suitable for work in a hospital setting." Strategic course planning requires an understanding of the three domains of learning: (1) the *psychomotor domain*, which includes physical skills and dexterity; (2) the *affective domain*, which includes attitudes, character issues, appreciation of beauty, and the like; and (3) the *cognitive domain*, which includes the thought processes. Your course may or may not have goals or objectives in all three, but it is likely to have at least some within the cognitive domain.

While you may identify only a few goals for your class, you will probably have many objectives. You may have from one to five (or even more) objectives for each main topic that you will address. The stem sentence for writing your objectives is very similar to the one given to help you write your goals. But there is one difference—the addition of the phrase "be able to," which yields a useful abbreviation in setting objectives: "As a result of being a participating member in my class this semester, *students will be able to (SWBAT)*_____."

Whatever you put in the blank must be a measurable activity or ability. A professor of a management course may write: "As a result of being participating members of my class this semester, students will be able to design a business plan for a small business that is suitable for presentation to bank officers." That professor would be able to measure whether or not individual students have written such a plan (or were making progress toward writing it). Knowing that this is one of the objectives of the course, the professor would continue the course plan accordingly. This is the "strategic" aspect of planning.

Before you begin to formulate your objectives, think about the levels of learning that you will expect of your students. The most widely accepted system of learning objectives was formulated by Benjamin Bloom (1956) and his colleagues at the University of Chicago. Their "taxonomy of educational objectives for the cognitive domain" (more popularly, "Bloom's taxonomy") delineates six levels of cognitive complexity, ranging from the *knowledge level* (lowest) to the *evaluation level*. Figure 4.1 depicts the taxonomy and some common behavioral words for each level. Take a few minutes to write some objectives for the course on which you are focusing, using SWBAT, followed by a behavior that is measurable.

1. SWBAT_____
2. SWBAT_____
3. SWBAT_____

8. Schedule

At this point in your course planning, it is helpful to at least think about what you will do on a week-to-week basis, even if you do not yet know how often or at what times your class will meet. It might be useful to take some individual pieces of paper and number them according to the number of weeks in your term, or to create the same number of pages in your electronic file.

Review your course objectives and begin to think about their logical sequence. That is, what should be taught first, second, third, and so on, and why? The objectives may display a discernible pattern that allows you to identify the

Evaluation
assess
defend
evaluate
predict
recommend
support

Synthesis
compose
create
design
formulate
plan

Analysis
analyze
appraise
categorize
compare
contrast
differentiate

Application
apply
demonstrate
illustrate
sketch
solve
use

Comprehension
arrange
classify
discuss
explain
interpret
sort

Knowledge
define
describe
identify
list
name
recall

Usage Guidelines:
1. Assess; then start where the learner is.
2. Set achievable learning objectives.
3. Move learning upward systematically.
4. Evaluate students at a level no higher than that at which instruction is delivered.

FIGURE 4.1   Bloom's Taxonomy of Cognitive Objectives

topic you want to address in each particular class period. To be most strategic, you should write in the objectives on the pages you numbered for each week. Keep these pages handy because you will need them as you work through upcoming portions of this chapter.

9. Textbooks, Course Packs, and Other Resources

Consider dedicating a shelf, file drawer, or storage crate to resources for each course (e.g., texts, journal articles, notes for ideas, handbooks, software). As you proceed with your detailed course planning and your individual class sessions, you can use this resource collection to finalize your planning. It also makes sense to set up a file in your computer for pertinent materials and Web addresses that you have identified for potential use.

Many colleges or universities expect professors to choose, or adopt, textbooks for their own particular sections of a course, while other institutions embrace a universal adoption for all sections of the same course. If your department has already chosen a book (with or without your input), then get that book out now and skip ahead to step 10, Possible Assignments and Activities. If you must make a decision about what textbook to use, the following can help:

1. Contact several textbook representatives, tell them the topic of the course for which you need to select a book, and request that examination copies be sent.
2. Once the review copies have arrived, determine whether the books are in their first edition or a subsequent edition, and whether this makes a difference for your course. Sometimes a new book will be the most fresh and appropriate one for your course but might contain some unresolved glitches; other times, a tried-and-true book will be the superior one for your purposes. Either way, in most cases, only the most current books should be considered.
3. Begin looking at the various books' tables of contents. How well do the topics seem to match up with what you plan to be teaching? The order does not have to be the same, but there should be a reasonable correspondence between your topics and the topics in the book.
4. Next, choose one or two particularly difficult concepts that you teach and find the explanations of those concepts in the textbooks you are still considering. Keep going through this process until you are satisfied that the book you are choosing does an excellent job of elucidating key concepts for your students.
5. Appraise all aspects of the book from a student's point of view. Remember that you are choosing the book for student use.

Once you have reached a decision, work through the following ideas:

1. Review the textbook as thoroughly as possible. Decide which chapters or sections you want to use. If you ask students to purchase a particular textbook, plan to use a significant portion of it. In this day of textbooks that cost a hundred dollars or more, students expect to get their money's worth from their purchases. If they buy a book and then find that the professor is using only a small portion of it, they rightfully feel cheated. Also, students will expect to have specific

assignments related to their reading; telling students to "just read along in the text for background" will signal to them that reading the book is not vital. You should present the book and clarify your expectations regarding the reading at your first class meeting. This step is more thoroughly addressed in Chapter 5.

2. After deciding which parts of the book to use, begin to match each reading selection with a particular week. Decide whether you want students to have read the material beforehand or whether you want them to wait until you have introduced the material in class first. Begin adding this information to your syllabus.

3. Formulate a strategy for how students will be held accountable for the reading. We will offer myriad possibilities in Chapters 7 and 8, but at this juncture start to think about whether a chapter lends itself well to a quiz, to a structured discussion, to a linked activity, and so on.

In recent years, many professors have created "course packs," or collections of instructor-developed materials and/or articles from journals and other sources that are more current or more detailed than the typical textbook. Creating a course pack involves making selections and securing permission to reproduce the items for students. To save time, you may use the services of a company that specializes in securing permissions, preparing documents, and printing and binding course packs. While course packs might be more expensive or narrower in scope than textbooks, they have potential benefits as well. Whether you have an extensive course pack of readings and learning activities for your students or not, it is highly likely you will want to use some supplementary materials. Begin developing a file of these materials.

In the section of your syllabus labeled "Readings," be sure to give all the information that students might need to locate and purchase materials. If you reserve readings in the library, include critical information about the policies and procedures of the library reading room. When you assign additional readings, provide students with a brief rationale (e.g., currency of information, special help with a difficult topic) for their selection.

10. Possible Assignments and Activities

Once you have identified your course goals and objectives, you can begin to design assignments and activities. One way we have found to do strategic course planning is to write down different ideas for assignments on separate Post-it notes and attach these to the numbered pages we have set up or to appropriate pages in the textbook. This allows for easy rearrangement of the ideas. You may also just type your ideas into the computer in a list, but actual or electronic Post-it notes are even easier to move around than text is. Whatever medium you choose, be sure to look back occasionally at your course goals and objectives.

Much more information on creating good assignments and classroom activities and learning experiences will be included in Chapters 7 and 8. For now, label a portion of your syllabus "Assignments" and be ready to come back to it after finishing more of this book (remember, the strategic planning process is recursive).

11. Assessments

Having written your objectives in measurable terms, you should design your assessments to match. The saying "What gets measured gets done" applies to crafting a course. Students assume that a concept that goes unmeasured must not be very important and therefore is not worth learning. If they do spend time learning information and never feel the learning is assessed, they will likely complain about this on the end-of-term instructor evaluations. It is not enough for you to say, "Well, someday you'll be glad you learned this, but I'm not going to assess it now." In the consumer-oriented environment in which we live, both real and perceived values count.

If you are new to teaching the course, you may want to ask colleagues to show you course examinations or other materials they have used with success. Most professors work well from models, and reinventing the wheel is inefficient. Besides saving you time, seeing your colleagues' assessment materials will also enable you to better gauge the level of your evaluation practices. Some people will be quite willing to share when asked, and will feel complimented by your request. Others, of course, may be more protective of what they have created, so respect their right to say no. Be sure to say thanks to those who help you, and to indicate your willingness to reciprocate. Chapters 10 and 11 provide numerous additional pointers on assessment practices.

12. Speakers/Guest Lecturers

If through the SWOT analysis you performed in Chapter 2, or some other means, you become aware of a weakness you have with regard to your course, you might consider having colleagues, community members, or students contribute their expertise. List their names and how you see them contributing (e.g., speaker for an hour, panel discussant, small group facilitator). In reaching your decision, consider whether the potential speaker will contribute meaningfully to the achievement of course goals and objectives; if a speaker just fills time, students will rightly perceive that time as a waste.

Invite your chosen speakers early so that they have enough time to respond. Once a particular speaker has accepted your invitation, add the name, date, and topic to the syllabus. Having several guest speakers during a term adds value to your course in students' eyes. See Chapter 7 for additional details on managing a class presentation by a guest speaker.

13. Classroom Learning Experiences

As you look over your goals and objectives, think about what learning experiences you want to offer your students. Are there potentially pertinent field trips?

What experiments or role-playing activities would enrich students' understanding of critical concepts? What videos or interactive Web sites would enliven their learning experience? How about small-group activities? Are student presentations appropriate for achieving synthesis and evaluation objectives? Many ideas for this section will be presented in Chapters 7 and 8; for now, just list ideas that come to you as you peruse your goals and objectives. You may also consider learning experiences that your professors employed when you were a student, as well as ideas that you have learned about at conferences or workshops.

14. Description of Yourself as a Teacher

When you were in college, you and your classmates probably exchanged information about professors as you tried to decide which courses to take. We think you would agree that expending energy on the class content is more profitable to students than using it to figure out the professor. So, in your syllabus, provide a short autobiographical statement that provides students some insight into your teaching style, beliefs, biases, and expectations.

Describing yourself also helps to establish your credibility. Emphasize achievements that the particular students in this course are likely to value. You can write the bio in narrative form or in bulleted points. Fill in some details during the first class meeting, and reveal others gradually throughout the term.

15. Communication Channels

Students will need to communicate with you in ways that fit their individual styles and schedules. What communication channels do you prefer? Do you want students to drop by during posted office hours? To call you on your office phone? To leave you voice-mail messages? To send you e-mail? Tell students how to contact you and what kind of response they can expect. Do you get back to students within twenty-four hours of their leaving a voice-mail or an e-mail message? Do you have obligations throughout the day and therefore need your students' evening phone numbers? Are you more responsive to seeing things in print than you are to hearing them? Generally, if you will tell students what works for you, they will try to comply. E-mail has helped many students feel more connected to their professors in part because it allows them to get questions answered rapidly.

16. Additional Catalog Information

You need to be reasonably familiar with information from your institution's catalog that may have an impact on the students in your course. Many instructors have found it helpful to include such key information as support for students with disabilities, academic dishonesty policy, procedures for withdrawal from the course or the university, and pass/fail options. While it is not necessary to reprint long portions of the catalog, it is worthwhile to include selected excerpts, with references to where students can go for additional information or clarification. Such practices not only provide information but also encourage students to become more aware of resources that enable them to become more self-directed.

17. Attendance Requirements

You should decide on your classroom attendance policy only after thorough research. Your own policy must be in line with the college and department policies, if any exist, as well as the common practices of the other faculty members. Students receiving scholarships and grants or participating in work-study programs may have attendance requirements that differ from those of other students; therefore, you need to be fully aware of guidelines set forth by your institution's financial aid department. You also should consider your students' lifestyles, which might be quite hectic, as well as your own values. The important thing is to set forth your attendance requirements in language that is as specific as possible without completely taking away your flexibility. It is difficult to defend a punitive action against excessive absences if that action is not spelled out succinctly on the course syllabus.

Given our collective experience and the recommendations of faculty from around the country, we recommend that you have attendance policies spelled out as clearly as possible right from the beginning. Consider the answers to these questions: Is attendance required or expected? Do you want excuses or reasons when students are absent? Will those excuses or reasons make any difference to you as far as penalties are concerned? Do you want to be notified when students know ahead of time that they will be absent? If so, how should they notify you? Are students allowed to make up for missed time? If so, how? Do a certain number of absences call for a lowered grade? What is your philosophy about late arrivals? Should students who are late slip in quietly and take a seat in a designated area, or should they go to their regular seat?

The clearer you are on the attendance policy, in your own mind and on your syllabus, the more smoothly your class will operate. Answer as many questions as possible at the beginning of the term so that you minimize challenges later on. Make it a point to refer students to carefully crafted passages in the syllabus if they ask you to clarify key policies.

18. Grading Policies and Procedures

Another area in which to be crystal clear is that of grading policies and procedures. After determining your unit's policies (if there are any) and talking with colleagues about the grading culture in the department, you can begin to specify your own policy. First, what will the grading scale be? Is there any flexibility? Are you using plus/minus or straight letter grading? Is your system based on points? If so, how do students earn those points? Do you accept late work and, if so, is there a penalty for lateness? Are there makeup exams? Will you offer extra credit? If students are not content with the grade they have earned, what is their recourse? What are the policies for students' getting an "incomplete" or withdrawing the class? How do you initiate expelling a student from your class, and what are the cultural issues related to doing so?

It may seem like a lot to investigate and consider, but the first time a sticky situation arises, you will be glad you invested the effort in advance to find out how to handle it. Although students may not agree with the rules, they derive a certain amount of security from thoroughly understanding them. Grading policies that are either unclear or inconsistently applied leave you open to extensive grade appeals (a time-consuming, disagreeable process), angry feelings, unpleasant reports by students, and sleepless nights for you, as you try to figure out what you should do. Over time poor grading policies also influence your student recruitment potential. You can always modify strict rules by granting leniency, but you cannot easily put a structure into place after the term has begun.

The components discussed above will make up the bulk of your syllabus, but there are several additions you may want to consider, in order to have the most complete syllabus possible. Providing students a complete syllabus is a start for helping them be successful—if they decide to take advantage of what you are offering. Your careful planning can provide them with some confidence and motivation to do just that.

Additional Syllabus Considerations

As you finalize your strategic planning, keep in mind that your syllabus should provide the increasingly overextended students who will populate your class with a complete and detailed course overview and agenda. Remember as well that you are preparing not only to deliver a single course but also to play a role in the future learning of students. As such, one of your goals should be to challenge students to assume greater responsibility for their own learning. A well-developed syllabus contributes to achieving that goal (Grunnert, 1997).

An extended syllabus can contain one or more of the following:

■ *Title page for course.* The official version of your syllabus may include a title page that displays the course number and title, a graphic related to the course, your name, a place for the student's name, the time and location of the course, and any other quick-reference information you consider important. It serves as a welcome page or an entry page into the extended syllabus and the course, so make it attractive and inviting.

■ *Table of contents.* With an extended syllabus that includes all the components we have addressed thus far, along with handouts or other support materials, you and your students will want a way to find information quickly. A table of contents allows for this. It takes only a few minutes to create, but it can save you and your students much time throughout the semester. Making the syllabus easy to navigate will show the students that you are aware of their time constraints and their need for fast retrieval of information. Going the extra mile for students can set you apart from others instructors, improving your student recruiting and retention success.

■ *Letter to students.* Consider writing a letter to your students. Introduce yourself (using some of the information you've previously generated), the course, your expectations, and so on. This letter may be the very first item in the extended syllabus and can set a friendly tone for the whole course.

■ *Resources.* Often there are resources instructors know about or have learned about from previous students that would help new students pursue the goals and objectives of the course. List these for students—and make the point that although these resources are not requirements, you endorse them.

■ *Course calendar.* In student focus groups recently conducted by one of the authors of this book, students made it clear that one component they want in their syllabus is a *distilled* version of the calendar—with dates, due dates, readings, and so on. It is not that students do not want the extended versions, too, but sometimes they need a quick reference page they can keep in their planners or grab when they are running to the library.

■ *How to study for this course.* One of the best ways to compile this section is to have students who have successfully completed your course write some suggestions for how to do well in it. Not only do they reveal ideas and clues that you would not think of, but they write in such a way that it is "heard" by the current students. The suggestions sound real because they *are* real. Obviously, if you are a first-time instructor, you will have to write this section yourself. But you can let students know in the syllabus that you will be asking for their input at the end of the course.

■ *Teaching methods.* Students with a consumer mentality want and deserve a clear idea of the instructional methods you intend to employ, especially if those methods are likely to be perceived as somewhat unusual. Listing your methods also serves as a good protection should a student later lodge a complaint about your teaching with the administration.

■ *Time estimates.* While it is impossible to tell students exactly how many hours they will be spending on your class (through attendance, homework, group projects, and other commitments related to course content), it is possible to give them an estimate. Students need to know up-front if a particular course's time requirements are going to exceed the time they have allotted. This information can help them in their planning; they can choose to take the class another semester or they can clear out adequate time in their schedule. If the class requires less time than they had expected, they can take an additional class or increase their commitments in other areas. Consider your own best estimates, but also use student comments from previous semesters to give a sense of student perspective.

- *Student organizations.* As Richard Light (2001) reports, student organizations often make a tremendous impact on the quality of the collegiate experience as perceived by students. For at least four reasons, you should identify and provide essential information (e.g., places, times, membership dues) for cocurricular organizations available to your students. First, they may not receive this information otherwise. Second, it shows that you value students' decisions about their discretionary time. Third, membership in extracurricular organizations promotes the development of students' social and leadership skills, which in turn contributes to academic success. Finally, student participation in such organizations fosters retention in degree programs and the institution as a whole.

Since your major goal is to facilitate your students' mastery of the course content, your syllabus should eliminate barriers to learning by anticipating reasonable questions. Be aware, however, that in recent years the syllabus has become more than a course plan. In our consumer-oriented and litigious society, it has evolved into a "binding contract" between the instructor and the student, with all the implications typically associated with that term. A well-developed syllabus that clearly outlines your expectations in all of the critical areas of the course can protect you if ever you are challenged.

Our society also emphasizes visual stimulation, so be mindful of how your syllabus looks. Typographical mistakes, poor-quality photocopies, and the like communicate to students that you lack professionalism—not an image you want to create during the first class meeting when the syllabus is distributed.

For the reasons given above, you should have your syllabus thoroughly reviewed, by colleagues or students, prior to having it printed for distribution. Other pairs of eyes can catch errors, inconsistencies, or problems with clarity.

Appendix 4.1 presents a model syllabus. It is not intended to supplant any guidelines that your colleagues might have provided or to address all aspects of every teaching assignment. It does, however, show you a grounded syllabus that may prompt you to consider critical points you may have overlooked. The model syllabus is general to consumer-oriented students. Reviewing it can help you save time and energy you might invest in other aspects of planning your course.

Planning Your Course Strategy

Many professors, particularly new ones, seem to view themselves and the textbook as the sole vehicles for delivering the material of the course. Accountable professors, in contrast, understand that they are facilitators of instruction; they must first discern how students process information and then use a range of appropriate instructional methods that allow for students to learn material in ways that are most efficient and effective for them. These professors also assess student learning regularly to ensure mastery of key material before progressing and to generate information to continually improve the quality of the learning experience, a strategy that Chapter 13 discusses in detail.

Because your students have probably been highly conditioned by a steady diet of electronic media, it is important to design stimulating elements into your class. Guest speakers, field trips, Web-enhanced instruction, and videotapes are each potentially powerful vehicles for your course. Begin early to accumulate resources, through your professional and community contacts, that lend credibility and panache to your course, and offer the opportunity for students to develop real-world insights that textbooks and other traditionally employed materials cannot provide. As you plan, however, remember to allow enough lead time to arrange experiential elements.

A course with a sound plan, communicated in an attractive syllabus, and enriched with special learning opportunities will have a marked impact on your students. Share your plan enthusiastically at your initial class meeting. Refer back to it throughout the course to provide students with enough structure to help them meet their goals in your course—and beyond.

Summary of Key Points

- Talk with other professors who have successfully taught sections of the course to which you are assigned.
- Develop a sound syllabus to serve as a blueprint for students, guiding them to success in your course.
- Plan your overall teaching strategy well in advance, drawing on resources beyond the classroom when possible.
- Plan guest speakers and field trips well in advance, and implement plans only after thoroughly assessing all of the inherent risks.
- Get organized from the beginning.

Through the Professors' Eyes

PAT: I've written course syllabi for years. Each year I find I get more and more specific with my explanations and expectations. We have changed our grading scale at the university this year to include pluses and minuses, so I need to rethink how to weigh my assignments. I keep trying to engage my students in higher-order thinking and perhaps need to reexamine assignments to ensure that I am accomplishing that goal. I am forever tweaking my syllabi to make them clearer, and I can't imagine why some of my colleagues never change their syllabi, except for test dates and assignment due dates. I have never been able to do that. I have recently found much material on the Web that my students can reference, so I'm developing a whole new online course packet for them. I know the students will like this, especially since they can download it at no charge. Textbooks and materials are getting so expensive that I feel guilty asking my students to buy more than one textbook.

DALE: I don't understand all this fuss about giving students treatises for syllabi. All they need to know is what their reading assignments are and the deadline for completing them. They need dates for tests and the final course project, and my grading scale. I give all directions in class. If they miss a class, it's their responsibility to find out how to do the assignments. I see no need to coddle the students—they are legally adults. One of my friends from graduate school still doesn't give his students a syllabus at all, saying it impinges on his academic freedom. He likes to enter the classroom, gauge the collective mindset of the students, and wing it. In spite of my strong appreciation for intellectual independence, I realize that approach invites a plethora of problems. Not completely a traditionalist, I have been thinking about creating a course home page, on the Web; this could eliminate unnecessary phone calls and e-mail messages from students and free up some additional time for my research.

KIM: I decided to base my first syllabi on those I obtained from another professor who has taught my classes for a long time. I think the first time it would be unwise not to take advantage of guidance that is offered by those who have taught so long. I will make a few adjustments to the assignments because of things I have heard from others. I would like to create more interactive work, but the syllabus from my colleague looks very good. I plan to set up a Web page that gives information about my background and also anticipates questions students may have. I have talked to my department chair about grading practices. I am used to grades being given only on tests, but I know other activities should be included in order to determine a final grade for the students. I am not sure how to weight tests, quizzes, and activities or how to write measurable objectives for all that I would like my students to learn. The department chair asked a second-year faculty member in our department to help me with this. Once I get the objectives done, maybe the assessment will make more sense to me. I met Dr. Zhang for lunch several days ago, and I liked him very much. He has taught for over twenty years in the same college where I am teaching, but in a different department. He said he would agree to be my mentor under five conditions. First, everything we say to each other would be kept completely confidential by both of us. Second, that I would agree to mentor a doctoral student, who is a graduate teaching assistant in his department, having recently arrived here from his country. Third, that all of our discussions be conducted in English, even though we speak some of each other's language. Fourth, that I would meet one of his classes while he is out of town in a few weeks. And last, that either one of us could end the relationship, without having to give a reason, at any time. I have thought very hard about these conditions and believe they are reasonable for what I will be receiving in return. I will call him tonight to accept his offer and schedule our next meeting.

Tips for Thriving

Regardless of profession, people in our society are becoming increasingly marketing-conscious. Instructors who seek to thrive in the classroom must contemplate the type of image they wish to establish in the minds of their students. By using the word *image*, we are not suggesting that you attempt to present a false persona but rather are encouraging you to focus on the qualities you truly possess in order to make your classroom efforts more effective, and thus achieve a greater sense of personal fulfillment.

Recall from the chapter our suggestion to give special emphasis to the visual quality of your syllabus. With today's desktop publishing software, you can incorporate graphics and other design elements with a minimum investment of resources. Such use of technology is likely to create a perception among students that you are contemporary in a wide variety of ways.

In addition, you might want to consider color-coding your materials. For example, if you were to teach two separate sections of the same course, you might want to have the materials for one section printed on blue paper and those of the other section printed on yellow paper. Should you make minor modifications in materials (e.g., different versions of essentially the same examination), your color-coding will enable you to keep materials well organized.

SUGGESTED READINGS

Diamond, R. (1998). *Designing and Assessing Courses and Curricula: A Practical Guide*. San Francisco: Jossey-Bass.

Duffy, D. K. and J. W. Jones (1995). *Teaching within the Rhythms of the Semester*. San Francisco: Jossey-Bass.

Eble, K. (1994). *The Craft of Teaching*. San Francisco: Jossey-Bass.

Grunert, J. (1997). *The Course Syllabus: A Learning-Centered Approach*. Bolton, MA: Anker.

Stark, J., and L. Lattuca. (1997). *Shaping the College Curriculum*. Boston: Allyn & Bacon.

APPENDIX 4.1

Model Course Syllabus

Principles of Management
MAN 2021 A1
Fall 20—

Class	Tuesdays and Thursdays, 9:25–10:40 a.m. Springfield Campus, Blair Building, room 111
Textbook	*Management*, 9th edition, by Burns and Schreiber, available at campus bookstore
Related Courses	Students would benefit from a prior knowledge of basic business terminology, gained through work experience or completion of an introductory course.
Instructor	Dr. Angel Torez, Professor of Business Management, received his B.S. in business administration and M.A. in marketing from Western Kentucky University, and a doctorate in business from the University of North Texas. Before entering teaching, he managed in the hospitality industry and in several sales organizations. He has been at the college since 1987, as instructor and department chair. His book *Managing the Diverse Workplace* is one of the nation's top sellers among titles focused on that workplace issue.
Office	Dr. Torez will be available to talk with students immediately following each class meeting. At other times, he can be seen in N 226 during hours posted on that office door. From Madison County, he can be reached by telephone at 462-4700, or at 930-4722 from Monroe River or Jefferson Counties. His e-mail address is atorez@mail.amc.edu.
Learning Methods	A variety of instructional methods are used to provide students with effective learning opportunities. These include role-play, group problem solving, and self-analysis activities, in addition to more traditional methods.
Learning Objectives	Upon successful completion of this course, each student will be able to:

1. Explain the basic management functions, skills, and roles.
2. Discuss management's role in enhancing efficiency and effectiveness.
3. Discuss the factors influencing changes in the manager's role.
4. Make ethical decisions that satisfy diverse organizational stakeholders.
5. Summarize the basic concepts of strategic planning.
6. Explain operating plans, policies, and procedures.
7. Explain the process for making effective management decisions.
8. Describe the function of commonly used decision-making tools.
9. Compare and contrast types of departmentalization.
10. Describe the dimensions and consequences of organizational culture.
11. Summarize the process of employee recruitment, selection, placement compensation, and evaluation.
12. Contrast common leadership styles.
13. Explain the manager's role in managing conflict and encouraging teamwork.
14. Explain the most popular theories of worker motivation.
15. Explain effective methods of overcoming communication barriers.
16. Summarize the methods of controlling.
17. Explain the principles of total quality management.

Attendance Policy	Although Dr. Torez is providing opportunities for each student's mastery of course objectives, students should realize the value that their experiences offer their peers. Therefore, it is critical that you attend class regularly to be a partner in this enhanced learning environment. Roll will be taken at each class meeting, and your participation will be taken into consideration in case of a borderline final grade. If class will be missed, it is each student's responsibility to personally contact the instructor in advance, regarding missed assignments. The instructor will not accept late work without valid reasons. Students are encouraged to contact the instructor anytime they are not achieving their intended level of success, prior to taking any other action. Students who need to withdraw must complete an official form, and submit it consistent with college policy, no later than November 9. "Incomplete" grades are awarded only when an emergency prevents a student from completing a minor portion of the course assignments.
Grading Criteria	3 unit exams @ 20% (45 multiple-choice questions, one essay) = 60% Research project (detailed standards provided at Sept. 17 class) = 20% Final exam (comprehensive, 100 multiple-choice questions) = 20%

Grading Scale	90–100%	A
	80–89%	B
	70–79%	C
	60–69%	D
	Below 60%	F

Methods of Achieving Success
Achieving success in MAN 2021 will require a time commitment outside of class that averages three hours per week. Students benefit from completing assigned reading prior to that content being addressed in class and from actively participating in classroom discussion, activities, and review.

Delta Epsilon Chi
Students enrolled in management and marketing courses benefit from participating in the college chapter of the national student organization Delta Epsilon Chi. This chapter has a rich history of success in state and national competitions, as well as service to our local communities.

Certificates & Degrees
Today's workplace values many certifications and licenses as "tickets to upward mobility." This course is required within the A.S. and B.S. degrees in business administration, marketing management, accounting technology, and office support technology.

Professional Standards
An atmosphere similar to that present in the most professional businesses should be displayed at all times. Thus, distractions such as personal communications devices and door slamming should be minimized, and consideration demonstrated to diverse opinions.

Principles of Management
MAN 2021 A1
Tentative Schedule

Week of:	Topics/activities/assignments
August 20	Introduction, review of syllabus. Building a learning community.
August 27	Chapters 1 and 2.
September 3	Chapters 3 and 4.
September 10	Chapter 5. Review for exam.
September 17	**Exam No. 1.** Return/review exam. Research project overview.
September 24	Chapters 6 and 7.
October 1	Chapters 8 and 10. **Project Proposal Due.**
October 8	Chapter 11. Review for exam.
October 15	**Exam No. 2.** Return/review exam. Chapter 12.
October 22	Chapters 13 and 14.
October 29	Chapter 15.
November 5	Chapter 16.

November 12   **Exam No. 3.** Return/review exam.
November 19   Chapter 19.
November 26   Chapter 20.
December 3   **Projects due. Presentations.**
December 10   Chapter 21. Review for final exam.
December 17   **Final Exam: Tuesday, December 18, 8 a.m.**

5 Launching Your Course Effectively

FOCUS QUESTIONS

- What objectives should you expect to achieve during your first class meeting?
- Why should you and your students perceive each other as collaborators in learning?
- Why is it increasingly critical to make your expectations clear to students?
- How should you follow up your first class meeting to ensure an effective launch?

As a college student, you completed dozens of courses. You can therefore probably remember at least a few terrible first-class experiences—a professor who was ten minutes late and obviously ill prepared; a classroom that was in disarray; or a professor who gave a minimal introduction, distributed a lengthy syllabus, and then dismissed the class as if its members were intruders. The stakeholders today who are clamoring for increased accountability in higher education may well have had similar or even more horrific first-class experiences—events that shaped their views markedly.

You might have had a few exemplary first-class experiences as well—a professor who took her post early and introduced herself to each arriving student; a table that contained alphabetized name cards for each enrolled student; or a passionately delivered introduction to the course material. For many students, such well-orchestrated initial classes planted seeds that grew into a learning community. These students were inspired to take a more active role in learning the subject matter throughout the term—sometimes in what they perceived beforehand as a boring discipline—than they ever believed they could (Lunde, 2000).

Replicating this kind of experience for your students is no more than you would expect if the roles were reversed. When you launch a course successfully, you will also manage successfully one of the two most significant mileposts for retaining students throughout the term (the other being the first exam). Providing you insights to do so is the objective of this chapter.

No matter how long you teach, meeting a class for the first time always entails apprehension. Even if your planning has given you a strong foundation for teaching the course, you may be nervous about encountering a fresh set of faces. How you and your students will perceive each other over the next ten, fifteen, or more weeks will depend largely on how you manage that first class meeting. One thing that can help is to try to see the occasion through the eyes of the students likely to be in your class. This chapter also contains many other suggestions intended to make the launch of your course successful for students and personally rewarding for you.

The first class meeting should serve at least two basic purposes:

1. To clarify all reasonable questions students might have relative to the course objectives, as well as your expectations for their performance in class. As students leave the first meeting, they should believe in your competency to teach the course, be able to predict the nature of your instruction, and know what you will require of them.
2. To give you an understanding of who is taking your course and what their expectations are.

Thus, the first class meeting needs to be carefully planned and conducted in a warm, enthusiastic fashion. Many professors believe that there is no need to conduct a full class meeting on the first day of the semester, because the enrollment usually does not stabilize until after the first week. However, in reality, few significant changes in enrollment typically occur during add–drop periods, and it is shortsighted to waste the time of most students enrolled for the benefit of a very few who might add the class later. Furthermore, conducting a solid first class meeting likely will create word of mouth among students that will generate a full enrollment—a win/win for your students, the dean, and you. There are eight specific objectives you should strive to achieve in the first week of a new class:

1. To orchestrate positive first impressions.
2. To introduce yourself effectively.
3. To clarify the learning objectives and your expectations.
4. To help students learn about each other.
5. To get to know your students.
6. To whet students' appetites for the course content.
7. To inform students of key facts about the course and instructional program.
8. To reassure students about their decision to enroll.

We discuss each of these objectives in a separate section. The last two sections of the chapter discuss assessing students' understanding of the starting position and following up on the first week of class.

Orchestrating Positive First Impressions

You probably know that your first impressions of people, events, and experiences are truly long-lasting ones. Thus, you want to ensure that the impressions students have of you and your course are positive. Richard Ailes (1995), the renowned communications consultant, believes you have fewer than ten seconds to create a positive image of yourself. Since students equate "the course" with you, then what you do, how you dress, how you communicate, and how you organize your class syllabus will be how they perceive the course and, ultimately, you.

Although most professors need not follow a preset dress code, we do know that how you dress conveys very distinct messages to your students. If your desire is to have a very casual classroom environment in which you perceive yourself as one of the class, then dressing in casual clothes similar to what the students may wear will serve that purpose. If you want to distinguish yourself from the students and convey a professional image, then you should wear clothing appropriate for professionals in your field. You may decide during the term to change your image according to the nature of the activities you will engage in with your students. For example, if you have lab days, you might wear a lab coat, protective eye gear, and latex gloves. If you have field days in which students will be working in real-life situations (e.g., schools, businesses, or medical facilities), your adhering to the organization's dress code will serve as an effective model for students. Nevertheless, how you present yourself that first class meeting will convey your intent for the classroom environment to your students.

Another factor that influences students' perceptions of your expectations is how you organize the learning environment. A clean chalkboard and desks in neat rows instantly convey a sense of professionalism and formality. Desks arranged in clusters or U-shaped configurations will prepare students for an informal, interactive experience. If you are assigned to teach in a classroom with furniture fixed in place, you will have to find other ways to communicate the degree of formality or informality you wish to maintain.

When students enter your classroom, there should be no question which class is meeting in the room. The course title and your name should be neatly and prominently displayed on the board or screen in front of the room. Students who might have entered the room by mistake can comfortably leave before the class begins. Position yourself at the door and greet entering students with a handshake and a smile. If such practice is out of your comfort level, be sure to make some attempt, whether verbal or nonverbal, with each entering student.

Introducing Yourself Effectively

Students register for particular class sections for either or both of two primary reasons: the convenience of its time slot and the reputation of the professor. Said another way, consumer-oriented students care most about fitting the class into their already busy schedules and having their needs met by a reliable professor. While greeting the students as they enter the classroom does much to establish the environment, your self-introduction is critical either to confirming the expectations students have already formed or to creating expectations from scratch. Many of today's students are skeptical toward authority figures—they question the motives, knowledge, and experience levels of those in charge. Some enter your class neither highly motivated toward nor enthusiastic about learning, and perhaps intolerant of activities they do not perceive as productive. So your introduction of yourself needs to be sensitive, yet highly focused on the particular course you are teaching. Convey your understanding of their limited time, while also reinforcing your expectations of rigor. You will have many opportunities throughout the term to reveal your broader background, but in your initial introduction you should strive for succinctness, humility, and a bit of enthusiasm and humor (Berk, 1998).

Your introduction should also clarify when and how students can contact you. Your syllabus will provide your office hours, phone and fax numbers, and e-mail address, but you might consider sharing your home phone number as well. One of the authors of this book has, for over thirty years, published her home phone number on all syllabi, and students have never abused that access. In fact, students are mindful to try to reach her in her office rather than bothering her at home, recognizing that the home contact is provided for true emergencies. You will also want to let the students know when you will be available to meet with them individually, particularly if your classroom is not located near your office. Regularly reserve fifteen or twenty minutes before and after class for discussions with individual students. Most students will not take advantage of these times, but your providing them conveys that you care about students' needs.

In today's technological world, many professors have established Web pages for their courses. These pages enable students who are not inclined to ask questions in class or to approach professors outside class to get to know you. Chapter 9 gives more detail on personal Web pages and other uses of technology.

In your introduction, avoid saying, "This is the first time I am teaching this course" or "I was only asked to teach this class two days ago." Although such statements may be true, they serve no useful purpose and will surely hamper your ability to establish a positive classroom environment. Even if you have not had sufficient time to fully develop your syllabus, you should provide an overview of the course and its learning objectives and then ask the students for feedback about their expectations. No later than the next class meeting, perhaps via e-mail before then, provide the class with a complete syllabus that includes a schedule of activities. If you do this right, students will feel that they had input into the planning of the class and perhaps will be more invested in its success (Carnegie, 1962).

Clarifying the Learning Objectives and Your Expectations

Students should leave your first class meeting with a clear understanding of the course goals, your expectations for their performance, and your philosophy of teaching and learning. Because today's students (and perhaps their families and/or employers) hold high expectations of what they will learn in college, and especially because they are likely to have heard horror stories of some poorly prepared graduates, you should also clarify how you perceive your role as the teacher and their role as learners. It is essential that you manage the expectations of students who view themselves as consumers by clearly explaining both the strengths and limitations of your course—that is, what you will and will not be able to accomplish because of time, space, finances, and other limits.

Your syllabus should present critical course information, and you should clarify that information as needed during the first class meeting. Review each section of the syllabus. For inexperienced students, you may want to create transparencies or PowerPoint slides that enable you to isolate each section of the syllabus. For academically mature students, you can simply distribute the paper copy and ask students to stay with you as it is reviewed. In either scenario, be sure to solicit questions from the students regarding the items on the syllabus, and draw specific attention to such critical items as attendance policy, provisions for makeup work, due dates of assignments, and grading procedures. If students do not raise questions, assure them that you will entertain questions about the syllabus via e-mail or at the next class meeting. Frequently, students do not process all the information from all their classes at the first meeting. Do not assume that a lack of questions means that everyone clearly understands everything. Revisit the syllabus at the second class meeting and after the first exam or assignment. As we said in Chapter 4, in today's higher education environment, the syllabus is viewed as a contract between you and your students. Thus, it is imperative that both you and your students have a common understanding of its content in order to ensure a successful class experience for everyone.

Helping Students Learn about One Another

The fourth objective for launching your course effectively is to help students get acquainted with one another. Some students might seem delighted if they never had to interact with you or their classmates. Whether they are shy or have some other reason for not wanting to break the ice, they may at first prefer to sit, listen, take notes, and leave. In doing so, however, they miss out on the opportunity to form study groups or share in conversations that will make their educational experiences richer and more successful. Students who actively get to know their classmates usually become more motivated to attend class and, in an age of accountability, are far more likely to be retained within the course, the degree program, and the institution. Furthermore, when students know each other, they maintain more positive attitudes about the class and participate more actively in classroom discussions and small-group learning activities—all of which serve to make your task much more rewarding.

How can you help your students to get to know each other? There are several options:

- Ask students to introduce themselves to the class. This can be ineffective, however, if students are more focused on deciding what they will say than on listening to the other self-introductions.
- Ask students to form pairs or triads whose task is to introduce each other to the rest of the class. Using pairs and triads provides the students with an opportunity to begin discussions with each other and keeps their attention focused. You might add some spice to this activity by having each student nominate a peer for a fitting award (e.g., "superwoman of the month") and then providing a token prize to the student making the most creative introduction.
- Take a refreshment break and tell the students that they need to get acquainted with at least two new people, whom they will introduce when the class reconvenes.
- Orchestrate a structured icebreaker activity, such as the one that appears in Appendix 5.2, that gets students up and moving around the room and encourages them to meet a large number of their peers firsthand.
- Ask students to form small groups and solve a preset problem related to course content. Be sure to make the activity enjoyable and to provide clear expectations of the outcome sought. After completing the task, each group can designate one reporter who will share solutions with the rest of the class and introduce the other group members.

Once you have completed one of these activities, it is critical to invest a few minutes to debrief it. The important question for students to answer is why you invested class time doing the activity. Students should eventually conclude that they are valuable resources for one another in their educational journeys and that not all knowledge will come directly from you or the textbook. They should also be encouraged to recognize several benefits from connecting with their peers (e.g., improved test scores, more effective matching of members in group activities). Said another way, by engaging students in group work during the initial class meeting, you plant the seeds for establishing a community of learners within your class and perhaps foster a long-term appreciation for collaboration in their workplaces and other arenas of their lives (Jones, 1991).

Getting to Know Your Students

You can probably remember a time when a person you perceived as important surprised you by using your name for the very first time. Many people consider their names to be their single most unique characteristic, one that defines them to everyone else within their environment. To establish a bond with each of your students, it is critical that you learn and use their names as early in the term as possible.

Prior to pursuing this objective, do what you can to obtain an up-to-date official class roll. It doesn't take long, and it's worth the effort, to read through the class list a few times to begin to familiarize yourself with the students' names. As you greet the students entering the room, you can verify the pronunciation of their names. When starting the class, read each name from the roll. If you see a name you haven't been able to verify, pronounce it as clearly as possible. If you're completely stumped, simply ask for help. Make phonetic notes as needed so that you can correctly pronounce all names at subsequent class meetings. Taking care to pronounce names correctly will convey your sense of professionalism and your sensitivity. After calling the roll, ask for a show of hands by those whose names were not called and instruct these students to meet with you after class or during the break to clarify their situation. If you have a large class, you may not want to call roll, but be sure to circulate multiple sign-in sheets so that you will have a record of who attended class.

Immediately following your icebreaker activity, distribute a student profile form or other information-gathering device to students. Appendix 5.1 shows a sample form that can be modified to fit your specific needs. Have students hand you the completed forms at the end of the class meeting. If you recall their names, say them aloud as you bid good-bye. If you don't have the names yet in your memory, you can read them off the completed forms. Improve your recall effectiveness even further—and add a high-tech touch in the process—by taking a Polaroid or digital picture of each class member and attaching it to the student profile form. Reviewing the profiles, with or without photos attached, before coming to class, and keeping them readily available while you teach, will greatly help you to remember each student in your class. In all but perhaps very large classes, you should achieve your objective of learning every student's name by the time you return the first exam or written assignment.

While learning students' names comes relatively easy for many professors, it can be a daunting task for others, especially when classes are large. Many professors assign seats for at least several weeks—a strategy that facilitates their matching of names with faces. Assigned seats also facilitate roll-taking, which is required by guidelines of many student financial aid programs, even for courses where attendance is not required. If you choose to assign seats, let the students know that you will be creating a seating chart and tell them why. Students with disabilities (e.g., poor eyesight or hearing) should be encouraged to work with you to reserve appropriate seats for the period during which the seating chart will be used (or for the whole term).

Many college professors believe assigned seating is demeaning to adult learners, even though it helps in learning students' names. There are other options, including name tents. Providing 5x8 index cards folded lengthwise and thick marker pens, ask the students to write their names clearly and in large print; fold the cards so that they stand up, and have students place them on their desks each time they come to class. With these portable cards, you can respond to students by name and, through repetition, master the names quite quickly. Arriving ten or fifteen minutes early to each class meeting and engaging in conversation with each arriving student will further sharpen your recall.

Whetting Students' Appetites for the Course Content

Depending on the length of your first class meeting, you may have some time left to whet the students' appetites for what they are about to learn. Because students may still add your class, you do not want to address too much content—especially anything that appears on the first exam and will not be addressed a second time—during the first class session.

A number of effective professors whet their students' appetites by asking open-ended questions such as "What do you think of when you hear [economics, sociology, etc.]?" This not only engages the students' interest but gives you something to work with. Students might not shout back what you would hope to hear, but take their answers at face value and do something with them.

An alternative idea, and one that also gets students to begin working in groups on the first day, is to do a no-book directed reading-thinking activity (DR-TA). The steps, which can be listed on the board or on the screen, are as follows:

1. On your own, list everything you can think of that might be in a book entitled
   _____. [Write the title of your textbook, or the title of your course if you do not use a textbook.]
2. Get with a partner, share your ideas, and then put the ideas you both generated for step 1 into categories.
3. Give each category a name.
4. Get with another pair and, together, combine your ideas. Then arrange the categories as a table of contents for this book and write it on the chart paper each group has been given.

This entire process takes about thirty to thirty-five minutes and is worth every second. Students begin to think about the class, they meet at least three other members of the class, and professors begin to have a sense of what their students know relative to the course as they walk around listening to the groups process the task and as they observe what students write on the chart paper for display.

Seeking to open students' minds to a new perception by asking additional, perhaps rhetorical, questions is also valuable. Sharing the front page of the morning newspaper, a video clip from a recent news broadcast, or the cover of a popular weekly newsmagazine is an effective attention-grabbing device for visual learners, while passing around examples of work appeals to tactile learners (Lunde, 2000). Experiential activities that require students to move around within the classroom engage the learning systems of kinesthetic learners. The key is to plant seeds to encourage students to examine their preexisting views, without trying to win them over to your views of the subject matter all at once.

You might also want to provide a cursory review of the textbook adopted for the class, acquainting the students with how the content is organized, what study aids are included, and how those aids might enhance their mastery of the course material. If you will be using supplementary materials, such as a course pack or a Web site, you may want to explore those with your students, making appropriate connections to the textbook and to the syllabus. If you have made arrangements to have materials on reserve at the library, you can review procedures for their use. Perhaps you have an extended reading list; reviewing it and highlighting specifically interesting or unique articles or books would be most beneficial to your students. Remember, your goal is to encourage students to establish a foundation on which they can build knowledge and skills throughout the course.

Finally, you want to be sure that the students have time to go to the bookstore and purchase the materials for your class. This is especially important if you teach night classes, if students have limited free time, and/or if the bookstore maintains limited hours. You also want to be sure that your students, particularly if they are new to your campus, know when, where, and how to access the resources of the library. Good teachers encourage students to use the library.

Informing Students of Key Issues

Like all clients that feel valued, students expect to be kept informed of key issues that might have an impact on their success. Therefore, immediately prior to your first class meeting, make yourself aware of key facts within the enrollment environment of your department's courses. These facts include:

- Number of spaces available in your course (and in other sections of it).
- Class sections that might have been canceled because of low enrollment or other factors.
- New class sections that might have been created because of unexpectedly high interest.
- Drop–add dates and procedures for making schedule changes.

As you approach the closure of your initial class meeting, you should make sure that students are aware of this information. It is quite possible that they, or their friends, have had changes in their schedules mandated by various factors. Presenting the latest information not only can give you an opportunity to recruit an additional few students (if you need to) but also demonstrates your concern for the best interest of your currently enrolled students. Consistently demonstrating increased enrollment in your course sections during the add–drop period may reflect well on you to your department chair and dean.

Reassuring Students about Their Decision

Whenever students start a new class, they typically experience a condition psychologists call "cognitive dissonance." This is a state of conflict that arises from trying to hold two contradictory ideas at the same time. In this mind state, students, like those who make any big decision in life, question the wisdom of their decisions. Tuition, fees for textbooks and other materials, opportunity costs, and other factors become the focus of their evaluation. Marketing professionals refer to cognitive dissonance as "buyer's remorse," and they invest a great deal of time and money in reassuring customers that their decisions were correct. Thus, they foster repeat business, or what higher education calls retention.

Before ending your first class meeting, briefly review with students the reasons why your course is a good investment of their time, energy, and money. Emphasize the important and relevant content they will learn, highlight the value of their peers, and share your enthusiasm for a dynamic classroom environment. Ensure that when they leave your classroom they will want to return for more. For many professors, the first class meeting is the most critical one to the retention of students throughout the term.

Assessing Students' Understanding of the Starting Position

As students conclude their first week in your class, it is wise to assess their perceptions in an anonymous, nonthreatening manner. Doing so at this critical juncture helps you identify stumbling blocks before they can grow into large barriers later in the term, which lead to withdrawals, and most of all, reduce the success that students could otherwise achieve.

Invest two minutes to distribute 3x5 index cards on which students may reply anonymously to several open-ended questions, such as:

- Who was the most interesting person you met in this class?
- What things are you most looking forward to in this class?

- What concerns you about your ability to be successful in this class?
- What questions do you have that are not yet answered?
- What has surprised you most about this class so far?

Ask students to place the completed cards at a convenient spot close to the door as they exit. Wish them well. Further details on processing this potentially valuable activity are addressed in Chapter 13.

Following Up the First Week of Class

Together, the face-to-face meetings, completed student profile forms, and ending assessments represent a rich set of data on the launch of your course. Closely review the student profiles and make notes in whatever form is convenient to you to help you better fit your course strategy to your students' needs. (Continue to use the forms to log results of conferences with students, reflections on messages received from them, and so on throughout the term.) Again, seek to fit the face with the form so that you can call as many students as possible by name when they enter your class the following meeting. Review the completed 3x5 assessment cards as well, and note any patterns in responses that seem especially significant. Reflect on the first week as a whole, and identify any actions that you might want to consider taking.

Finally, send a carefully crafted e-mail message to all members of the class. Share with them some positive reinforcement of their performance in the first class meeting. Clarify any issues that might have arisen through your review of the student profiles, the 3x5 assessment cards, and/or your reflections. Tell them how much you are looking forward to the term and why, and then remind them of the reading assignment and activities for the following class meeting. Invite students to reply with questions or comments. You will likely be very surprised by the quality of feedback that you obtain from the quiet leaders within your class. Use that feedback to open your second class meeting and continue the positive momentum.

Summary of Key Points

- Plan for a substantive first meeting that addresses students' needs and gives you useful information and insights.
- Create a positive visual image of yourself and the classroom for arriving students.
- Extend a personalized welcome to as many students as possible.
- Learn and begin using students' names right away.
- Earn the right to teach the class by introducing yourself convincingly, yet humbly.

- Clarify your course objectives and performance expectations by reviewing the syllabus effectively and embellishing it with useful detail.
- Orchestrate an enjoyable way for students to meet each other.
- Whet students' appetites for the course by sharing material they will perceive as interesting and pertinent.
- Provide students an overview of the textbook and other critical course resources.
- Reassure students that the course will be a wise investment of their time and resources.
- Gather feedback that will enable you to identify potential problems early.
- Provide e-mail feedback prior to the second class meeting.

Through the Professors' Eyes

DALE: Over the course of the term, I usually get to know all I want to know about my students. There's no need to know too much about them—I can't solve their personal problems, anyway. I believe if I let students know what I expect out of them, those who really care about their education will live up to my expectations. I have other obligations, particularly my research, which takes up all my campus time. My research is particularly lucrative to me and to my college, and essential to my career advancement. I see no need to spend lots of time with the students, most of whom can participate in campuswide initiatives developed to meet their assimilation needs. They can ask me questions during class time and during the three office hours that I keep each week. I give them my office phone number and the hours they can call me—what else should they want or need? One of my colleagues has set up "virtual office hours" during which he will read and answer e-mails. I will have to think about that— it may be more efficient than having to hold real office hours, and it could help me manage my research more efficiently.

PAT: When I first started teaching, students rarely dropped out of my classes. Now I have three to five students each term who seem to just disappear. I try to talk to my students before they get into academic difficulty, but sometimes I don't see the problems coming. While I don't want to make it my responsibility to solve all their problems, I realize many of my students come to the university with more baggage than we had back in the 1960s. I'm pretty open-minded, and have never really encountered students with problems that could not be resolved with some creative thinking—if they would just come talk to me! I applaud the mission of such institutional initiatives as the "Freshman Experience" to help retain our students, but I realize an increasing number of my students reside a distance from campus and are therefore not able to participate. I try to convey to my students my concern for their success, and I establish an open-door policy so that students feel free to contact me or wander into my office if I am not busy. I am in my office a lot more than the required office hours, because often students' problems can't wait until posted office hours. For my introductory class this term, I'm going to experiment with an idea I recently read about—requiring students to visit me once in my office during the first two weeks of the term. I will use the information form each student completes to guide the discussion and, I hope, establish a better relationship with students right from the start. My dean is really concerned about FTE (full-time equivalent) production, and although I never felt like I had to recruit students, I do feel responsible for trying to assure that those registered in my classes do actually complete them. The office visits early in the term just might help increase my student retention.

KIM: My first class met today and I was very nervous. As I reviewed my syllabus with the students, I realized I was simply reading from it and probably being perceived as stiff. During the review of my biography, I put down my syllabus for a moment and became quite direct with my students. I told them that I have been in this country for only five years and that my English is not yet what I would like it to be. But I also said that they could choose to focus on superficial things like my accent and let it bother them, or focus on the major points that I am making and understand the material from a new perspective. As my department colleague tells me, success in this country is about making good choices from the many that are available. One international student came up to me after class and shared with me his challenges. After he finished, I supported him and shared some of my very similar challenges. It felt good to have an understanding person do that so freely. I am looking forward to getting to know him and each of my other students. I want to know all about them, why they are taking my class and their goals and aspirations. My mentor suggested that I identify a few students in each class on whom I can count to be honest with me about my presentations. Concerned about my language skills and the clarity of my speech, I believe asking their reactions would be very smart. When I get excited about what I am teaching, I talk really fast—and when I talk fast, my English is not always that clear. My mentor keeps telling me to keep my language simple and direct, use PowerPoint (which has been easy to learn), and provide class notes to my students to help them focus on my lectures. Following this advice will keep me from worrying so much about my language. Several of the textbook publishers provide visual materials that can be used with the new projectors in my classrooms.

Tips for Thriving

Leo Buscaglia (1990), the late popular author and professor at the University of Southern California, launched each of his courses in a very effective way that markedly influenced the retention rate of his students. He required each one to visit him in his office, for what he called a "voluntary-mandatory" office visit. His goal was to simply establish a rapport prior to the time when any kind of "bad stuff" (e.g., failing exam grades, excessive class absences) might occur. His actions obviously served to prevent many students from experiencing that bad stuff.

One of this book's authors has replicated Buscaglia's practice in recent years. At the first or second class meeting of each course, a sign-up sheet with fifteen-minute time blocks is circulated throughout the class. All students are asked to commit to a convenient time and to bring with them any questions they might have regarding the course. The information that students have divulged during these office visits has been not only illuminating but also critical to the professor's ability to address each student's specific learning needs. Once a personalized bond with each student is created, open sharing has become commonplace. Why not try this proven strategy in your classes this term?

SUGGESTED READINGS

Ailes, R. (1996). *You Are the Message: Getting What You Want by Being Who You Are.* New York: Currency-Doubleday.

Berk, R. (1998). *Professors Are from Mars, Students Are from Snickers.* Madison, WI: Mendota Press.

Fisch, L. (1996). *The Chalk Dust Collection: Thoughts and Reflections on Teaching in Colleges and Universities.* Stillwater, OK: New Forums Press.

Jones, K. (1991). *Icebreakers.* San Diego, CA: Pfeiffer & Associates.

Lunde, J. P. (2000). "101 Things You Can Do the First Three Weeks of Class." Tomorrow's Professor Listserv, Message 168, Stanford University Learning Laboratory, http://sll.stanford.edu/projects/tomprof/newtomprof/postings/168.html.

APPENDIX 5.1

Student Profile Form

The information you volunteer below will enable me to meet your individual needs more fully. All information will be kept in strict confidence.

Date _____

Name _____ Course _____

Complete mailing address _____

E-mail _____Tel. (day)_____ (night)_____

Employer/title _____ Avg. hrs./week _____

Goal in taking course _____

Ultimate educational goal _____

Background _____

Hobbies/interests _____

Personal accomplishments _____

_____

Special situations _____

_____

Most memorable learning experience _____

Learning challenges _____

_____

How do you learn best? _____

Signature (indicates receipt of syllabus) _____

Questions/concerns related to class? (Use back if necessary.) _____

_____

APPENDIX 5.2

Icebreaker Activity

The objective of this exercise is for you to become acquainted with at least twenty other students in this class. Find one person who fits each of the following criteria (or a creatively modified version), and neatly enter his or her name in the blank beside the clue.

1. Is a fan of (local sports team) _____
2. Has seen (name of musical group) in concert _____
3. Regularly surfs the Internet _____
4. Has traveled outside the country in the past year _____
5. Has shaken hands with a governor or senator _____
6. Recently saw the movie (title) _____
7. Has two or more siblings _____
8. Is an avid reader of Stephen King novels _____
9. Has flown on an airplane within the last month _____
10. Has viewed a lunar eclipse _____
11. Can identify what D. W. Griffith did for a living _____
12. Has been skiing within the past year _____
13. Once read *The Diary of Anne Frank* _____
14. Has driven over the Golden Gate Bridge _____
15. Has never had a broken bone _____
16. Is a regular viewer of (name of TV show) _____
17. Can tell you in which country the current Pope was born _____
18. Can tell you the latest winner of the Stanley Cup _____
19. Owns a dog named Jake _____
20. Voted in the last presidential election _____

6 Managing the Context of Your Course

FOCUS QUESTIONS

- How do you get effectively organized and remain so throughout your course?
- How should you organize a class session to ensure efficiency and effectiveness?
- How can you manage communications and challenging situations with students?
- What are the critical professional practices for you to display consistently?

> *We never educate directly, but indirectly by means of the environment. Whether we permit chance environments to do the work, or whether we design environments for the purpose makes a great difference.*
>
> —John Dewey

"**M**om," frustratingly cried the new freshman, phoning home from the dorm hundreds of miles away, "three of my five classes have over four hundred students. We're afraid to raise our hands, even when we're totally lost. One professor jumped all over a guy yesterday for asking an 'ill-conceived' question. The students who get there late sit in the aisles or stand in the back of the room. There's always chatter going on around me—people trying to figure out where the professor is in the textbook—so I can't hear half of what he's saying up front. And after class, the professors walk right out of the room—like totally unapproachable."

At the beginning of each new academic year, thousands of students on hundreds of campuses no doubt make such phone calls home. The same kind of frustration that causes them to drop classes and change majors has made parents angry and caused them to question rising tuition costs. It has also fueled the account-ability movement. While some factors are beyond the control of professors, others are clearly within their spheres of influence. This chapter is dedicated to helping you develop strategies for effectively managing the context of your courses.

Once you have launched your course successfully, your next challenge is to maintain the momentum you have worked so hard to establish. As a student, you probably worked with well-organized professors as well as with absentminded types who had to scramble to locate a copy of a handout or syllabus from among a pile of unsorted papers. Even if such experiences were decades ago, you can very likely describe the frustration you felt when your reasonable requests were not met. The expectations of today's students are every bit as high, if not higher, than yours were then.

If your course planning was thorough and the first class meeting went well, then getting fully organized for the remainder of the course will be relatively easy—if you attend to it immediately. Waiting until the first student assignments are submitted or your first examination is administered will make getting organized far more challenging and time-consuming. Heed the often-repeated admonition of effective managers from varied fields: "Plan your work, then work your plan, and most problems will be minimized."

Organizing Your Course Materials

Organizing your course materials is critical to achieving optimal student learning. Through their decades of teaching, the authors of this book have exchanged information with scores of professors whose organizational strategies can be plotted along a broad continuum, from zero to exemplary. We will highlight three of the most effective strategies we have found and, realizing that courses and students vary, leave it to you to identify variations that best meet your needs.

1. One systematic way to organize course materials is to insert all critical documents into a large binder, using tabbed dividers or simply a blank sheet of colored paper between sections. You would include several copies of the course syllabus, as well as the official class roll and the completed, alphabetized student profiles. Insert, as they are developed, the lesson plans for each class session, any pertinent notes, and extra copies of materials you hand out to students. Students inevitably will lose materials or ask for those distributed when they were absent. Having these materials immediately available reinforces your peace of mind and displays your concern for your students' success.

Another section of your course binder should be designated for copies of your examinations, quizzes, answer keys, and study guides, to which you may refer during class when checking for thoroughness, as well as when reviewing for the exam. Include as well all project assignment handouts, with their respective grading rubrics, which you will want handy when your students ask specific questions about examinations, projects, and grading.

2. An organizational strategy that many mobile faculty members employ is to file all course materials into a single briefcase, plastic file cabinet, storage crate, or expandable cardboard file. Any of these is likely not to exceed ten pounds and can be transported—using a small wheeled carrier, if necessary—to the professor's office, classroom, automobile, or home office with great convenience. The storage unit might contain file folders or large manila envelopes that hold exams, handouts, extra copies of the syllabus, and so on. This method also provides a place for you to store a copy of the textbook, assignments collected from students, and videos or other instructional materials to be used during class. Professors who employ this strategy report that—even when picking up a ringing telephone on the way out of their offices—they feel secure knowing that all of their materials for each course are in one convenient, reliable place.

3. A growing number of professors are setting up Web pages on which they post the syllabus, assignment directions, handouts, and so on for each of their classes. Students can view the materials in the privacy of their living quarters and print hard copies as needed. This strategy, which will be further highlighted in Chapter 9, not only provides students with around-the-clock access to critical documents but also reduces the amount of paper that the professor needs to transport to each class meeting.

In each of the strategies described above, the key factor is being well organized. If you handle the course materials properly, your students will perceive you as a professional and caring teacher. The systematic, consistent use of an organization strategy will also free your mind to manage other aspects of your teaching more effectively, including the important one of interpersonal communications.

In Chapter 4 we emphasized the development of a sound syllabus, and in Chapter 5 we discussed the importance of the initial class meeting on student retention. As you move deeper into the term, revisit your syllabus in class to provide focus, direction, and guidance in your decision making. Abrupt changes, especially those perceived by students as inconsistent with the foundation you have already built, engender confusion and frustration. Although you will no doubt recognize changes you would like to make in the delivery of the materials, the nature of the assignments, the content of the exams, and so on throughout the term, note those changes without making dramatic deviations from the syllabus of the course you are presently teaching.

Lesson Planning

Lesson planning is another important organization function. Although establishing an agenda may keep your class flowing from activity to activity, what you plan to accomplish in those time segments must be clear in your mind and must facilitate the achievement of the overall goals and objectives of your course. The degree of detail in your lesson plans is directly related to your teaching style, experience with the material being taught, and comfort level in the classroom. Strategic lesson planning focuses on four elements: establishing objectives, planning learning experiences, identifying required materials, and evaluating student progress. Each of these is discussed below.

1. Establishing Objectives

In Chapter 4, we provided an overview of Bloom's taxonomy of cognitive objectives—the most widely recognized system for guiding the development of learning outcomes. You might recall from Figure 4.1 that with each of the six levels, we listed common verbs used to describe student behaviors consistent with that level. During your preterm planning, you developed the broad areas of student performance. Prior to each class meeting, your task is to identify the specific expectations of student performance to be attained by the end of the lesson. Writing your objectives with respect to Bloom's levels will help you identify effective classroom activities and an evaluation process that measures student success.

2. Planning Learning Experiences

Focusing as best you can on your students' existing knowledge levels, their learning styles, their overall maturity, and related factors, the next task is to identify activities and teaching methods to match the objectives you clarified above. Chapters 7, 8, and 9 will help you make better decisions related to learning experiences, but it is critical here to answer some foundational questions: What content do you need to present, and what is its appropriate level of complexity for this course? Does it lend itself to using an overhead projector, a PowerPoint presentation, or some other form of visual device to focus students' attention? How do you intend to keep the students engaged in your lecture? Would it be desirable to have students immediately apply their knowledge in a group activity? If so, how will you structure that activity? What is the ideal size of groups for this activity, and how will you select members? What directions do you need to provide so that students can be successful in their group work? How will they share their group findings? What key points do you need to make in debriefing the activity? Do you plan to engage students in discussion? If so, what are the key questions you want to ask? What cognitive level of learning should they reach?

Bloom's taxonomy can be used to formulate questions, just as it can to clarify objectives. Professors typically aim at the higher-order cognitive functions, so plan to evaluate at that level. You should be mindful of the concerns of such education stakeholders as employers, professional groups, and legislators—who complain that college graduates have trouble with higher-order thinking—and ensure that students' higher-order thinking skills are developed to the fullest extent.

3. Identifying Required Materials

When planning your in-class learning experiences, make a list of the specific materials you will need. Are you planning to show a video? Do you have the video close by, or must you retrieve it from someplace else? Do you need to reserve it ahead of time? Is a VCR always available in your classroom, or do you need to order it? If you are planning group work, do you have all the materials you need to share with the students? Make a list of resources you need for each lesson in advance. We have found it worthwhile always to have a tool kit of materials: whiteboard markers, Post-it notes, name tags, a three-hole punch, index cards, scissors, and so on. You may or may not need all in any given class period, but it promotes a sense of security to have them already packed, just in case.

4. Evaluating Student Progress

How are you going to know if the students accomplished the objectives of the lesson? Your evaluation strategies should not only be appropriate for the objectives of the lesson but contribute to the overall evaluation process for the course. If your evaluation strategy indicates that students did not achieve the objectives of the lesson, you can review the material or try a new approach the next time the class meets. It is far better to reteach missed concepts than to continue to plow ahead without the comprehension of the students. An important adage for many professors to remember is "Less is more." Rather than "cover" the material, we should be more concerned with students "learning" the material.

After each class, note what worked and what did not work. Such reflection will allow you to make adjustments in your plans for the next class meeting and will give you a head start when you rethink your class for another term. Reflecting on your practice can also help you focus on problems with clarity, potential examination questions, and alternative sources of materials. Although we do not advocate that you "teach the test," we do believe that what you teach and what you assess must be correlated. Too often students complain that a test did not measure what they studied. If this is a legitimate complaint, it can be traced back to the professor's not planning the instruction and assessment concurrently.

Inevitably, students will ask you, "Is this on the test?" That question may annoy you, but you should be able to answer it honestly. Answers such as "This specific problem won't be on the test, but I will expect you to be able to demonstrate the process used to solve the problem" or "I will not ask you to write out definitions of these terms but rather to use the terms appropriately in your explanation of related phenomena" convey to the students what is important (concepts and process) and what is not important (specific facts).

Developing an Agenda

To ensure that each class meeting is managed efficiently and effectively, it is critical to have an agenda that divides your scheduled time into segments. Such organizing will assist you in pacing the class. Some professors like to write the time allotments on the chalkboard to provide structure for those needing it and to encourage the students to stay on task as well. A typical agenda may look like the following:

1. Reflections on last class meeting (10 minutes)
2. Review of homework assignment (10–15 minutes)
3. Overview of new material (10 minutes)
4. Lecture on new content (20 minutes)
5. Break (10 minutes)
6. Group activity over new content (25 minutes)
7. Group debriefing (15–20 minutes)
8. Explanation of assignments (10 minutes)

Note that the above agenda reinforces mastery of material addressed in the previous session and does not address new content until twenty or twenty-five minutes into the class meeting. Students are not required to be "on" the minute they step into the classroom, allowing some time to transition from their previous class, their workday, and other challenges. In addition, students whose schedules or last-minute conflicts might have delayed their arrival would not be severely penalized by this schedule. Coverage of the most critical content is focused in the core period of the session, when students are most likely to experience optimal mental engagement.

While strategic agenda preparation requires that you spend some time with your course plan to identify activities that foster the achievement of course objectives for a particular group of students, it will enable you to experience the sense of self-satisfaction all teachers need. The personal security that an agenda provides also enables you to focus on fostering a personalized relationship with your students.

Managing Your Class Time

Establishing an agenda and a good lesson plan for each meeting should enable you to keep your class on target. However, unpredictable events sometimes affect even the best planning. To minimize their impact, and to provide you with the optimum amount of time to address your objectives, you would be wise to adhere to the following guidelines:

- *Begin each class precisely on time.* When students know that their tardiness will not affect your class management, they will typically extend themselves to arrive on time. On occasion (e.g., when there is severe weather), you might decide to begin slowly by reviewing previously taught material or even by talking individually with students regarding their progress, but start on time nonetheless.

■ *Adhere to your agenda.* Students frequently complain that professors go off on tangents and tell irrelevant stories. Adhering to your agenda and lesson plans, perhaps by writing the plan on the board or sharing it a day in advance via e-mail, should keep you on target. Remember, however, that you have developed your agenda and lesson plans on assumptions about your students' ability to learn. If they are exhibiting comprehension difficulties, you should adjust your agenda and lesson plan and regroup, rethink, and perhaps reteach on the spot.

■ *Schedule breaks.* In a class lasting longer than one hour, schedule a ten-minute break midway through the session. For classes of three or more hours, schedule two breaks of ten minutes each or a midway break of fifteen or twenty minutes. The starting time of the class and its proximity to typical mealtimes, the walking distance to various facilities, and so on should be factored into such decisions. (It might be wise to assess your students' preferences on this decision at your first class meeting, thereby fostering the perception that this is their class.) Announce and write on the board what time students should return from a break, and start your class on time afterward. Otherwise, students are likely to get caught up in conversations or activities that prolong your starting time, affect instructional effectiveness, frustrate highly focused students, and foster ill will. You might also want to double-check attendance after the break. If students use the break as an excuse to skip out early, address the situation proactively at the following class meeting by explaining its impact on your management of the class and requesting that anyone who must leave early tell you so at the start of the break.

■ *In discussions, shut off nonproductive talk.* Whether with the whole class or in small groups, discussions must be targeted to your learning objectives. When a student makes a tangential comment, you can confirm the interesting nature of the point and then redirect discussion to the central issue. When students are working in small groups, circulate among them actively, especially at the beginning, to ensure that everyone fully understands the goals of the activity and remains on task to accomplish them. Chapter 8 presents more details on using small classroom groups effectively.

■ *Whenever possible, relate course content to everyday events.* Integrate the news from the international, national, and local scenes, as well as from pop culture and sports into your content if you can. Add relevant cartoons or quotations to your presentations. Find props to enhance your students' engagement. Pay attention to your voice projection, volume, enunciations, and variety—for example, when properly employed, dramatic elongated pauses can engender student reflection. Use gestures to emphasize important ideas and concepts, and move throughout the room to nudge the disengaged into the dialogue. Communication theory tells us that nonverbal cues are stronger than verbal cues, so be sure that your nonverbal gestures do not detract from or negate what you say. Most important, plan to make your class relevant to the specific group of students enrolled and exercise a bit of levity. Even if you are "humor-challenged," you can probably apply your points by telling a story to which your students are likely to relate. The idea is to provide students an extra reason to attend when their lives hold so many diversions that they might be tempted not to come to class.

■ *Use the class time in its entirety.* Avoid being swayed by some students' requests to go home early. Usually such requests are made by a few highly vocal but relatively unmotivated students. Your most motivated students silently reject the suggestions from their counterparts to cut classes short. Which students would you want to reward for their behavior—the motivated or the unmotivated?

■ *End class on time.* If you become sidetracked from your agenda, do not expect students to remain after the scheduled ending time of the class to make up the lost time. You will have to use the next session for catch-up. Many of your students have family, work, or other school obligations to meet after class, and making them late discounts your standing in their eyes. Being overly free-flowing does not foster a positive learning environment in your classroom.

■ *Before dismissing the class, remind students of what they can expect during the next session.* If you have a special event planned, such as a guest speaker or a highly controversial video, convey that information enthusiastically to the students, so that they will look forward to returning. Their energy will feed the occasion.

Ineffective professors often mistakenly view the class period as time to fill so that students stay busy. Strategic professors realize that with clearly established learning objectives, well-chosen resources, and strong teaching and learning methods, time management is a relatively easy issue to master.

Managing Your Classroom Environment

Managing your class time strategically will prevent or help you overcome most of your challenges. There are, however, several additional practices that will help you to ensure that the environment is conducive to maximum learning, perceived as fair by students, and supportive of your own peace of mind. Depending on the characteristics of your students and your own comfort level, you might be able to allow students to contribute to one or more of these practices.

First, develop a workable system for taking roll. Most student financial aid programs require participants to attend class regularly, so record keeping is a must. You might want to circulate a roll sheet, reminding students that they are responsible for neatly entering their names. As mentioned earlier, seating charts can help you check attendance at the start of each class meeting. Whatever method you choose, follow it systematically and explain it orally and on your syllabus so that each student fully understands your policy.

Next, plan somehow for the arrival of latecomers. Locking the door behind you as you enter the classroom is no longer considered a defendable option at most institutions. A viable possibility, however, is to designate specific seats within the classroom for late arrivers and admonish those who do so to enter quietly and follow the attendance record-keeping protocol you have established. This strategy minimizes distractions and allows you and your students to remain focused on your learning objectives.

Finally, institutions of higher education are increasingly engaging their students in "service learning," in hopes of their developing a more grounded understanding of their obligations to their communities. As their exemplar, you should model such behavior in the most basic of ways, by demonstrating responsible housekeeping practices in your classroom. No professor or class should have to follow another class into an unkempt classroom. You should accept the responsibility to leave the classroom in at least as good a condition as you found it. Boards should be erased clean, furniture properly arranged, and trash placed in a proper receptacle. Besides modeling responsible behavior for students, you will also maintain the respect of the housekeeping staff. If you are tempted to underappreciate the custodian's role, imagine having to ask a custodian to unlock your office because you have left your keys on your desk. The custodian whose area of responsibility has been consistently well treated by your students is likely to come to your aid generously.

Improving Interpersonal Communications

As we have emphasized throughout this book, the reality in the highly competitive life of today's postsecondary institutions is that professors have some obligation not only to motivate students to continue in their pursuit of higher education but also, to some degree, to "sell" their programs such that their reputations serve as effective recruiting tools.

Besides being well prepared for your classes and conducting efficient and interesting lessons, you can develop positive reactions from your students through good interpersonal communications. There are several guidelines you can follow:

- Listen to your students—free of preconceptions. You should spend at least as much time listening as speaking. Students want to communicate; give them the opportunity to do so.
- Perception is important. Choose your words carefully to be respectful of social and cultural differences in your classroom.
- Both praise and criticism of individual student's work are best given privately. Excessive praise in front of the class can be as devastating to the student as excessive criticism—either can be embarrassing. However, written praise or criticism can be personal and helpful, particularly when the comments are constructive.

- Do not argue with your students. Students frequently like to engage in arguments with you or their fellow students and in doing so can push you to the limit. Arguing in front of the class rarely works; although you may win the verbal battle, ultimately you will lose the battle for control. If there is disagreement, encourage the student to stay after class or come to your office to continue the dialogue. Both in class and in private, control your emotions.

An especially effective tool for managing your communications with students (and others) is transactional analysis (Stewart and Joines, 1987). Developed by psychotherapist Eric Berne (1964), this theory recognizes that each of us has developed three ego states that determine the communications patterns we regularly employ. The first ego state is that of "child." It is a totally emotional state characterized by self-absorption and dependency on others for need satisfaction and is often observed as either pouting or being rebellious. Language is very *I* centered: "I want," "give me," "I expect," "I need."

The second ego state is that of "parent." This is also an emotional state, one characterized by either judgmental or nurturing language, such as: "You made me very proud," "You make me angry," "You cannot seem to do anything right," "You demand a lot of attention," "You will not graduate if you do not start applying yourself." Note that the parental ego state uses *you* language.

The third ego state is that of "adult." This is an objective, analytical ego state that emphasizes higher-order and critical-thinking language: "Let's analyze what we have said here and determine where we are," "We have been very creative in our thinking—let's examine our thoughts," "We have been doing a lot of evaluating here—can we look again at our criteria and see if we are applying them equally and fairly?" Language in this state is frequently *we* language and indicates the equality of the people involved in the transaction.

Only one ego state predominates in an individual at a given time. However, all three might come into play during any single class session given the range of individuals in the class. The effective professor will seek to elevate interaction to adult ego states and to keep the class dialogue objective and collaborative. Enjoying a resurgence of popularity among those in the helping professions, transactional analysis is a practical tool that can help you cope in your classroom with the variety of challenges students will pose.

Transactional Analysis Exercise

For each scenario below, identify the ego state from which each of the three statements that follows is generated. Then select the most effective statement for the situation.

1. At the end of the first meeting of a new class, a student asks: "This class really has a lot of work required. Do many students flunk?" The professor responds:

    a. "Only the lazy ones who don't get with it right away."

    b. "I do everything I possibly can to make sure everyone passes."

    c. "The course material is challenging, but I provide many resources for helping everyone learn it. Nearly all students are successful in this course."

2. During the second class meeting, the professor states a well-developed position on a controversial topic. A student heatedly attacks the professor's position. The professor responds:

    a. "It's clear you've been brainwashed by one side of this issue."

    b. "Can I see a show of hands of those of you who support that position?"

    c. "You've stated a viewpoint that many people believe to be true. One of the most important reasons we attend college is to be exposed to divergent points of view; this exposure helps us make more grounded decisions throughout our lives."

3. Thirty minutes into the third class meeting, a student's cell phone rings, and he gets up to go into the hall to answer it. The professor says:

    a. "Oh noooooooo!"

    b. "I told you not to let that happen! See me after class!"

    c. Nothing at the time, but before dismissing class says, "Now that we're up and running, I want to remind everyone that our syllabus asks you to keep personal communications devices in the mute position. If you're in a potential emergency situation of some kind, please let me know before the class starts."

4. During the review of the results of the first exam, a student emotionally states that a certain question was tricky. The professor says:

    a. "Tricky? If you really knew the material, you wouldn't say that!"

    b. "Really? I used the test bank. You'd think all the questions would be good."

    c. "Hmm. What about that question do you believe is unfair?"

5. At the end of a class during which the professor returned the first scored papers, a struggling student approaches to question her less-than-perfect grade. The professor says:

    a. "You look disappointed. Would you like to talk about the paper?"

    b. "Cheer up, it's only one grade."

    c. "You made above the class average, a very acceptable grade on the first paper."

Exercise Answers and Discussion

Communications experts say that when messages are mixed, only 7 percent of the meaning is attributable to the words themselves, while 38 percent is attributable to the tone of voice, and 55 percent to the body language used. Thus, in the above exercises, since you have only words on which to base your answers, your choices might vary from ours given below.

Our perception is that in scenario 1, *a* reaction comes from a judgmental parent, *b* from a nurturing parent, and *c* from the adult ego state. Using *c* prevents the parent from being hooked by the question and fosters an objective communications dynamic as the course gets launched. Note that the parent ego state reacts emotionally, whereas the adult ego state responds objectively.

In scenario 2, response *a* comes from a judgmental parent, *b* from the irresponsible child, and *c* from the adult ego state. As in the first scenario, *c* is clearly the most effective response.

In scenario 3, response *a* comes from the child, *b* from the judgmental parent, and *c* from the adult ego state. Again, the adult response is the most effective, reminding students of the agreed-on policy while also recognizing that there might be legitimate reasons to have a personal communications device. If the professor controls his or her tone of voice carefully, the dignity of the student is protected.

In scenario 4, response *a* comes from the judgmental parent, *b* from the irresponsible child, and *c* from the adult ego state. Again, the adult response is clearly the most effective.

In scenario 5, response *a* seems to come from a nurturing parent, *b* from a child or perhaps a judgmental parent (seeing only the words prevents us from knowing for sure, but it is definitely from an emotional ego state), while *c* comes from the adult ego state. In this case, however, the adult response is probably not the most effective for a struggling student. The nurturing parent response demonstrates a sensitivity that the student would likely perceive as helpful.

Although our discussion of transactional analysis is limited, you can see that it has great potential to impact the effectiveness of your course management. Like other concepts we present in this book, it is one of many tools that you might employ to improve outcomes with students and make your teaching more consistent and rewarding. Stay open to trying new approaches, even if they feel uncomfortable at first. Such openness is extremely critical in an age of accountability.

Special Strategies for Managing Large Classes

Over the past few decades, finances have constrained academic decision making. The strategy of employing large introductory classes to subsidize small upper-division and graduate-level classes is now a fact of life at many institutions. At the same time, the accountability movement will no longer permit some of the common shortcomings of large classes—such as students' disengagement and easy tests that measure only surface knowledge—because these lead to low evaluations from students and other stakeholders and a perception of reduced learning. Besides dealing with security, confidentiality, and other logistical issues, those who teach large classes must markedly scrutinize their management of the learning process to ensure student success.

While true in a class of any size, the planning and organizing functions are especially critical in the effective management of large classes. Issues that should be addressed prior to the first class meeting to maximize student focus and minimize unproductive time include:

- Visiting the classroom well in advance so that you can leverage its size and equipment to orchestrate compelling "events" that could not be duplicated in a small classroom.
- Staggering dates of exams and submission dates for papers with those of your other courses to avoid bottlenecks in paper flow and delays in returning scored projects.
- Developing systems for expediting roll-taking, distribution of handouts, collection of student assignments (you might think about a slotted lock box), and other logistical tasks (Davis, 2001).
- Dedicating a seating area near the door for late arrivers and early leavers, and stressing noise minimization.
- Selecting a cadre of student aides, from previous proven students or new ones who visit your office prior to the start of the term, and providing a system of incentives that will foster their high achievement of quality service to students.

In your decision-making process, consult with other professors in your area to see what has worked well and poorly for them. Your strategies on the points that directly affect students must be clearly communicated in your syllabus, orally at the opening class meeting, and reinforced in other early meetings and as needed throughout the remainder of the term. Be cautious about ignoring negative feedback on your systems or changing them because a few students complain. Instead, conduct an informal evaluation by all students in the class partway into the course to ensure that the policies and procedures are workable in the majority of students' eyes. (See Chapter 13 for more information on informal evaluations.)

Often, professors believe that the only workable instructional method in a large class is the lecture. After all, the rooms where we teach large classes are called *lecture* halls. We would like to propose, however, that the lecture is only one of the methods that can be used effectively in a large class. Research conducted by Graham Gibbs (1998), of the Open University, indicates that the effectiveness of large introductory classes is increased when the focus is on learning rather than on teaching, when assessment is strategically employed to foster focus on learning objectives, when students do for themselves and for each other some of what the professor once did for them, and when peer support and peer pressure are fostered. So, rather than employ the common authoritative approach, whose judgmental-parent ego state is likely to trigger students' surreptitious rebellion and irresponsibility, you might want to consider an alternative instructional strategy. Another critical key to success in large classes is making them at times "psychologically small," by dividing the large class into small groups for some of the learning experiences—starting from the very first day. Students thus have a smaller number of classmates to get to know and can feel safe. When larger groups are needed, the professor can combine two or more smaller groups, gradually expanding the number of students who interact comfortably.

Part of making a class seem psychologically small is to learn as many students' names as possible. As we discussed in Chapter 5, although learning names in a large class is more challenging doing so encourages participation by students who are more likely to feel anonymous. Consider having students make a note of every time they participate by asking a question, making a cogent comment, and so on, then direct them to turn in the notes, with their names, at the end of class each day, with enough description to allow the professor to identify the comment or question. The professor can then write back to each student with encouragement, answers, or whatever else is appropriate. A professor can also choose to give participation points to those students who take advantage of this learning opportunity.

A variation on this idea of participation notes allows you to take attendance as well. All students are given an index card on the first day. They write their names right on the top, and from that day forward they pick up their cards as they walk into class. The professor can see which cards are left in the box and thus can mark down absences. Either during the class or as a closure for the day, students are to write on their cards a question, a comment, a summary, or a point they would like to see reviewed in an upcoming class. After class, the professor can quickly read through these cards and get a sense of what was understood, what might still be muddy, and where an appropriate starting place for the next class period would be. They can also write back to the students to heighten the sense of connection that is so important to learning.

Earlier in this section, we mentioned dividing the class into small groups or teams. Teams of four to six students are typically large enough to provide diversity of experience and motivation, while being small enough to manage. In a class of several hundred, you might designate the teams with names of states or other geographical regions or the names of well-known political figures (e.g., Pierre Trudeau or John F. Kennedy). Allowing students to pick their own team members, following an icebreaker exercise (see Chapter 5), would reduce logistical challenges. You might also allow individuals to opt out, in which case they would do the entire team project themselves or with fewer partners. In giving broad assignments, make it clear that team members must divide the work equitably. Team members could then evaluate the contribution of their teammates by assigning shares of a total allocation and communicating this allocation to you by private e-mail. For example, if you use five-member teams, each member would be expected to divide 400 points among the other team members (i.e., the rater excludes him- or herself). The scores from one member for the other members might be 120, 110, 90, 80. All of the team members' scores will be averaged, creating the individual team member's score on the project. (To protect an individual student's grade, a minimum threshold of 50 points might be imposed.) You or one of your teaching assistants should probably meet early in the term with each team to clarify understanding of the syllabus, assignments, and so on. Or you might have the teams select captains with whom you will meet. You can also create e-mail lists for each team, and the class as a whole, to dispense information throughout the term and to facilitate feedback as projects move along. Such a setup can establish a didactic environment not only between you and your students but also among the students themselves.

You need not limit the use of teams to outside assignments. Learning within the classroom is greatly enhanced when students are expected to play a more active role than they typically play in a large lecture-driven class. For example, after delivering a certain amount of material from the front of the room, have students discuss that material in pairs or "buzz groups." Display several questions to be answered within the small group and then shared with another group across the aisle. In such a process, students advance in Bloom's taxonomy toward a greater understanding of critical course concepts.

Employing teams and group discussions not only facilitates management of the large course but also creates opportunities for support and competition that will likely make the course more enjoyable for students while improving the quality of their learning. Working in teams also gives students an opportunity to develop their interpersonal skills and fosters learning beyond the classroom. Finally, this strategy helps you manage your time effectively by allowing you to focus on issues that emerge throughout the term as teams meet, rather than dealing with an array of questions all at the same time. Once you have experienced the results of this approach and have worked through the loss of ego gratification that comes from being the "sage on the stage," you will likely ask yourself why it took you so long to understand that education is more about student learning than it is about teaching.

Managing the First Exam or Major Assignment

No event demonstrates your success as a teacher more than does your first major examination or assignment. As we noted in Chapter 2, the first exam or major assignment is often the most critical milepost in students' deciding to remain in a course through its conclusion. Therefore, it is imperative that such assessment tools are well designed, fair, and deemed relevant by the students—issues that will be addressed comprehensively in Chapter 10. In addition, it is essential to view this critical milepost in a context that recognizes both student responsibility and professors' accountability. We do not believe the first exam or assignment should be made artificially easy—in fact, it should reinforce high standards. However professors should provide students with clear expectations of the exercise so that their study time is focused and that the scores reward those who are most effectively prepared.

First, as you teach, clue students in to important concepts and ideas that you intend to include on the examination. Provide an ample review—both in writing and orally, and perhaps a short sample exercise that includes questions similar to those that will appear on the exam. Also tell them what format(s) the examination will use—multiple-choice, short-answer, essay, or some combination of these formats—and how much time they will have to complete the examination. If you intend to use essay questions, you should provide sample questions and a rubric for how you will evaluate the answers. Remember, examinations should not serve the purpose of catching the ill-prepared student but should instead help you and your students evaluate their understanding of the content they have been studying.

The first true psychological milepost for retention is the students' perceptions of their first exam or assignment results. Some students will inherently know how they did, while others will need to see the scored document. Typically some will underperform and be the most likely to drop the course. Anticipating this result, strategic professors must decide what, if any, action they will take to deal with the situation. "Curving" the test results—in which students are awarded unearned points so that the total class results more closely approximate a bell curve—is in our minds indefensible in an age of accountability. When students underperform on the first exam, you should conduct an analysis of the test results—perhaps facilitated by a Scantron system or other technological tactic—which identifies the test items most frequently missed, then evaluate each frequently missed item for its clarity, validity, and other salient features. The presence of poorly constructed questions, answered correctly by only a few students, might indicate that you should omit those questions and recalculate the scores. Another possibility that one of the authors has employed with great success is to offer students the opportunity to drop their score on the first exam. He reasons that some students add the course late, are delayed in purchasing the text, or have somewhat valid reasons for not being as prepared as they might be. Since his syllabus lists five total assignments, each weighted at 20 percent of the final course grade, he allows students to exercise "Plan B" by simply writing that phrase on the next scored assignment. He goes on to explain that there will be no "Plan C, D, or X." Each term he is convinced that several students are retained who would have otherwise dropped the class (Lyons, Kysilka, and Pawlas, 1999).

If your scored assignment is a major paper or project, you should break the assignment into several chunks and provide feedback to your students on each of them. For a major paper, you might have students develop a theme statement and an outline of the argument to submit for review and scoring. The second chunk might focus on the resources they intend to use to build their argument, and the final piece may be the completed paper. Every major written assignment or project should be coupled with a rubric (see Chapter 11) that is shared with the student at the time the assignment is made. By giving students the scoring criteria up front, you indicate what is important to you; students can then expend their time and energy in positive ways to complete the assignment. If students perceive that you are fair in the assignments and feedback you give, they will be more likely to persist in your course.

Surviving When You Are Not Prepared

At one time or another, all professors face a class for which they are not prepared, because of an emergency illness, family problems, or last-minute demands by administrators. Most students are reasonably understanding the first time this happens. However, they do not tolerate a consistent lack of preparation and are not shy about expressing their dissatisfaction either on student evaluations or directly to institutional leaders. The following strategies can help you to cover for yourself when you are unprepared to meet your class:

■ Seek help from a colleague who has an area of expertise that can fit into your curriculum. Fellow faculty members are often willing to become a last-minute guest speaker in a pinch and may even enjoy conversing with your students on a topic they are really excited about.

■ Have students engage in brainstorming activities regarding a concept or an idea you presented in a previous class. Through the brainstorming, they can examine ideas from a variety of perspectives and perhaps gain a more thorough understanding of the concept or idea.

■ Break students into small groups and have them develop questions they think would be appropriate on their next examination. You might even suggest that they write sample exam items. You can then incorporate their suggestions into the examination you give. Such an activity not only serves as a review for your students but also provides you with information about what they perceive to be the most important concepts to learn.

■ Locate a video at your institution's media center or a video rental store that can embellish what you have been teaching. The video may provide an opposite viewpoint, emphasize important concepts, raise specific questions, or simply clarify for students what they read.

■ Have students work in groups on an upcoming project. You might even excuse them to go to the library or computer lab to work on their project. Students, particularly if they are busy adults, appreciate having some class time to work on projects. Have them report on their progress at the next class meeting so that they do not take advantage of the released time to do other things.

■ As a last resort, admit to students that you are not as prepared as you intended to be, and ask them how they could best use the class time. Whenever you give students the authority to make decisions, you are obligated to abide by those decisions even when you do not approve of them. If students say, "Let's cancel class," you may find that you simply lose class time. In letting students plan activities, you can set parameters saying, for example, "Why don't we do some brainstorming—anything but canceling class is a valid option—then select the one that would be of greatest value."

Being spontaneous and relaxed can usually help you through awkward moments. If an emergency arises that causes you to miss class, be sure to notify the administrator who is designated, in turn, to notify your class. When you return to class, apologize to your students and adjust your syllabus accordingly. Having collected e-mail and phone numbers of all the students in your class, you can notify them easily in advance about your impending absence and later follow up with them about how you plan to make up the lost time. Even if you notify your students directly, remember to notify your administrator as well.

Adhering to Ethical Standards

Like all professionals, college professors must adhere to a code of ethics that serves as a guide to fair and equal treatment of all students in their classes. Behaving in ethical ways is easier if you familiarize yourself with your institution's policies regarding students' rights and responsibilities, and if you attempt to view situations through the eyes of the stakeholders. Read both the student handbook that outlines students' rights and the faculty handbook that indicates your rights, responsibilities, and rules of conduct. In the absence of written rules provided by your institution, the following guidelines related to commonly occurring challenges could serve you well:

■ Discuss student progress or problems *only* with the student. If a student is a legal minor, you may be asked to speak to a parent or guardian, but this should be done in the presence of the student. Remember, your students are adults and the Federal Educational Rights and Privacy Act (FERPA), enacted in 1974, protects them against disclosure of critical information.

■ If students share troubling information with you—such as details about illegal activities or mental/emotional distress—encourage them to access support resources available to them on campus, such as free counseling services. If students are hesitant about contacting these services, you might ask if they would prefer that you make an appointment for them. In that way, you can help them avoid the awkwardness of having to call a stranger for help. If a student refuses to get help, and you believe that student can become dangerous to him- or herself or to others, seek the advice of your administrator. Between the two of you, you can research institutional policies and procedures to find a way to help the student, or at least to protect other students and yourself.

■ Do not accept payment from students for tutoring, consulting, or similar duties that are a logical extension of your role. Similarly, if you use books you publish or other materials you own in your classes, you need to be certain that any royalties you earn from those materials are given to your institution's foundation. Books and materials sold to students enrolled in other institutions can of course contribute to your income.

■ Be careful about socializing with your students. Many professors like to celebrate the end of a term with their students, particularly if the class was an exceptionally good one. Bringing snacks to class is probably acceptable (but check with your school policy). Planning to go to a restaurant or pub, however, may be a little more risky. If you meet at an establishment where alcohol is served and any of your underage students is caught drinking, you could be held liable. Even when all of your students are legal age, in today's litigious society you may find yourself involved in a lawsuit if, during or after a party you arranged or sanctioned, any student is injured or injures someone else. Decline any invitations by your students to parties with them away from the campus. Another note of caution: Under no circumstances should you ever celebrate with only one or two students. Not only could your reputation be tarnished, perhaps irreparably, but you also risk putting students in an extremely awkward situation vis-à-vis their families, peers, and campus or community authorities. This precept certainly precludes dating students, even if they are single and close to your age. Dating students can put both parties into very uncomfortable situations and can jeopardize your future at your institution.

Professional Practices Exercise

Since professional challenges arise suddenly, let us present some potential situations, give you an opportunity to respond, and then debrief with some useful insights regarding each scenario.

1. At the conclusion of your Tuesday-morning class, you return to your office to find an adult female whom you don't know reviewing the office hours posted on your door. After you introduce yourself, she responds in a nervous tone, "I'm Mary Smith, the mother of April Miller, who is a student in the class you just completed." You invite her into your office, ask her to have a seat, and offer her some water. She continues, "April didn't come home last night, and we're worried sick. For the past couple of weeks, she has been behaving erratically. Has she been having problems in your class?"

2. In your largest class, Chris is clearly one of the brightest students. Seemingly without having to exert himself, Chris was able to achieve scores on the first two exams in the low 90s. Earlier today, as Chris submitted the first term paper, you overheard a conversation between him and one of his friends that led you to believe that his paper might be inappropriate. Giving

it a quick review in your office, you notice that although it is well written, the paper does not fit several of the specific performance standards you identified at the time the assignment was made.

3. Samantha struggled the entire term in your class. She came by your office nearly every week to get tutoring on difficult issues. By the end of the term, she had made very good progress, scoring an A on the last unit exam. On the last day of the term, barely an hour after completing her final exam, Samantha appeared at your office door with a gift-wrapped package in her hands. Holding the gift toward you, she expressed how thankful she was for the help that you had provided her in the course and asked that you accept the gift as a symbol of her appreciation.

4. Your Wednesday-evening class has been an absolute joy to teach. Mostly working adults, the students have arrived promptly and been well prepared for each class meeting, worked cohesively in small-group situations, and performed well on all of your assessment activities. Tonight, as you distribute the final exam, one of the informal leaders announces, "We're meeting down at the Campus Pub to celebrate after the test is over. Won't you join us?"

Debriefing

1. Unfortunately, Ms. Smith's situation is becoming increasingly common. When her daughter was younger, she may well have had the child's behavioral issues addressed proactively by the teachers and administrators of schools that April attended. Now, however, April at least eighteen years old, is no longer considered a minor. FERPA protects even immature adults from unwarranted disclosure of their educational progress. While using your emotional intelligence to demonstrate genuine concern for Ms. Smith, it is critical not to divulge information that would put yourself, or potentially April, at risk.

2. The challenge this situation presents has been complicated greatly by the advent of the Internet, the rise in the number of classes with large enrollments, the changing perceptions of what cheating means, and other factors. The potential problems here are many and varied, but it is critical to address the situation soberly, without accusing Chris of cheating. The possibilities include, but are not limited to, Chris's having downloaded a paper from a Web vendor of such products, his resubmitting a paper written for a previous class, and his using material provided by his peers. Your most responsible strategy might be to ask a colleague to be present in your office when you bring Chris by after your next class for a clarification meeting. Broach the topic clearly by stating what you actually saw and heard. Then say, "Chris, I have questions about the goals and direction of the paper you recently submitted. Would you help me understand how you approached it?" As you listen closely to his response, you might—rather than asking additional, pointed questions too quickly—rephrase and reflect

his explanation so that you become clear on all salient issues. While submitting downloaded papers is clearly plagiarism, and likely subject to your institution's disciplinary policies, it may well be that Chris did not understand the implications of his resubmitting a paper with few or no changes.

3. The acceptance of any gift from a student enrolled in your class jeopardizes your being viewed as objective in the determination of final grades. Thank Samantha for her thoughtfulness, but tell her that your help was provided with no expectation of reward. Encourage her to extend the gift to a family member or friend for whom such an expression of gratitude is appropriate.

4. Never drink with students while they are enrolled in your classes. Besides the absence of professionalism that the acceptance of this invitation would demonstrate, there are at least three major risks to you. First, if you attend, your students' pub outing may well appear to an administrator, a judge hearing a drunken-driving/injury case, or some other official to be a sanctioned class event. Second, if even one of your students is underage, your pub appearance could make you liable for contributing to the delinquency of a minor. Finally, if even one of the students has a history of substance abuse, you do not want to support an event that may contribute to his or her difficulty. You can either ask the class to move the celebration to a venue that does not serve alcohol or to politely beg off.

Dealing with Disruptive Students

In all areas of society—higher education included—many people feel that incivility has escalated in both degree and frequency. Remember that students arrive in classrooms with increasing amounts of baggage; you cannot expect your teaching to be immune from disruptive incidents. Although we offer no guarantee, we believe that the suggestions we make in this book about getting to know students and understanding their learning styles will go a long way toward preventing the frequency and degree of disruptive behavior.

We nonetheless realize that some situations arise that inevitably trigger unacceptable reactions in some students. Such reactions are likely to include loud excessive talking, profane or defamatory language, or physical invasion of others' space. In an increasingly accountability-minded and litigious society, you cannot fail to respond when students cross the line with you or with their fellow students. Not responding to unacceptable behavior from a student creates a hostile environment for other students, reduces the effectiveness of instruction, and detracts from your standing with students. We encourage the following practices become a part of your style addressing such situations:

- Refer students to campus support resources.
- Confront students quietly outside of class.

- Employ your adult ego state and refuse to become angry, sarcastic, or accusatory.
- Go the extra mile to preserve the dignity of all concerned.
- Keep private issues private.
- Document actions and words immediately, and inform those who have responsibility for student affairs.

Summary of Key Points

- Develop a means to organize your materials that works effectively for you.
- Plan your daily agenda and have lesson plans for each class meeting.
- Provide feedback to your students—privately and in open classroom settings.
- Start and stop your classes on time.
- Plan breaks accordingly and restart your class on time.
- Plan for such environmental factors as roll taking, late arrivals, and housekeeping.
- Develop alternatives to the lecture format for large classes.
- Strive to engage your students at adult levels of conversation.
- Prepare the first exam or major assignment carefully to ensure fairness and relevance.
- Have alternatives in mind when you are underprepared or have to cancel a class.
- Adhere to a code of ethics and professional practices.
- Address disruptive students proactively.
- Remember to have fun!

Through the Professors' Eyes

PAT: I am always trying to improve my organizational strategies. Years ago, I found that keeping separate notebooks for each of my classes really works well for me. I have developed sets of transparencies that I have labeled according to my course objectives. I keep them in plastic page protectors, secured in notebooks so they are handy and ready to use. They also don't get messed up that way. I also have identified videos that can be used for each course and keep a list of them filed with each course notebook so that I can remember their specific strengths and weaknesses. I'm always on the lookout for new materials, and I ask my students to help too. Many times they will see something on television that directly applies to what I am teaching, and they let me know or even bring me a recorded video clip. I put a lot of stock in student recommendations and try to use those that are a good fit for the course. The more organized I am with respect to my class, the more comfortable I am about exploring beyond the course objectives. Sometimes, the spontaneous discussions are much more fruitful than the activities I planned for class. I like the freedom to adventure into unplanned tangents and can nearly always relate such escapades to my class objectives.

DALE: I have never really had much problem with course organization. I have identified the essential information and have found the most efficient way to present it is through well-designed and well-orchestrated lectures. I've developed a very effective presentation of my course content. The students don't complain when they get an excellent lecture. Being highly organized in my teaching provides me with the time I want to do my research and work on my publications. Since I teach the same class every term, I don't need to worry about how I manage my course. It's all in one notebook. The only time I really need to make adjustments is when new versions of textbooks come out—I usually vote to adopt the texts that have been used the previous year. Why reinvent the wheel? Most are very good books, though perhaps not the best on the market. Students do increasingly complain about the costs of textbooks.

KIM: I am having some conflicts in my thinking about how to teach my classes. I know what needs to be taught, and my department colleagues and mentor have really helped me. I have discovered, though, that they are all busy with their own work, so I try not to ask trivial questions and use up their goodwill. I am trying to meet my students' expectations and my college's student-centered learning goals, but I am really more comfortable in the more formal lecture format. After all, that model is what I know best. I also note a difference between the learning goals of my younger and older students. When I do plan some student-centered activities, my older students do not participate as well as my younger students do. One of my older students seems to feel that a lack of English language skills is synonymous with lack of intelligence, and I am challenged not to become angry with him. Other older students seem to think they can be very informal with me and can call me by my first name. Although they are my elders by several years, I do not think that is good and sometimes worry that what they are doing does not show the respect a professor deserves. One of my Eastern European colleagues allows her students to call her Dr. D. Maybe I can let my students call me Dr. Kim. I am trying so hard to find a "best way" to organize my classes and to establish rapport with my students. I am getting so frustrated. There is so much to think about and to plan for—I thought teaching would be easier than this.

Tips for Thriving

Interacting with students in class can be one of the most rewarding aspects of your career. In order to be highly successful in that endeavor, you need to answer a few important questions:

1. What would you expect from the class if you were the student?
2. What activities would you enjoy most if you were a student in your class?
3. What other activities should you plan in order to meet the needs of the diverse students in your class?
4. How can you make large classes seem small?
5. What were the communication strategies of your best professors?
6. What are the fundamentals of ethical practice?

By answering these questions, you will have guidelines that can make you successful in your classes. If after you plan your course, you reexamine your efforts by thinking as a student, you should be able to make your classes both enjoyable and challenging. Remember, students really do like to be fairly challenged. Also keep in mind that a good teacher is a good listener who can alter conditions of learning as necessary to ensure good learning by the students.

SUGGESTED READINGS

Hativa, N. (2000). *Teaching for Effective Learning in Higher Education.* Dordrecht, Netherlands: Kluware Academic Publishers.
James, M., and D. Jongeward. (1996). *Born to Win.* Cambridge, MA: Perseus Books.

CHAPTER

7 Instructor-Directed
Learning Methods

FOCUS QUESTIONS

- What methods can you direct that will help students learn most effectively?
- How do you create an environment in your classroom that is conducive to learning?
- How can you enhance the effectiveness of lectures with today's students?
- What measures should you take to maximize learning outcomes from video presentations and guest speakers?

For decades, many professors were concerned about what they "covered" in their classes. But let us take a look at how *The American Heritage Dictionary of the English Language*, fourth edition (2000), defines the transitive verb *cover*. Skim through the following definitions asking yourself which ones describe what a professor is doing when "covering" material classroom:

> **1.** To place something upon or over, so as to protect or conceal. **2.** To overlay or spread with something: *cover potatoes with gravy.* **3a.** To put a cover or covering on. **b.** To wrap up; clothe. **4.** To invest (oneself) with a great deal of something: *covered themselves with glory.* **5a.** To spread over the surface of: *dust covered the table.* **b.** To extend over: *a farm covering more than 100 acres.* **6a.** To copulate with (a female). Used especially of horses. **b.** To sit on in order to hatch. **7.** To hide or screen from view or knowledge; conceal: *covered up his misdemeanors.* **8a.** To protect or shield from harm, loss, or danger. **b.** To protect by insurance: *took out a new policy that will cover all our camera equipment.* **c.** To compensate or make up for. **9.** To be sufficient to defray, meet, or offset the cost or charge of: *had enough funds to cover her check.* **10.** To make provision for; take into account: *The law does not cover all crimes.* **11.** To deal with; treat of: *The book covers the feminist movement.* **12.** To travel or pass over; traverse: *They covered 60 miles in two days.* **13a.** To have as one's territory or sphere

of work. **b.** To be responsible for reporting the details of (an event or situation): *Two reporters covered the news story.* **14.** To hold within the range and aim of a weapon, such as a firearm. **15.** To protect, as from enemy attack, by occupying a strategic position. **16.** *Sports* **a.** To guard (an opponent playing offense). **b.** To defend (a position or area): *cover third base.* **17.** To match (an opponent's stake) in a wager. **18.** To purchase (stock that one has shorted). **19.** *Games* To play a higher-ranking card than (the one previously played). **20.** *Music* To record a cover version of (a song). **21.** *Obsolete* To pardon or remit.

We feel fairly confident that none of them do! While we are hopeful that this brought a chuckle, the more sobering point is what sort of learning is being orchestrated when the professor's approach to teaching is covering material? Today's professors realize they are no longer held accountable for what they cover, but for the grounded learning they foster in students. As you begin this chapter, we ask you to examine your fundamental teaching and classroom paradigms and open your mind to a new perspective.

A Continuum of Methods

One of the primary aims of this book is to help you develop a teaching style that is not only effective with students and accountable to other stakeholders, but also personally rewarding to you. Most college professors, early in their teaching experience, teach as they were taught. Unfortunately, these models and techniques may not be effective with some of the students you read about in Chapter 3. Helping these students achieve learning success requires you to understand your own philosophical base as discussed in Chapter 2. It also obliges you to become familiar with various teaching methods built on sound principles, as well as to understand how students perceive and process the information flow that you create within your classroom (Ericksen, 198).

This chapter and the next address the seemingly opposite ends of a continuum. At one end are instructor-directed learning methods—at the other are student-driven learning methods. The strength of instructor-directed learning methods lies in their potential to provide students with structure, organization, and sequence, and so it is with these that we begin. They do have their limitations, though, which we discuss at various points in this chapter and the next. Keep in mind as you read both chapters that ultimately, deciding which methods to use will depend on your determination of the most effective way to achieve a particular learning objective through your instruction.

As you begin to conceptualize how you will approach your teaching, you will likely reflect on your own student experiences. You may have had deeply traditional professors who, in a misguided effort to stress their high standards, boasted how few students ever earned A's in their class. Such a boast indicates a paradigm in which the professor is the sole intellectual resource in the classroom and bears the entire burden of imparting knowledge to students—those who were characterized by Professor Kingsfield in the 1973 movie *The Paper Chase* as having "minds of mush." Teaching, in this paradigm, entails having students avail themselves of the professor's perception of the course material, integrate that perception into the formulation of an "enlightened" view, and then regurgitate that view in carefully crafted essays—or else!

Our purpose is not to denigrate any particular position on teaching. However, those who are most knowledgeable about teaching and learning have concluded that employing the traditional paradigm as a primary strategy is untenable in the contemporary environment. This conclusion is based on (1) a change in the generational conditioning of those who are now college professors, (2) an increased focus on accountability for what happens in the classroom, and most important, (3) new research findings about how human beings learn.

Today's Teaching and Learning Paradigm

Chapter 3 detailed an array of factors that have had an impact on how today's students process information. It serves little purpose here to debate whether that impact is good or bad—it is fact. Currently, most television ads run only fifteen seconds, and companies are experimenting with three-second advertisements. Compare this with ads of a generation or two ago that lasted thirty to sixty seconds (without even discussing life before television), and factor in computers and other forms of technology that provide instant feedback to users, and you can see why "lecture-as-monologue" should no longer be the primary vehicle of instruction in higher education. Today's students do not learn very effectively from such a format (and yesterday's students would likely have learned a lot more from varied formats, as well).

An even more important argument for a contemporary paradigm, however, is that recent brain research has fundamentally changed what we know about how students learn: the student-as-receptacle model does not match any of the up-to-date research (Ratey, 2001; Restak, 2001). The healthy human brain has a virtually inexhaustible capacity to learn—to detect patterns, to remember, to self-correct from experience, and to create. Achieving the learning outcomes that you have established for your courses requires an ongoing understanding of, and attendance to, students' learning systems and styles.

A strong argument for employing strategic teaching is that students come to colleges and universities to work with professors who are on the cutting edge in their fields. Is it not also critical that professors be on the cutting edge in fostering student learning?

Let us assume that you do believe that you are accountable for the student learning that occurs as a result of your teaching—in other words, that *student learning is paramount* to your role as a professor. You try to make every decision about how you teach and what you teach fit with the ultimate goal of maximizing learning in all of your students. If so, then when you strategically choose to use instructor-directed teaching and learning methods, you are deciding that, in order to reach a certain goal, you will be the director, creator, supervisor, and manager of the learning experiences. You must be cognizant of the focus and the level of engagement, both on your part and the part of your students.

Teaching and learning situations can be divided into three different dimensions: (1) who is directing the teaching/learning experience, (2) who is engaged in the teaching/learning experience, and (3) how deep the level of engagement is. As with any model, these dimensions are not absolute, but they will serve as a guide for thinking about the ideas we will present throughout this chapter and the next. Strategic professors learn to think of themselves as masters of their craft. Not unlike a master cabinetmaker or surgeon, professors must develop a wide variety of tools for completing the total job most efficiently and effectively. Generally, craftspeople who reach the level of master employ the largest variety and most effective tools currently available. In higher education, the instructor-directed tools of a master professor include lectures, video presentations, guest speakers, and controlled whole-group discussions. The following sections present each of these tools, along with ideas for using them most strategically (Reis, 1997).

Strategic Use of Lectures

In spite of mounting evidence of decreased effectiveness, lecturing remains the most common method used when teaching adults (Bligh, 2000). We do not suggest that all lectures are bad, but, like any other kind of ineffective teaching, poor lectures need to be eliminated. Our purpose in this section is to help those who choose to use lectures as part of their strategic teaching to be able to do so more effectively. While traditionalists and revisionists vary on the value of lecturing, the following are widely accepted as reasons one might choose to use lectures (Brookfield, 1995):

- To establish the broad outlines of a body of material.
- To provide guidelines for independent study.
- To model intellectual attitudes you hope to encourage in students.
- To encourage learners' interest in a topic.
- To set the moral culture for discussions.

As you can see from Figure 7.1, lectures can fall anywhere along a continuum anchored at one end by completely one-way lectures (monologues) to highly interactive lectures at the other end. Given the limited attention spans of most of today's students, relying primarily on lectures that fall at the far left of the continuum is likely to be an ineffective strategy. Therefore, when you choose to lecture, be sure to (1) limit the length of your lecture segments to no more than

Lecture Continuum

monologue—
completely
one-way lectures

highly
interactive
lectures

*Lectures are designed and delivered anywhere along this continuum.
Where do yours fall?*

FIGURE 7.1   Lecture Continuum

fifteen minutes at a stretch, (2) use a variety of visual and auditory stimuli, and (3) engage students frequently and actively in processing the lecture information.

One of the best ways of lecturing in fifteen-minute segments is to use what Middendorf and Kalish (1996) call *change-ups*. The purpose of a change-up is to reset students' attention clocks. Before giving multiple examples of change-ups, let us list some explanations and suggestions:

- Change-ups can be brief interludes (up to two minutes) between two portions of a longer lecture. The idea is to direct students' attention elsewhere and then to redirect it back to your lecture.
- Change-ups can be shifts to entirely different portions of the class. You might lecture for fifteen minutes, then show a fifteen-minute video clip, and then conduct a structured, small-group debriefing that relates the video to the previous lecture.
- Change-ups must be tied to your learning objectives. Telling an unrelated joke or taking a ten-minute break does not contribute to the achievement of learning goals and thus is not considered a change-up.
- Change-ups can eventually become a habit, but their use must be deliberately planned and scheduled. We recommend that you include plans for change-ups as you develop your lecture notes.

Change-ups can be done with individuals or groups, and their purpose can vary from having students reinforce ideas presented in the lecture to having them make connections between a new concept and a previously learned one. The following are some common change-ups and how they might be used.

- *Whip-around Pass.* The idea with Whip-around Pass is to pose a question to the entire class and then to call on a specific student to respond. The "whip-around" comes from calling on other students quickly for rapid responses, not lingering on one or two students who want to give long-winded answers with supplemental comments. The pass part of the strategy allows students who don't have an answer, or whose answer has already been stated, to "pass." There are times, especially with a small class, when so many fresh answers are coming that you might choose to whip around through the class more than once. If a class is very large, you may whip around one segment of the class for the first question, another segment for the second question, and so on. The goal is to keep it active and fun. One professor who uses this strategy threatens students that she will actually bring in a whip to crack to remind them that they are to be quick.

■ *Graffiti Boards*. At certain points in the term, you may want to plan change-ups that involve physical movement. In Graffiti Boards, you tape a large piece of butcher paper to the wall before class. You may write a question regarding the day's content on the paper or leave it blank until time for the change-up. At the appropriate time, ask students to go up to the graffiti board and write answers to a given question, write a response to a statement you have made, or compose a witty saying that reflects their understanding of the content presented thus far. If the class is too large for everyone to be up at the graffiti board at once, you can hang several long pieces of paper on different walls of the room.

■ *Quick Questions*. Hand out index cards at the start of class. When you sense the need for a change-up, ask students to read through their notes quickly and write one question that they have regarding the lecture on the card. Collect the cards, read some aloud, and answer the questions. You can also have students exchange the cards, read them over, and then return them to the asker—with an answer.

■ *Question, All Write*. Ask a question regarding some of the content just addressed in the lecture. All students are to write an answer—having them write it on a Post-it note or an index card adds to the novelty. After everyone has had a chance to respond, ask a few students to read what they have written, ask all students to compare their answers with someone else's, or collect all the answers and read a few of them to the class, commenting and extending the ideas as needed.

■ *Note Review*. A change-up that requires no additional materials is the Note Review. For this, stop at an appropriate juncture in the lecture and ask students to get with a partner and compare notes. They are to find differences in what they wrote down—these might include different omissions, differences of opinion or perception, or differences in style. The comparison helps students make sure their notes are complete, review the content, and reset their attention clocks so that the lecture can proceed.

Uppermost in your mind as you are planning your lecture and the possible use of change-ups should be student learning. You must ask yourself what you can do to ensure that your students are learning the concepts you are trying to teach them. Investing time in a change-up of some sort can help you be more certain that the material in your lecture will make it into your students' heads.

If you feel rushed when you are teaching, the thought may cross your mind that you better hurry up and "get through" the material and dispense with the change-ups or other means of refocusing the students' attention clocks. Remind yourself, though, of the ultimate goal, student learning, and that to get there you must provide refocusing time. Your just getting through the material does not mean that the students learned it. As a strategic professor, keep your eye on the learning target, always considering and reconsidering the best way to reach it.

Augmenting Your Lectures with Visuals

Today's students have grown up with high-tech, high-color, high-intensity, high-speed visuals. Even the formerly staid national evening news reflects the change in viewers' habits and preferences. "Talking heads" like the venerable Walter Cronkite have been replaced with news commentators who are on the screen for no more than a minute at a time, surrounded all the while by constantly changing visuals.

To achieve effectiveness with today's learners, you will need to supplement your lectures with compelling photographs, graphics, footage, and so forth. So much is available for essentially every topic anyone might ever want to teach that it is not difficult to find visual and auditory stimuli to accompany a lecture. If you have student assistants familiar with your content, consider enlisting them to produce some visuals for you. You will want to preview their efforts, but you might be surprised at how creative and effective they can be.

Many faculty members are using PowerPoint or similar presentation software to supplement and/or guide their lectures. For strategic teachers, presentation software neither replaces the lecture nor serves just as a backdrop—instead, it enhances learning by providing visual cues for students' mental organization. Think twice about using features of the software that create sizzle but add little to genuine learning. If you are a novice, be sure to consult with those on campus who have responsibility for effective use of such technology—many colleges now employ specialists to help faculty integrate technology more effectively.

Most contemporary faculty members who at one time used slides have converted those slides to some type of presentation software. There are two primary benefits of doing so: (1) the PowerPoint slides are much easier to reorder or reconfigure than traditional slides and (2) the lights can be left on while students are viewing the slides that are projected using presentation software. Neither benefit should be discounted. Remember, though, that just because the lights are on, you are not guaranteed students' unflagging attention. The faculty member who presents slides with a lecture must still be cognizant of the need for periodically resetting students' attention clocks.

Video and sound clips can serve to keep students focused on the content of a lecture. They can illustrate a point, demonstrate a concept, clarify a confusing notion, provide background information, or deliver a figurative punch. A clip may be as short as thirty seconds or as long as twenty minutes, but used strategically, it helps reinforce the lecture in students' minds.

Props are underutilized in most college classrooms. Some would view props as unsophisticated or superfluous, but we disagree. We have found them valuable in helping students connect with particular concepts and know other professors who would concur. Props can support the powerful teaching techniques of analogy and metaphor. For example, when helping students understand that people are able to learn more easily when they already have background knowledge on a topic, one of us used Velcro as a metaphor. When students participated in a demonstration with a Velcro-covered paddle, a foam paddle, and a tennis ball covered with the loop side of Velcro, and discovered the Velcro ball did not stick at all to the foam paddle but stuck easily to the Velcro paddle, a lasting point was made. From then on, asking students whether they had the Velcro for a particular concept she was teaching, the insight was obvious—they remembered that background knowledge allows people to be able to learn more easily and efficiently.

Transparencies shown on overhead projectors enable you to prepare presentations in advance and can be quite colorful and appealing. They also allow you to remain facing the class as you use them. Publishers sometimes provide transparencies to professors using their company's textbooks, which makes this kind of prop especially convenient. PowerPoint and other presentation software (discussed earlier in this section) are gradually replacing transparencies, however.

From a psychological perspective, flip charts (large pads of paper set up on an easel) provide a bit warmer tone than transparencies and seem to facilitate student participation. They are most effective in small classes that focus on interpersonal issues and skills. From a logistical perspective, visuals on flip charts can be prepared in advance or can be constructed during the course of the lecture. Either way, you can keep the chart intact or tear off sheets that can then be thumbtacked or taped around the classroom, providing students the chance to refer back to previously addressed material. Since they do not require electricity and are portable, flip charts are especially convenient and reliable.

The chalk or marker board is best used in situations in which spontaneity is critical to the success of your lecture, such as in involving students in identifying material for class review. Avoid writing long passages, which require you to keep your back turned to students for extended periods. You would be wise to start at the very top of the board and to print in letters viewable to those farthest away. Keeping extra chalk, markers, and erasers on hand is prudent, to say the least. An easy-to-remember acronym for effectively using the board is SUE: S = *Say* it before writing; U = check for *Understanding*; and E = *Erase* energetically before introducing new material. (It is also thoughtful to erase the board energetically before leaving the room so that it is ready for the next group to use.)

Professionally produced maps, charts, globes, or other props have great potential to enhance your lectures as well. Assess in advance whether students can easily see these materials from their normal seating positions so that you will be prepared to reposition chairs or make other adjustments to the classroom during your lecture, thus maximizing the effectiveness of these learning aids.

Other Considerations for the Strategic Lecture

The change-ups discussed earlier help students frequently in processing the information in your lecture. Alternately, you might ask students to indicate their agreement or disagreement with an idea by nodding or shaking their heads or by doing a "thumbs up/thumbs-down" response. When having them work problems, you can ask them to hold up their answers. Tell the students that it is important to you to make sure they are following and understanding your presentation and that you will need them to provide that feedback. Some professors and students are comfortable with using more outrageous techniques than those mentioned above (e.g., giving students noisemakers that they can use when they stop understanding), but you will have to determine what you want to use. The idea is to keep students engaged and to keep you informed of their engagement.

The astute teacher reads students' body language. It is astonishing to us that we can walk by a classroom where, judging by the body language, the only person engaged in the lecture is the person delivering it. What amazes us is that the professor either has not noticed or does not care that students are not paying any attention to the lecture. It is perfectly acceptable to stop and say, "Hmmm, apparently I'm interested in this, but I haven't sparked any interest in you" or "Wow, I guess I got carried away all by myself. I want to pull you back into this. What do I need to do?" or the like. You can be honest with your students, and generally they will help you.

An extension of reading students' body language is discerning their facial expressions. Although the "whatever" visage of some younger students is difficult to read, most students send clear signals. Students whose eyes are alight, who are smiling when you are, who are looking pensive when you ask them to reflect, who are wrinkling their brows over a difficult problem or situation you have posed, who have rolled their eyes or closed them, or who even have "closed" their faces altogether are all signaling you. Read the signals and respond appropriately.

Feel free—no, feel compelled—to teach students what you mean by participation during lectures. Challenge, through your actions, those who seem to think that by merely showing up they have done their part for class. Since you are holding yourself accountable for your students' learning, always expect much more than just showing up. Consider providing a handout that explains what you mean by participation. Reasonable expectations include:

- Coming to class prepared (having done whatever was assigned).
- Sitting so that learning will be optimized. Considerations include sitting where you can see the professor and interact with others in the class, avoiding distractions (certain people, sounds, sights), and maintaining an alert physical stance (not leaning back against the wall with feet stretched out).
- Offering comments that are pertinent to the material.
- Asking questions when you have them.
- Supporting others in the class who are asking questions or making contributions.
- Disagreeing constructively when appropriate.
- Attending regularly (that means all the time, barring physical illness or the like).

Some professors have found it valuable to demonstrate what they mean by participation. For example, Hal Blythe, in *It Works for Me* (1998), writes that when his questioning is met with a deafening silence, he uses a form of role-playing. Leaving the lectern and taking an empty seat in the classroom, he raises his hand, and says, "Dr. X, I've got an answer," then gives it. He then returns to the lectern and thanks his alter ego for the valuable insight. He then finds another empty seat and asks the lectern another question. Blythe reports great success engendering a dialogue that real students enthusiastically join. Benefits of this technique include the following:

- It stimulates everyone in the class.
- Once you invade students' space, they no longer feel secure in their silence.
- Once "one of their own" responds, the rest of the class is often willing to join in the fun.
- Your alter ego allows you to pose questions students never do.
- Your alter ego speaks in their language, which makes the rest of the class feel part of the discussion.
- Your movement is kinetic. A body in motion tends to create other movement.
- The technique offers variety. Your student alter ego can either ask or answer questions. Blythe says that he has even sent his alter ego to the board and that, on one occasion, in sort of an exchange program, a real student wanted to move to the podium.
- It creates a more open, dynamic class atmosphere, in which the professor is perceived as having ingenuity and a sense of humor.

This section has introduced you to a variety of techniques to use to make your lectures more effective. You can add even more variety to your lectures by interspersing them with some of the other instructor-directed methods explained in the following sections.

Strategic Use of Video Presentations

Video presentations can contribute to the richness of your courses, but you must select them carefully to ensure an appropriate fit with the curriculum and to prevent students from perceiving them as time fillers. In some courses, videos are not appropriate at all. They tend to be most effective in introductory units of instruction (by providing appropriate contextual information) and in conclusions (by providing applications of concepts studied).

To effectively use a video in your classroom:

- Check with colleagues to ensure that the video is not commonly used in another course within the curriculum.
- Limit the length to twenty-five minutes or less. If it is critical to show a longer work, divide the showing into segments with debriefing sessions interspersed. As with lengthy lectures, students can become disengaged during a long video. Remember to do change-ups or other quick checks.
- Preview the video shortly in advance of using it in class to ensure that its content is appropriate to the instructional unit and your particular group of students and to check its quality.
- Order viewing equipment well in advance so that you know it will be available during the class period in which you intend to show the video. Keep handy the names and phone numbers of the technology staff at your institution so that you can call if there is a problem.
- Check the equipment before class, to make sure that it is working properly and that you understand its controls.
- Give students an "advance organizer" (or viewing guide) that lists specific things you would like students to look for as they watch the video (see Appendix 7.1).
- After showing the video, debrief and synthesize its content with the other activities of the instructional unit.

No matter how convenient, well done, or appropriate they are, it is especially important that you not overuse videos in your class. You do not want to develop an image among students and fellow faculty members as an instructor who is taking shortcuts and failing to provide sufficient rigor to the course. Unless you are teaching a course in film, journalism, or other media studies, you probably want to limit yourself to showing no more than two or three lengthy videos during a term. However, interspersing video clips of a few seconds to several minutes is often an effective technique.

Although Web-based demonstrations are not video per se, there are some similarities in terms how powerful they can be in many situations. Obviously, you must have either Internet access in your classroom or a Web-capture software program. As the technology has advanced, glitches have become more rare, but our recommendation is to have a "plan B" when using the Internet as part of a lecture. The connection may be down, the Web site may have disappeared, and so on. When they work, Web demonstrations can be fabulous with today's tech-savvy students; but when they don't work, standing there without another option is frustrating and lonely.

Strategic Use of Guest Speakers

Occasionally having a guest speaker can be an excellent way to increase student learning. As in the case of video presentations, be careful not to overuse this tactic. Observe the following guidelines in using a guest speaker:

- Clearly identify your objectives in inviting the guest speaker. A common objective is to have the speaker address an important issue on which your knowledge and/or the textbook is relatively weak.
- Obtain a resume or biographical sketch in advance so that you can prepare an appropriate and enthusiastic introduction that energizes the speaker and prepares the class for the learning opportunity.
- Clarify explicitly with the speaker, well in advance, exactly what the time parameters are and what you want him or her to address.
- Encourage students to ask questions but also indicate areas that are out of bounds—the last thing you want is for the speaker to be embarrassed.
- Several days in advance, confirm by telephone or e-mail the guest speaker's appearance.
- Develop a contingency plan in case the guest speaker cannot come—meetings get called at the last minute, traffic accidents occur, and so on.
- Play an active nonverbal role during the presentation, maintaining consistent eye contact with the speaker and encouraging students to do the same.
- If the speaker exceeds the time limits, simply stand and move to the side of the classroom.
- At the conclusion of the presentation, thank the speaker aloud, and reinforce key points made during the presentation and provide specific linkage to critical concepts.
- Announce a short break, during which time you may deliver a personal thank-you.
- After the guest departs, discuss the presentation with students to positively reinforce instructional objectives. Deal positively with any student criticism of the speaker, should it arise during this discussion.
- Promptly mail the guest speaker a professional letter of thanks, with a photocopy to his or her designees, if appropriate.

Afterward, talk with students to determine their perceptions of the guest speaker's effectiveness. You may decide to ask the speaker to return for subsequent terms, but be cautious about asking for too much. Many guest speakers feel an obligation to serve their local communities by talking to students, but most have their limits (Lyons, Kysilka, and Pawlas, 1999).

Strategic Use of Controlled Whole-Group Discussions

Students learn best when their minds are actively engaged. Research indicates that mental engagement during discussions is superior to that which occurs during one-way lectures (Sousa, 2001). Some degree of lecture or demonstration *may* be required to present new material, but a controlled whole-group discussion can help that information take root in the students' minds. Discussion is appropriate for enabling students to:

- Apply information delivered through instructor-directed means to situations they perceive as relevant;
- Analyze the perspectives of other students within the class—a significant goal for younger students especially.
- Synthesize material delivered from diverse sources—the textbook, the lecture, the visual presentations.
- Evaluate the validity of their previously held beliefs.
- Evaluate the evidence and logic provided by others against their own developing knowledge base.
- Gain motivation for pursuit of additional learning.

To make controlled whole class discussions most effective for meeting the learning objectives of the class, Davidson and Ambrose (1994) make the following recommendations for balancing content and process functions:

1. Ask effective questions that push students to higher-level thinking (see again the discussion of Bloom's taxonomy in Chapter 4) and that encourage them to respond to one another's comments.
2. Listen proactively by hearing not just the words but also the tone and the underlying message.
3. Use your peripheral vision to make sure that all class members are as engaged as you want them to be. You can then use your eyes, your body language, and other questioning techniques to pull in and address what your peripheral vision has told you.
4. Empathize with speakers and encourage the class to do the same. Make sure that ideas are not simply dismissed out of hand.
5. Keep your sense of timing, knowing when to ask a question, when to summarize, when to make a connection to an earlier comment, and when to be quiet.

6. Help clarify ideas that are poorly explained by either restating them or using visuals to give them structure.
7. Separate yourself from the discussion part of the time. Although you are the director of the discussion, in this case, you need to let the students take the lead sometimes and not try to restate every comment or respond to every idea.
8. Vary the pace and tone of the discussion. Keep the tempo brisk when needed or slow it down when appropriate. Encourage and allow levity if that's needed, and stay focused on a more serious tone when that is needed. Support or confront, when necessary.
9. Make connections with both individuals and groups. While this is challenging when you first try it, or before you know the students better, it fosters active engagement for all.
10. Share relevant personal information—remember that self-disclosure can be powerful when it is done appropriately but perceived as self-serving when it is not.
11. Be flexible in allowing the discussion to take off even, if it does so in a direction you originally had not intended. If necessary, change the format to affect learning outcomes positively.

You can see that making sure a whole-class discussion is productive involves a great deal of energy and focus. Inexperienced faculty often think that holding a discussion will let them off the hook for a while and might be something to do if the lecture has left them drained or if they haven't had time to plan adequately. This is far from the truth. A productive discussion takes both advance planning and careful, keen orchestration throughout.

Students retain information most effectively when discussions are frequent, nonthreatening, lively, and mentally challenging. Leading discussions with all of these qualities is a significant challenge in contemporary classrooms, populated as they are by diverse students with varied experiences. Large classes are probably the major obstacle to orchestrating effective discussions. Fear of embarrassment, lack of knowledge, low self-esteem, and the desire not to stick out from the crowd are among the many reasons students are reluctant to participate actively in large-group discussions. You can probably relate to those reasons from your own experience, so be sensitive to your students' feelings. To achieve an atmosphere in which classroom discussions achieve their fullest potential, employ the following commonsense practices:

Strategies for Early in the Term
- Break the class into groups of no more than five students (sometimes called buzz groups) to discuss a critical question.
- Decide what the purpose is for the small group.

- Establish ground rules for discussion groups, such as "value all opinions" and "each member must participate."
- Before discussion begins, have students introduce themselves to each other and select a spokesperson for reporting their collective conclusions.
- Monitor the discussion within groups to ensure that students understand and follow the ground rules.
- Prompt participation from all students by posing nonthreatening, open-ended questions.
- Have each group report their findings in an orderly way, encouraging amplification of key points.
- Summarize the overall activity by citing appropriate points you heard within groups and asking for illumination from individuals making those points.

Strategies for Later in the Term
- Expand the size of discussion groups incrementally.
- After establishing an appropriate class culture of tolerance and openness, begin posing relatively broad yet not overly abstract questions to the entire class. Then encourage applications of course concepts through subsequent questions.
- After posing a question, pause to allow students ample time to process it and form a thoughtful answer. Doing so will help build students' confidence and heighten their engagement.
- Call on respondents who have raised their hands or indicated a willingness to participate through some less obvious nonverbal signal.
- When calling on subsequent respondents, create a more dynamic atmosphere by scanning the room and choosing people who are physically distant from each other.
- Avoid calling on those whose body language indicates they are not mentally engaged—it will only stifle the discussion and their future involvement.
- When you encourage involvement of nonparticipants, do so out of earshot of other students.
- Provide feedback on the positive components of responses, especially from those who had previously been reluctant to participate.
- Avoid calling a response incorrect; instead, ask whether anyone sees another way to answer. Be sure, however, to clarify correct objective information before moving the discussion along.
- Be extremely careful about providing the correct answer to a factual question before students are ready to hear it. Doing so will condition students to wait for you to find them answers in subsequent discussions.
- When a discussion bogs down, summarize appropriate points before posing an additional question.

- Close discussions positively by asking if someone would like to have the final word or by stating how the conclusions apply to the course objectives (Lyons, Kysilka, and Pawlas, 1999).

Even the best discussion leaders occasionally experience challenges in achieving a free-flowing, highly engaged dialogue. Four of the most common problems are (1) lack of general participation, (2) overparticipation by a small number of students, (3) diversions into areas inappropriate for your course, and (4) highly personal or emotional reactions by students. These problems are likely to occur, especially during the early stages of your teaching, but anticipating them can help you reduce their frequency and severity. Some tips for dealing with each of these challenges are presented in the following paragraphs.

1. Even after you have achieved a positive environment for classroom discussion, you sometimes will sense passivity from the majority of the class. This is especially common as the course winds down and students are overwhelmed with assignments due at the end of the term. Avoid the tendency to slip into your judgmental parent ego state and punish students for their nonparticipation. Instead, build common ground by saying something like "You look a little reserved" and giving students a chance to vent some emotion. If the discussion still lags, you might shift the order of your lesson plan slightly and provide more instructor-directed activities. Later in the class meeting you might elicit discussion most effectively by initially employing the small-group strategy, which you used early in the term, and a debriefing that is more humorous and engaging than normal. Also, providing increased positive feedback to individual students, as well as comments to the whole class, such as "I'm really proud the way this class has . . ." will likely pay big dividends.

2. Discussions that are dominated by only a few students cause noncontributing students to become disengaged, take the focus off your learning objectives, and risk establishing a pattern in the class. In the interest of building a positive classroom atmosphere, many new instructors are reluctant to silence those who overparticipate but then spend the remainder of the term feeling a loss of control. To avoid this, speak in private with those who tend to dominate, first thanking them for their involvement in class discussion but then going on to ask their help in encouraging the less involved by allowing you to seek their participation.

3. Occasionally, permitting a degree of wandering can make the discussion more lively and engaging. At the same time, you must be willing to step in early to refocus on your objectives. Do so by first acknowledging the collective experiences of the speakers and then asking a transitional question that returns the discussion to its proper focus. If such measures prove ineffective, be proactive and remember the Pareto rule, which warns you that 80 percent of your challenges will come from 20 percent of your students. For the student who repeatedly makes unrelated comments, you might say something akin to "That's an excellent point, and one that we will explore further when we get to Chapter 14." The key is to intensify the students' focus on the learning goals. As with most problems, the best solution is prevention. Clarify the parameters of the discussion at the outset, and reinforce them through use of a whiteboard, an overhead projector, a Power Point slideshow, or another visual aid. If the discussion starts to wander, a simple reminder of the parameters is usually effective and nonthreatening.

4. Perhaps affected by sensationalized news coverage and confrontational interview programs on television, today's students sometimes contribute highly emotional or personal reactions during classroom discussions. Some of these reactions lead to arguments that divide the class along gender, racial, political, or religious lines. Furthermore, students may directly challenge your authority. The keys in such situations are anticipating potential outbursts, knowing your personal comfort level with such situations, and knowing your students' limits. If discussions become heated, stay appropriately involved with your most calm and rational tone of voice, asking questions designed to return the focus to objective points made in the textbook, lecture, or discussion. Using a visual aid to list points or summarize facts can deescalate the emotion, minimize repetition and engender objectivity.

Like so many other activities in teaching, orchestrating effective classroom discussions is a balancing act that stretches students' comfort zones and content understanding, while recognizing reasonable professional boundaries. Stated once again, discussions are most effective when carefully planned with your learning objectives clearly in mind.

Summary of Key Points

- Strategic professors must develop a wide array of instructor-directed tools.
- Instructor-directed teaching/learning methods are comfortably familiar to many professors and students and can provide structure, organization, and sequence.
- Lectures occur along a wide continuum, from the one-way monologue to what appears to be a free-flowing interchange between students and the professor.
- Learners must have their attention clocks reset through the use of change-ups or other quick-check techniques designed to help them focus. This is true for all learners, regardless of age or sophistication.
- Visual stimuli—including but not limited to presentation software, props, transparencies, flip charts, and Web-based demonstrations—are essential in strategic lectures.
- Video presentations must be selected carefully, limited in length, and synthesized with other course material.

- Incorporating guest speakers into a course requires careful planning and follow-up to increase student learning.
- Controlled whole-group discussions can push students to higher-order levels of thinking and require a great deal of energy on the part of the professor.

Through the Professors' Eyes

KIM: Delivering lectures in my classes has been very difficult for me. In my culture, students only listen and take notes. No one would dare interrupt the professor during a lecture to ask questions. But students here do it all the time. The first time it happened, I was shocked, and asked the student to see me after class to answer his questions, which is the common practice everywhere I went to school. I talked with my mentor about this, and he has shared with me some techniques for answering students' questions, and about "engaging" my students in their learning. When I was first exposed to "active learning," it seemed disorganized and confusing, but it is becoming more comfortable. I can see where it could be more effective for student learning and more personally rewarding. I cannot change my lecturing style too quickly, because it is the most efficient way to address large amounts of content. But I can develop more effective lectures if I prepare overheads and use PowerPoint to enhance my lectures and to clarify complex ideas. When using that technology, I can be more certain that students take good notes and understand my lecture content. As I gain confidence, I will start to use other techniques. I will be sure to master them, though, before I use them in a lecture because it would be very easy for the class to get out of control if I do not use them properly.

DALE: I know that the recent trends in higher education are to create more student-centered classrooms, but I think those methods can get out of control and the students don't learn what they need to learn. I never really liked group work when I was in school. In groups, not everyone carries his load, so some students learn while others just piggyback on the work of the best students. I also don't have the time to rethink and redesign my classes. I know my lectures work. I like to be in control of my classes, and my better students appreciate that. I have very few students who ever complain about my teaching. They know they will get what they expect in my classes. If they don't learn in my class, it's because they simply don't work hard enough.

PAT: For a number of years, I have experimented with both teacher-centered and learner-centered methods of instruction, and feel that I have reached a good balance. There is clearly some content that I must teach through lecture and discussion, especially the introduction of new material. I've designed really good presentations and am very comfortable with them. My students certainly appreciate the anecdotes I use to emphasize major ideas, and they appreciate my perspective, from years of experience, on contemporary issues.

On a recent evaluation, one of my students wrote, "Having a living legend share information from firsthand historical perspective is awesome." Other than my fear of being perceived as a dinosaur, I suppose that is a compliment.

Tips for Thriving

There is something very special about watching true professionals work, be they physicians, carpenters, or teachers. In many ways, teaching is a craft like so many others, which requires the development of a core set of values and vision of a desired outcome. It also requires the mastering of a growing kit of tools. Each tool has a specific purpose, and when used in situations for which it was not designed, it loses its effectiveness. A carpenter who uses a wrench as he would a hammer will not only lose efficiency but also risks damaging the wrench in the process, causing it to lose its effectiveness in the tasks for which it was designed. Instead of relying only on straight lecture—the hammer of many professors—continue to develop an array of tools that fit best for increasingly precise tasks. In the process, you will develop a far more effective and rewarding teaching style. Keep thorough notes throughout your course, evaluating the strengths and weaknesses of teaching tools you employed in each component of your course. Like a good carpenter, continually look for new tools that will increase your effectiveness. Trade techniques with colleagues not only to increase your own success but also to build the type of learning community that improves the environment for all.

Invest also in developing the types of communications skills that differentiate the truly effective instructor from others. Vocal energy and variety are qualities you can develop when your focus in sensitized. Carefully observe and, where appropriate, begin to adopt the effective behaviors you see. This chapter has provided only the most essential information on the major instructor-directed vehicles available for delivering your course. Many articles and even entire books have been written on instructor-directed methods, and you will want to review these over time. It is especially critical to talk with colleagues to ensure that you continually improve the quality of the product you deliver to students and the personal rewards you receive from teaching.

SUGGESTED READINGS

Bligh, D. A. (2000). *What's the Use of Lectures?* San Francisco: Jossey-Bass.

Ericksen, S. C. (1984). *The Essence of Good Teaching*. San Francisco: Jossey-Bass.

Golding, J. (2001). "Teaching the Large Lecture Class." In D. Royse, ed., *Teaching Tips for College and University Instructors: A Practical Guide*. Boston: Allyn & Bacon, pp. 95–120.

Reis, R. M. (1997). *Tomorrow's Professor: Preparing for Academic Careers in Science and Engineering*. New York: IEEE Press.

Sample Viewing Guide for Videos

Please complete the following viewing guide as you are watching the videotape "The Reading/Writing Connection." You are not expected to get every single bit down during the viewing; we will take time after the video to talk about it and share ideas. Continue your ideas on the back of the sheet when there is not enough room provided on the front.

1. Where is the classroom where this videotape is filmed?
2. What is Ms. Martine's teaching philosophy?
3. Does Ms. Martine remind you of any of your professors? If so, who and why?
4. What do you think the purpose of "Morning Message" is?
5. What are some of the ways that you see the reading/writing connection being made for the children? (Continue to add to this throughout the videotape, and continue onto the back if necessary.)
6. What do you think the purpose of "Vivian Ven" is?
7. Damien's story is similar to what other story? Does Ms. Martine consider that acceptable? How do you know?
8. Describe what makes this classroom a "community of readers and writers."
9. When all the children wanted to talk about their nightmares, what was Ms. Martine's solution so that everyone got to talk?
10. How does Ms. Martine address the teaching of skills in her room?
11. What struck you as most interesting, or what surprised you most, in this videotape? (Please be specific.) Write your answer below.

CHAPTER

8 Student-Driven Learning Methods

FOCUS QUESTIONS

- Why do students benefit from directing their own learning activities?
- What are the proven student-driven learning strategies?
- How can classroom discussions be made effective for today's students?
- How can you incorporate contemporary strategies into your teaching?

> *Good teachers possess a capacity for connectedness. They are able to weave a complex web of connections between themselves, their subjects, and their students so that students can learn to weave a world for themselves.*
>
> —Parker Palmer

Think back to a time when a magical curiosity drove you to pursue the understanding of a particular idea. Perhaps it involved a science experiment you devised yourself, a historical figure with a shrouded past on whom you developed a presentation, or a seed planted by a guest speaker in one of your classes—whatever it was, it dramatically pushed the limits of your known world. The pursuit of knowledge for the sheer pleasure of knowing is a powerful force. The best teachers demonstrate an awareness of this fact in their teaching and, moving at a pace that fits their students, seek to move each learner toward greater self-direction of their learning.

Extending the attention on learning methods begun in Chapter 7, this chapter focuses on those methods primarily controlled and directed by students themselves. We should note, first, that we understand why many professors would question the wisdom of employing such methods. After all, today's students appear to need a great deal of structure to guide their learning—in and outside the classroom. Extensive research (Dunn and Griggs, 2000; Light, 2001) has identified some common learning challenges, many of which we discussed in Chapter 3. Traditionalists might ask, "If students are so capable of directing their own learning, why are colleges and universities even needed?" The answer might be that the ultimate goal of higher education in today's world is to enable students to access and process rapidly changing information—in effect, to become their own lifelong teachers. Keep this complex philosophical context in mind as we describe the potential benefits of incorporating an appropriate ratio of student-driven versus instructor-controlled teaching and learning activities into your courses.

As we said in Chapter 7, ultimately, of course, which methods you use will depend on your determination of the best way to achieve a particular learning objective. Here we will add that, although you will initially make the strategic determination of which instructional method to use, it is your students who will take on much of the responsibility for what happens in the future.

The Contemporary View

At several earlier points we stated that the strategic teacher must start where the learner is, and we suggested that many learners may not be where you hope they would be. At the same time, other students will be well beyond where you might expect them to be. Television, the Internet, and other forms of rapid-turnaround information-delivery systems have expanded the quantity and enriched the realism and currency of information to which students have been regularly exposed. In the 1940s, Americans read newspapers or listened to radio accounts of World War II battles—sometimes days after they occurred. Today people watch battles on live television, complete with instant analysis by commentators knowledgeable about the strategies of each warring party. Personal computers—in schools, in homes, and at work—have empowered today's college students to pursue information of their own choosing and at their own pace. Web searches are far more efficient than the library visits of earlier generations.

Several decades ago a professor could assume that students would arrive in the classrooms without much knowledge of the subject at hand and that he or she could shape and control the information flow that influenced the students, categorizing information into discrete compartments. In contrast, today's instructors typically face students whose greatest need is to *sort out* and *make sense* of the vast torrent of information that rushes all around them—this sorting out is a paradigm commonly referred to as *contextual* or *constructivist* learning. This approach flows from the research decades ago of renowned educational psychologist David Ausubel, who identified the single most critical factor influencing learning to be what the learner already knows (1978). He cautioned all educators to ascertain students' existing knowledge base before developing their strategies. This dynamic shift change in the flow of information, along with discoveries about how people learn, has fueled a movement that emphasizes helping learners make connections between their preexisting knowledge bases and new information or perspectives.

Active Learning

Student-driven learning methods are based on the concept of *active learning*. So that you better understand that term, let us once again employ a continuum, as we did in Chapter 7. If at one end we put active learning, what might we call the opposite extreme—passive learning?—or is that a state that does not exist? Do lectures, video presentations, and guest speakers engender passive learning? After 15 minutes or so for most learners, does the mind typically become occupied with other thoughts? The research would indicate that it does (Stage et al., 1998).

We define *active learning* as an approach selected by a professor in which the teaching and learning environment is designed for the learner to be actively engaged in the acquisition and processing of knowledge and information. In an active learning environment, students are doing much of the work, at their own pace, to achieve their individual learning objectives (Silberman, 1996).

Richard Hake (1998), a professor of physics at Indiana University, prefers a synonymous term: *interactive engagement*. He says that such learning involves methods "designed in part to promote conceptual understanding through interactive engagement of students in heads-on (always) and hands-on (usually) activities which yield immediate feedback through discussion with peers and/or instructors" (p. 65).

Although different theorists and practitioners give different definitions of this approach, those definitions commonly include students' drawing on prior knowledge to make mental connections at ever-higher levels of learning. Whatever sources you consult on the topic, and whatever differences you find among them, keep your individual conceptualization of active learning in mind as you progress through this chapter.

Those of us writing and those of you reading this book have accepted the challenge of accountability for the student learning that occurs as a result of our teaching. We have all agreed that *student learning is paramount*. Every decision we make about *how* we teach and *what* we teach is made with the ultimate goal of fostering learning in students. Therefore, when you strategically choose to use student-driven methods, you are deciding that, to reach the ultimate goal of student learning, (1) students will be directing the learning along a continuum that fits their abilities; (2) the primary focus will be on a unique collection of students; and (3) students will be doing the majority of the work in the classroom and classroom-related activities. Your work comes before class when you are designing and preparing the learning experiences.

The operative word in the phrase *active learning* is the second one: *learning*. According to Angelo and Cross (1993), "Learning can and often does take place without the benefit of teaching—and sometimes even in spite of it—but there is no such thing as effective teaching in the absence of learning" (p. 3). We agree wholeheartedly. As a professor in the age of accountability, you must make the extraordinary effort it often takes to ensure that students are actually learning what you are trying to teach.

Unfortunately, sometimes it is easier to convince professors of this than it is to convince students. But convince them we must, because students must now also accept this axiom, and thereby accept at least as much responsibility for their learning as we have. In a compelling article in *The Chronicle of Higher Education* (June 4, 1999), Mark Benvennto offers the following, in response to a comment a student had written on an evaluation ("Get up to the f---ing board—that's what we pay you for!"):

> Although many students may not want to hear it, for most of them, interactive learning is the same thing as taking your medicine. You may not like it, but it is good for you. You will learn more by being engaged in a class rather than just listening to a lecture. You will learn more by teaching your classmates, and asking them and the professor questions, than by just listening and answering others' questions. You will learn more working in a group than working alone. You will learn more if you use your mind than if you come to class simply to be entertained. (p. B9)

We need to upgrade students' perceptions of their responsibilities as learners. When we are strategic teachers and they are strategic learners, the teaching/learning experience is incomparable in its efficacy.

Strategic Teaching Using Student-Driven Methods

Teaching exclusively as you have been taught may be comfortable for you, but it is often not very effective with today's students—nor is it preferable given what is now known about the brain and learning. Wherever you are in your teaching career, you can enhance your success by developing a teaching style that regularly employs some student-directed learning methods. You will need to experiment, analyze, and reflect on your efforts. You will also need to have regular discussions with colleagues experienced in these methods.

To begin, consider ways to promote learning both inside the classroom (when the students are right there with you) and outside the classroom (when the students are far away). The primary student-directed learning methods for use inside the classroom include open discussion, learning in small groups, role-playing, case studies, and student presentations. Methods for outside the classroom include experiential learning, fieldwork, and focused study time. Each of these broad areas will be explored in the following sections. The suggested readings made at the end of the chapter are only a small sample of the works that have been written on these and similar topics.

Strategic Use of Open Discussion

In Chapter 7, we discussed the type of discussion led by the professor as a whole-group activity. In the open discussions we describe here, students lead the activity and direct the learning for themselves and their peers. The following are some techniques to use when you are having the students direct whole-class or large-group discussions themselves:

- Designate an item as the "speaking stick" or some such moniker. The person holding the item is the only person who may speak. Different rules may govern when and how this person passes the item to the next speaker, but the key factor is that total control of the speaking and the turn-taking is literally in the hands of the students.
- Even without a speaking stick, students can be in charge of calling on the next speaker. They should, of course, be encouraged to include as many different speakers as possible and to make sure that all parts of the room and both genders are represented fairly. (Men tend to be called on much more frequently than women, even by other women.)
- Use speaking chips. Purchase several sets of poker chips to distribute at the beginning of a discussion period. Either you or the students decide what each color represents and how many of each color the students should receive. For example, blue might represent questions, red could represent disagreements, and white could represent clarifications. Participants must give up a chip when they want to speak. They must be clear on which color they are using and then channel their comments to stay within that category. Limiting the number of chips keeps the discussion focused and prevents people from dominating.
- Conduct a fishbowl discussion. A reasonable number of students sit in a circle in the middle of the larger class. They are asked to discuss a question, a topic, or issue. The other students observe the discussion but may not speak until it is their turn in the middle. Whole groups may take turns in the fishbowl, or students can form tag teams whose members trade off as the situation requires. There is a lot of movement and engagement in this process.

The following are a few suggestions to make student-led small-group discussions productive:

- Present questions or problems for the group to discuss simultaneously. You may have generated these, or the students may have. Give them adequate time to formulate answers. Then have them either "report out" one group at a time or confer with another group to share what they determined.
- Present different questions for each group. This works particularly well if the questions are ones that the students brought to class—questions for which they want answers. Then, after adequate time, each group can give their answers to the whole class.
- Provide groups of six to ten students with a controversial statement related to course content. Each group then prepares both "pro" and "con" positions. After adequate time, the group is randomly divided and must conduct a debate for the class. Thus, the members do not know ahead of time which side they will have to take. You can expect high energy on this.

Invest time reinforcing the learning that has occurred during a discussion period. Too often, students are conditioned to take notes only when the teacher is talking, so they fail to record critical information during discussions. Emphasize the amount of learning that has occurred, the excellent points that were made by fellow students, and the new ideas you have garnered as a result of hearing the discussion. Of course, you can always say something to the effect of "I made some excellent notes today for ideas that I want to address in our next exam. I hope that you made extensive notes as well." If they didn't take notes this time, they will next time!

Strategic Use of Small-Group Learning Strategies

A popular instructional development of recent years has been the use of small groups within classrooms to provide students an engaging, nonthreatening learning experience. The strategy leverages the tenets of the *constructivist approach*, whose adherents believe that students, rather than coming to the course with a "blank slate," construct new knowledge within the parameters of their existing knowledge. Although purists differentiate *cooperative learning* (teacher controls activities, monitors work closely) and *collaborative learning* (students direct their own learning, while the teacher serves as a resource) along a continuum, many practitioners treat the terms as largely synonymous (Panitz, 2001). While there is value in considering the connotations of each term individually, we will focus initially on their common elements:

1. *Positive interdependence of goals, roles, resources, and rewards.* Students must believe that they are linked with others such that one cannot succeed unless the other members of the group also succeed.

2. *Face-to-face promotive interaction.* Students must help, assist, encourage, and support one another's efforts to learn.
3. *Individual accountability.* Each student's performance is assessed, and the results are given back to the group and the individual.
4. *Social skills.* Taking the lead, making decisions, building trust, communicating, and managing conflict are all practiced in small groups.
5. *Group processing.* Members monitor how well goals are being achieved and how well effective working relationships are being maintained.

It is these five elements that differentiate cooperative/collaborative learning groups from traditional discussion groups and a well-structured cooperative/collaborative learning lesson from a poorly structured one (Johnson, Johnson, and Smith, 1991).

Strategic use of cooperative/collaborative learning groups contributes to an egalitarian environment in the classroom and shifts the role of the instructor to that of a *facilitator of learning.* To facilitate means to draw upon the existing collective knowledge base of a given assemblage of students and to then integrate additional sources when appropriate. A cooperative/collaborative classroom is a more participatory and flexible learning environment than is an instructor-centered classroom. Since cooperative/collaborative learning mirrors the movement within the American workplace toward use of self-directed work teams, many professors who prepare students for occupations employ it widely.

Like any tool, cooperative/collaborative learning has both strengths and weaknesses. Its advantages include:

- Engaging the learning systems of each student actively, through positive interdependence.
- Empowering students to pursue learning that each perceives as relevant, thus creating individual accountability.
- Building the interpersonal skills necessary for success in the larger society.
- Developing solutions that integrate multiple perspectives.
- Allowing the instructor to effectively manage the learning environment by monitoring group work and interceding where most appropriate.

The major disadvantage of cooperative learning is that some students (typically a small minority) may take advantage of the ostensible freedom of this approach to piggyback on the efforts of other group members. To prevent this, the instructor must:

- Teach students how to be effective members of cooperative groups.
- Decide on group sizes and numbers, placement of students within groups, room arrangement, and planning materials.
- Specify objectives for the learning experience.

- Monitor student behavior, including assistance with the task, processing of discoveries, and bringing closure to the exercise.
- Structure win/win outcomes, individual accountability, and intergroup cooperation.
- Intervene, when necessary, to ensure that students are behaving and contributing as appropriate.
- Evaluate the quantity and quality of students' learning.

Before employing a more collaborative approach that provides students greater input into these tasks and responsibilities, the professor should assess the comfort level of students with a looser approach. Collaborative approaches typically extend learning to outside the classroom, where students are conducting research and holding meetings (albeit some in cyberspace) to accomplish project goals (Millis and Cottell, 1998), (Matthews, 1996).

The time you invest in additional planning for cooperative/collaborative learning activities is usually rewarded by the freedom you gain to monitor implementation and the opportunity you gain to provide individualized coaching for students whose needs are greatest. While your initial efforts at employing these strategies might leave you wondering if you have performed your duties, you will likely soon realize the advantages of being able to circulate around the classroom to become more familiar with the needs of individual students.

The size of the groups will vary according to the tasks, but groups of four to seven students typically work most effectively. The smaller the group, the less information and experience there is upon which to develop solutions. The larger the group, the smaller the opportunity is for individual students, especially shy ones, to contribute. Larger groups also lend themselves to being dominated by one or two students, yet they can also be more diverse. Discussions are livelier and solutions more broadly based when members are diverse in age, gender, race, and other factors. To ensure diversity, it is typically more effective to assign students to groups, rather than allowing students to select for themselves.

When the group work will be done in class, random assignment usually works well. Simply divide the total number of students in the class by the number you want in each group to determine the number of groups. Then, beginning at a convenient place within the class, have students count off up to the number of groups you need. Then have all the "number 1s" gather to conduct their discussion. Proceed with the "number 2s" and so on. You can also form random groups by having students draw numbers or items of a particular type or color from a container.

Random assignments do not work well for groups that will be meeting outside of class because of students' disparate schedules, areas of residence, and other factors. One of the biggest complaints that students have about cooperative/collaborative groups is the difficulty finding time to meet. Such activity typically also does not foster the spirit of collaboration that is intended to maximize student learning and also sometimes leads students to divide the work too narrowly and piece it back together at the end, resulting in insufficient mastery of the total project. Therefore, strategic professors take students' schedules into account as they assign groups. Proactively creating groups that *can* meet will significantly increase the likelihood that they *do* meet and will lower what David Yamane (1996) calls "transaction costs," that is, the prices students pay for having to work collectively.

The effectiveness of small-group learning depends largely on the quality of the learning experience you design or have students design with your review and approval. Having students group together to answer the review questions at the end of the textbook chapter may be only slightly more effective than assigning the same material as individual homework. Using a custom-designed case problem with interesting characters and situations is more likely to provide a dynamic learning opportunity that cannot be duplicated at home or in the library. Employing a competitive classroom activity—such as the Circle of Knowledge in Appendix 8.1—can lead to a far greater mastery of course material than you otherwise would be able to achieve. Learning experiences that require students to explore their personal values and discuss them with those of diverse beliefs create a truly synergistic environment. As always, think about why you are having students take part in a particular learning experience. Never use group work for its own sake. Rather, use it because it will lead to outcomes superior to those of another instructional method (Colberg et al., 1996), (Dunn and Dunn, 1999).

Regardless of their size, composition, and place of meeting, it is critical to monitor the groups' progress. When you are using groups within the regularly scheduled class meeting, move quickly throughout the entire classroom during the initial phases to gauge all groups' understanding of the assignment and outcome to be produced. Then, observe from a distance and circulate more deliberately to help any groups that get stuck. Rather than simply providing information, ask questions that will stimulate students to uncover clues for solving their own problems. You will no doubt see some students emerge as teachers of their peers within each group. This benefits all students—teaching others helps students synthesize their own masters of concepts, and learning from peers helps students understand information and concepts they might not have understood from a lecture or textbook.

When students are involved in small-group learning outside the regularly scheduled class meetings, you must be diligent to ensure that everyone understands the tasks, roles, objectives, time frame, and so on. Some professors make time to meet with individual groups working on long-term projects. Others establish specific times for the group leaders to consult on challenges. Still others use e-mail to allow student teams to convey overall progress, problems, issues, and the like.

Following any group learning experience, it is essential to facilitate a debriefing that enables students to develop a sense of accomplishment and place their discoveries in a proper context. Ask questions—both rhetorical and pointed—to bring the activity to a satisfactory level of closure. A debriefing might include additional out-of-class research to develop a more comprehensive solution, which the group can present at the opening of the following class meeting.

Another small-group strategy coming into widespread use is Problem-Based Learning (PBL). John Cavanaugh, vice-provost for academic programs and planning at the University of Delaware and principal investigator on the Pew grant, sorts out the place of PBL among the various learning strategies as follows: "Imagine a family tree: Active Learning would be at the top. Cooperative/Collaborative would be a subset of that, and I see PBL as a subset of Coop/Collab based on cases. All forms of group work do not center on cases; problem-based groups do" (Rhem, 1998).

Whereas typical cooperative/collaborative groups are set up to reinforce learning of material that an instructor has already presented, PBL introduces students to new material through a problem addressed in small groups. The goal in doing so is to stimulate higher-order thinking. PBL is used extensively in health sciences education because it gives the students in that field opportunities to continually *apply* preexisting knowledge and build on it, rather than just trying to learn new material that has no link to what they already know. Professors in other disciplines as well have begun writing PBL cases for their students because the power of this learning format is enormous (Spence, 2001).

In your first efforts to employ one of the various modes of small-group learning, you are likely to feel unnecessary once the groups get going. You may even feel guilty about either not being "in charge" of the classroom or not "covering" more material. A few students, imprinted by a consumer mind-set, might imply that you have somehow shirked your responsibilities by not directing the class. After observing the quality of the discussion, monitoring students' overall reaction, and speaking with experienced facilitators, you will likely overcome your negative feelings rather quickly and find yourself looking for additional opportunities to employ small-group learning strategies (Fallows and Ahmet, 1999).

One last recommendation concerning small group work: Evaluate group cooperation and collaboration along with the final product. Students consider graded activities to be important. Therefore, if professors do not assess their cooperation and collaboration along with other aspects of their work, students will not attend to increasing their team-building and emotional intelligence skills. You must determine what percentage of the overall grade will be for teamwork and provide it in writing at the time the assignment is made. A handout for the project could say, for example:

> There is a reason why I am having you complete this task as a group. I believe that in many cases two or more heads are better than one. So that you know I am serious about what I am saying, 40 percent of your grade will be based on the effectiveness of your collaborative effort. I will make that judgment by considering the following:
>
> ■ Observations of your group interactions when you are in the classroom.

- Explication of the role(s) that each group member played in the final product. Each member of the group will write an explication of what everyone in the group did (including self).
- Weekly scores given by each member of the group to the rest of the members. Those scores will be divided as follows: Assuming that you have four members in your group, each member of the group will have 100 points to divide up among all the members of the group. Each person MUST give him- or herself 25 of the points and then award the other 75 points based on a rubric-driven evaluation of how well each of the other members of the group contributed to the project. Sharing the aggregated scores on a weekly basis provides invaluable feedback to individual members of the group, which provides increasingly specific focus and motivation.
- The overall sense that the rest of the class and I have about whether or not you are working seamlessly as a team when you do your final presentation. We have all, unfortunately, witnessed group presentations that were done by a minority of members who had divided up the workload and never communicated about what was being done or what was being learned. What I want to see is a group presentation that showcases each member's ability to take over any one of the other roles, because you are so familiar with all parts of the material and those parts fit together.

More and more students arriving in college and university classrooms are used to working with other students—but they may not know how to be members of a true team. Employers and community leaders are looking for people who can be contributing members of true teams. There is much professors can do to give students this experience within their programs.

Strategic Use of Role-Playing

As a learning method, role-playing attempts to help students discover personal meanings in a given subject or resolve personal dilemmas with the aid of their social group. Whenever students take risks, as they do in improvisation, they typically achieve a valid educational payoff. In a more intensive and personal way than other teaching-learning methodologies, role-playing:

- Allows students to develop an understanding of others' perspectives.
- Encourages students to work with others in analyzing situations and developing workable solutions.
- Provides students an opportunity to apply concepts they have learned in a rich, realistic environment.
- Gives students the chance to gain insights into interpersonal challenges they are likely to face in their careers and private lives.
- Enables students to effectively contrast problem-solving methods or take on diverse perspectives.

- Offers a constructive channel through which to express feelings and process feedback.
- Presents students with a forum for building self-esteem and confidence.
- Helps students realize that college courses can be fun (Lyons, Kysilka, and Pawlas, 1999).

Whether the scenarios selected are deadly serious or lighthearted or whether they focus on the affective (i.e., emotional), psychomotor, or cognitive learning domains (or a combination of these), role-playing can have a dramatic impact on student learning. It can make an important contribution to the long-term retention of fundamental concepts. The varieties of scenarios and learning goals are endless, but in each case the instructor must:

- Identify and introduce to the class a sufficiently explicit problem and the surrounding issues.
- Explain the rules that will guide the role-playing exercise.
- Match and orient students to the roles within the activity.
- Involve even extremely shy students, perhaps as chief observers or evaluators.
- Set the stage for students, which includes establishing observation tasks.
- Monitor the activity to ensure it takes an appropriate direction.
- Debrief the participants afterward to ensure accomplishment of desired learning outcomes.

Role-playing is an especially effective teaching/learning tool within the social sciences and occupational disciplines. What more effective way to learn about the judicial system could be found than by conducting a mock trial? Or what more valid means of understanding entrepreneurship could be used than developing a business plan and presenting it to a (peer) group of potential financial backers? How might students better develop conversational foreign-language skills than by role-playing an everyday situation staged in an appropriate location?

When they know they will be closely scrutinized by their peers, many otherwise passive students will prepare extensively to deliver an authentic representation of a given role. With prompting, they will ask themselves all sorts of "what-if" questions, continuously improving the quality of their learning up through and including the presentation. Such learning activities clearly have the potential for enriched learning unmatched by other instructional methods.

Strategic Use of Student Presentations

Students master and retain learning quite effectively when they present their work to others. Many people can remember details of a school presentation they made long ago. Regardless of the discipline area, your students will likely benefit from making presentations also—that is, as long as you follow sound practices.

First, remember that the number one fear of adults is public speaking, so your students, whatever their age, are likely to need a great deal of reassurance. One key form of reassurance that many professors overlook is providing students with an adequate overview of the assignment. As a result, students commonly make unfocused, disjointed presentations—which contributes to feelings of inadequacy the next time around. Therefore, students should be provided—in writing and well in advance—the objectives of the presentation, as well as a detailed scoring rubric. In a large course or when building teamwork is an especially desirable goal, you might consider having students make presentations to a subset of the class, or in a group setting—for example, as a member of a forum or panel discussion. Presenting to a small group is less frightening than presenting to a large group, particularly if the chosen subset of the class has been working together on various projects through the semester.

If yours is an introductory course and/or students voice considerable anxiety, provide individual coaching or model presentation skills, showing students how to gain viewers' attention, use visual aids, form a powerful conclusion, and so on. You can also have a student with a proven track record in another professor's class demonstrate effective presentation skills. Videos on how to develop an excellent presentation are another possibility. A final, but far less desirable, option is to deliver a full presentation yourself, emphasizing in advance the key techniques students should look for. Some students would likely have difficulty separating such a presentation from a regular lecture or demonstration, while others might view such a presentation as *the* model and work so hard to duplicate it that they appear unnatural.

Viewers and speakers can derive full value from presentations only when feedback is plentiful, objective, and consistent. We recommend allowing viewers to contribute to the evaluation of their peers. One frequently used method is to give viewers index cards on which they are asked to do a "three by three"; that is, they are to write down three strong points and three suggested improvements for each presentation. These are turned in at the end of the presentation and then attached to the evaluation form completed by the instructor.

The student who makes the presentation should not be the only one who is engaged and learning. Therefore, you should measure the learning that occurs among the audience. This helps to indicate to the student presenters the effectiveness of their efforts. It is sometimes worthwhile to base at least a portion of the presenter's grade on how much the other students learned. Remember, what gets measured gets done, and most students value those measurements (i.e., grades) highly.

Deliver praise for student presentations in public, and give constructive criticism in private. This way of delivering feedback is part of creating a supportive environment. Keep in mind that such an environment increases students' retention of the material they have already presented, as well as what they have heard their fellow students present. It also contributes to the enhancement of student efficacy and self-esteem.

Finally, remember that nearly any good idea can be overdone. Unless yours is a public speaking course, resist the increasingly common tendency, especially in graduate courses, to have students learn the majority of the course content through various types of presentations. Consumer-oriented students are likely to perceive that such an arrangement denies them access to the expertise of a professor for whom they invested considerable time and financial resources.

Strategic Use of Experiential Learning

For decades, occupational programs have placed students in internships and externships, jobs in actual work settings, to link course content to the demands of the real world. Many can attest to the learning value of those experiences and to the accompanying opportunities they provided to make valuable career-building contacts. Experiential learning is highly motivating to many students and offers them a rich opportunity to develop the higher-level skills of Bloom's taxonomy. It has the potential to change students' perceptions of their communities and their roles within them, and it assuredly helps participants make informed career and lifestyle decisions. This section briefly introduces experiential learning, which includes not only internships and externships but also fieldwork and service learning. In all of these experiences, students direct their own learning outside the classroom, while the professor assumes the role of resource and mentor.

In the late 1960s, when student idealism led to the demand for increased relevancy in higher education, various types of experiential learning projects became a significant part of the curriculum in many discipline areas. Now called "service learning," that practice has returned in full force to most campuses—holding promise for the inspired Millennial Generation members to contribute to the betterment of many entities. Campus Compact—an organization whose mission is to assist institutions of higher education in providing young people with the values, skills, and knowledge of active citizenship—promotes service learning as the most recognized and effective teaching method available to help students become active responsible citizens. Service learning exposes students to the needs of the larger society, engages them in addressing those needs through community service, and connects what they learn in the classroom to real-world situations. At its best, service learning is a powerful teaching method that allows students to reflect why such conditions exist and what their democratic responsibilities are in addressing them. A study by the Higher Education Research Institute comparing service participants with nonparticipants showed that participation in community service positively influenced every one of the thirty-five measured student outcomes, which fell into the broad categories of academic development, civic values, and life skills (Astin, 2000).

The challenge with experiential learning lies in ensuring the legitimate role of each experience in achieving predetermined learning objectives. While students will value the independence and the personal satisfaction they receive from internships or fieldwork, we must strive to ensure what they learn is transferable to an even wider arena. Thus, the instructor must not only select sound learning activities carefully but also build reflection and analysis into the learning experience.

If you plan to include experiential learning projects in your class, a tool that you should strongly consider using is the *contract*—a written document that spells out the pertinent issues and responsibilities of the student and professor, and is signed by both parties. Generating a contract generally involves a three-step procedure:

1. Develop the parameters of the experience. These include the product that you expect students to generate (e.g., a reaction paper, a journal, a video oral report), its evaluation criteria, and related logistical requirements. Provide a printed copy for each student, along with a list of possible topics.

2. Create a proposal form that students will submit for your review before actually beginning the experience. This form will give you the opportunity to provide direction and minimize the chances that the experience will be nothing more than wasted time.

3. Return the proposal, along with your comments, to the student. At this point, the proposal becomes a binding contract. That is, for a certain body of work, submitted according to stated time parameters and performance standards, you agree to award a particular grade.

You might want to consult with others in your department prior to finalizing the contract to ensure that it meets commonly accepted standards of your situation. Even after you have determined their value to students, fieldwork experiences need to be examined for their impact on the overall curriculum and the goals of the department and institution.

Faculty members who choose to involve students in service-learning projects need to develop ways to combine service to the community with student learning in a way that improves both the student and the community. Doing this effectively takes time, effort, and detailed knowledge of the situation into which students will be sent. A growing number of campuses are offering workshops and support for faculty who want to take advantage of this learning strategy.

Strategic Use of Focused Study Time

Remember the definition of the strategic learner? Strategic learners are deliberate and conscious. They are mindful of their strengths and weaknesses as learners and of what they must do to be effective and efficient during the learning process. As a professor, you should facilitate your students' learning by ensuring that they know *how to learn* and are *intentional* in their learning. Becoming strategic learners will serve your students well, both while they are students and through-out the remainder of their lives.

Often, professors say, in one way or another, "Harrumph. You know, nobody ever taught me how to study, and I did okay. By the time students get to col-lege, they should know how to study." We have a number of responses to these sentiments:

- As professors, we are not necessarily typical of the students who are pop-ulating our classes. Although some of us were first-generation college stu-dents, others of us had college-educated parents who schooled us, directly or indirectly, on how to be effective in college.
- Maybe no one did teach us to study, but what if someone had? How much *more* could we have learned, and how much more quickly could we have learned it?
- Students may have learned how to study before they got to college, but col-lege is different from high school. Also, general study techniques may not be sufficient for the type of learning students need to do in a given spe-cialty. Should we not do everything we possibly can to ensure the learning of the students we have, even if this means including letting them in on the secrets we possess about learning our subject area?

That being said, the following list presents a few student-driven learning methods that will facilitate the focused studying that students do outside of the classroom. Although the instructor does the prep work, the students are respon-sible for seeing each method through.

- Ask students to keep a study log in which they write down what they are involved in while studying and how long they spend on each task. Tell them that there is a participation grade attached to this activity because you are interested to see what they are doing. Also suggest that if they eventually have some trouble in the course, the diary might help you advise them on different ways to study. The first semester you do this, you can suggest which tasks they should be doing and estimate the time they will take, but after several semesters of collecting actual student logs, partic-ularly of those students who were successful in the course, you can give actual examples.
- An alternative to the study log is the exam log, in which students record what they studied, how they studied, the time they studied, and what they think will be on the exam. Just after the exam, they record how well they believe they did—and why. After the exams are returned, they can reflect on why they scored as they did and why their estimate was on target—or not so close. This is especially effective with younger, lower-division stu-dents who may have little practice in studying for difficult exams and in assessing their readiness for an exam.

- Complete study sheets as they do the assigned reading. Your work may consist of nothing more than listing chapter objectives and leaving an adequate amount of space for students to list what they find in the reading to amplify each objective. You can collect the study sheets weekly or on exam day. Once the exams are graded, you can compare—and encourage the students to compare—the study sheets of those who did well on the exam and those who did not do well. The differences may be plain to see.
- Have students complete a "wonder, interpret, tie-in" (WIT) sheet while they are reading. Students write down concepts, words, or facts that make them wonder; they write down their interpretation of at least one idea presented by the author; and they make statements about how what they are reading ties in with other concepts from the class. In class, students can form small groups to talk about what is on their WIT sheets.
- Require students to do what Russ Moulds (1997) calls "interactive annotations." Students may highlight and underline their text, but they must also go further and add meaningful margin notes where they interact with the author—arguing, commenting, reflecting, asking, agreeing, referring to other portions of the text or other sources, making connections with personal experience, reacting, comparing, and so on. Students can turn in their whole textbook so that you can read through and check their annotations. It is a heavy workload, but to avoid having to carry all the books on any one particular day, you can stagger due dates, do all the checking in class, or use some other alternative.

The time you spend helping your students learn represents an investment in their future success. You will be repaid, with interest, but larger dividends also accrue—for the students as they move through college, and for society as these students move on from college to work, and beyond.

Summary of Key Points

- Resist the trap of teaching only as you have been taught yourself. Today's students are likely to possess a knowledge base on which you can build through student-driven learning methods.
- Work to convince students that active learning carries many benefits to them.
- For classroom discussions, use small groups until students attain a satisfactory comfort level.
- Use collaborative/cooperative learning techniques to enable students to effectively process and apply material from your presentations.
- Employ role-playing to enable students to understand diverse perspectives.
- Experiment with experiential learning initiatives to increase student engagement and higher-order learning.

- Integrate student presentations into your course to increase students' retention of material and to build their self-esteem.
- Plan to teach students how to become strategic learners. Doing so fosters their learning efficacy, which benefits them in your course and in their future learning.

Through the Professors' Eyes

DALE: All this emphasis on student-centered learning is interesting, but most of my students don't want to teach themselves. They expect me to teach them what they need to know, and I am very comfortable with that. After all, that is my job as a teacher—to direct them to what is important to learn. I also like an efficient classroom and don't like to waste my time or the students' time. A couple of my students have shared their interest in doing a project, and I might explore that option with them. They are mature and very good students and perhaps could do some independent work that might provide an angle for looking at my research and other issues in a new way. I must confess to a bit of an eye-opening experience this week, however. Out of the clear blue, my major adviser, Orwin Luke, called me. We hadn't spoken for nearly ten years. He's getting ready to retire and, of all things, has joined the Peace Corps! He put up with a lot of my bravado in graduate school, and once he came to my defense when it looked like I might be washed out of the doctoral program. The conversation we had this week has been rattling around in my mind, and it has me asking myself some pretty profound questions.

KIM: There is a great deal of interest within my department for using group work in instruction. In my culture, groups are used a great deal, but we tend to be very guarded about that type of work. Those working in a group would be ostracized for sharing insights and conclusions achieved within that group. I realize this culture is much more liberal about this issue and am beginning to overcome my resistance to the widespread use of groups in my courses. One advantage of group work is that it takes the pressure off of me to perform and reduces my anxiety over my language skills. The first time I used group work in a class, I was surprised how much the students enjoyed solving the case problem that my mentor had helped me develop. The students were very engaged in solving it. I just walked around helping them clarify the issues. I must admit that I even felt a little guilty that first time, because most students really did not need me to help very much. But they were so engaged and creative! I still need to organize my group projects better so that my students are sure to learn all that I want them to learn. But I think I can make this work. My students seem to like working this way. By listening to discussions in their groups, I am also increasing my own language skills, particularly the idiosyncrasies and the slang the students use so much.

PAT: For many years, I have liked having my students do group work and individual projects. Sharing their work with each other really extends the excitement in the class, boosts their individual confidence, and helps me learn new perspectives from my students. They actually help me keep up-to-date in a number of areas related to what I teach. Most students excel in this format, but those who are prone to slacking must be managed. I use peer evaluation in which each team member allocates a given number of points to each of the other members of the group. That really reins in the few who might otherwise take advantage of the efforts of strong students and also motivates them to get involved in the early planning of group projects. Many potential slackers have turned out to really develop a liking for the course material. My students increasingly view my classes as a learning community, not just a place to sit and listen.

Tips for Thriving

This chapter has offered information on only a few of the widely used student-directed learning methods. There are dozens of additional tactics and strategies available for enabling students to "discover" things worth learning. Many of these are activities that students can complete in a relatively short amount of time but that can add considerable flavor to your course.

Besides being the manager of the context of the class you deliver, you may find that your greatest role is that of champion of your discipline. Your passion and creativity are the sparks that ignite the fuel of your students' minds. When you demonstrate that fact genuinely and persistently, your students will become far more effectively self-directed than you ever could have imagined.

SUGGESTED READINGS

Colberg, J., P. Desbery, and K. Trimble. (1996). *The Case for Education: Contemporary Approaches for Using Case Methods*. Boston: Allyn & Bacon.

Fallows, S., and K. Ahmet. (1999). *Inspiring Students: Case Studies in Motivating the Learner*. London: Kogan Page.

Johnson, D. W., R. T. Johnson, and K. A. Smith. (1991). *Cooperative Learning: Increasing College Faculty Instructional Productivity*. ASHE-ERIC Higher Education Report, no. 4. Washington, DC: The George Washington University, Graduate School of Education and Human Development, pp. 6+.

Matthews, R. S. (1996). "Collaborative Learning: Creating Knowledge with Students." In R. J. Menges and M. Weimer, eds., *Teaching on Solid Ground: Using Scholarship to Improve Practice*, pp. 101–24.

Millis, B. J., and P. G.Cottell, Jr. (1998). *Cooperative Learning for Higher Education Faculty*. Phoenix: Oryx Press.

Silberman, M. (1996). *Active Learning: 101 Strategies to Teach Any Subject*. Boston: Allyn & Bacon.

Stage, F. K., P. A. Muller, J. Kinzie, and A. Simmons. (1998). *Creating Learning Centered Classrooms: What Does Learning Theory Have to Say?* ASHE-ERIC Higher Education Report 26, no. 4. Washington, DC: The George Washington University, Graduate School of Education and Human Development.

APPENDIX 8.1

Circle of Knowledge

The Circle of Knowledge (Dunn and Dunn, 1999) is a highly motivating small group strategy for reinforcing learning of factual material, prior to moving to upper levels of Bloom's taxonomy. The steps are as follows:

1. Divide students into teams of three or four, and distribute the teams throughout the classroom.
2. Pose a brainstorming question to the teams (e.g., list countries in Asia), providing a specific time frame between two and three minutes (e.g., two minutes, thirty-five seconds) for completion of the task.
3. Taking turns and moving clockwise, each team member is to whisper to teammates an answer that meets the criteria of the question.
4. One member is designated as the recorder, using paper and pencil to record each response.
5. The recorder participates as a member and provides responses in his or her turn.
6. No member may skip a turn or give more than one answer in a turn.
7. If a member becomes stumped, teammates are allowed to draw or to act out an acceptable response, but not to say it out loud or write it.
8. Progress cannot continue unless each member satisfies his or her obligation to whisper an answer not already on the growing list.
9. At the end of the predetermined time, the facilitator calls a halt and makes all recorders put down their pencils.
10. Using a board or an overhead projector, the facilitator writes each team's number at the top of a column.
11. The first team's recorder calls out an answer. The facilitator writes this answer in that team's column.
12. On each team, the recorder should then scratch out that answer from his or her team's list, to avoid a possible penalty as the activity progresses.
13. After the last team calls out its answer for the master list, a new round begins. The team that went last in round one goes first in round two, and so on.
14. A team may call out only those answers that appear on its list.
15. When a team runs out of answers on its list, it calls out "Pass" but should stay active in the game.

16. All team members should watch the master list as it builds. If an answer is given that essentially matches another answer already on the board, or is an incorrect fit with the criteria, anyone may yell out "Challenge."
17. If the facilitator determines that the challenge is valid, the challenging team receives a bonus point (written at the top of the team column), and the team providing the duplicate or incorrect answer is denied credit for the answer.
18. If the facilitator determines that the challenge is incorrect, the challenging team is penalized one point (written at the top of the team column).
19. The rounds finish when all teams have passed. Each group may then discuss missing correct answers, and the first team to call out a missing correct answer is given one additional point.
20. The game is concluded, and the facilitator tallies the points for each team—correct answers, plus challenge points, minus penalty points—in full view of the teams. The winning team is the one with the most net points.

9 Infusing Technology into Your Teaching

FOCUS QUESTIONS

- How can popular technology be employed to improve accountability measures?
- How can employing instructional technology improve your teaching?
- How can technology be used to engage students more actively in their learning?

One of the authors of this book recently had an experience that frames the issue of using technology in your instruction. Paying the monthly bills, he discovered he had reached the final coupon in the payment book for his automobile loan. According to the coupon, he would have to call the bank to determine the amount of the last payment. He did so expecting to receive a recording telling him to call a new number, because his bank had merged with another and then had been acquired by an even larger bank since the loan was obtained. (Mergers, acquisitions, joint ventures, and the like have become quite common in business, but increasingly in higher education as well. But that is another story.) Rather than receiving a hoped-for human voice to help celebrate the achievement of this financial milestone, he received an answering menu. The computer-generated voice recording went through the options ("Press 1 for . . .," etc.) without any mention of automobile loans. After hitting 9 to go through the options a second time, he decided that his needs fit the "consumer loan" category. He pressed that number and received a second menu ("Press 1 to check your balance," etc.). Reviewing the entire list, he finally heard "Press 9 for loan payoff details." When he was connected to a third menu, as you might imagine, he was ready to "go ballistic."

This story points to the huge potential for technology to improve the *efficiency* of instructional and accountability processes. But to achieve *effectiveness*—the raison d'être of accountability—institutions of higher education must give appropriate attention to the human dimension. We use the term *high-tech/high-touch paradox* to describe the dynamic between society's increased use of technology, while at the same time expectations of increased emotional intelligence are rising. Today's students tend to be very sophisticated about technology and have come to expect its use within the educational environment. While some have resisted its use, technology has become a fact of life in the teaching and learning enterprise. How we use it, when we use it, and with what expertise and quality we use it is crucial in our strategic decision making. We believe that high-quality technology can enhance the effectiveness and efficiency of our students' learning and when employed strategically holds tremendous potential for improving student retention and program completion.

For many tasks, instructors can use the same popular technology employed throughout the larger society. For others, technology designed specifically for use within higher education holds potential for improving the quality of interchange between you and your students. Its functionality has increased dramatically in very recent years, largely in response to increased enrollments, the shortage or high cost of space in which to hold traditional classes, and the rising expectations of students and other stakeholders. Regardless of the complexity of the technology, it is imperative that you learn to use it appropriately and effectively—technology use for technology's sake is not an effective model to employ. Instead, the technology should be used strategically to have as its ultimate purpose the improvement of teaching and learning, which are the most significant contributing factors to meliorating institutional effectiveness.

To highlight the potential of technology's use in the classroom, we will once again employ a continuum to guide our discussion. Imagine at one end professor-initiated, teaching-focused tools, and at the other student-managed tools that focus on student learning. Leveraging the full range of technology can help you organize your class instruction, develop more effective learning relationships with students, enhance your presentations, facilitate your students' learning, improve your assessment of students, and manage your grading systems.

Organizing Class Instruction

As a strategic professor, you no doubt begin each term by providing your students a syllabus that—increasingly viewed as a contract with students—addresses the array of functions highlighted in Chapter 4. During your initial class meeting, you likely follow up the syllabus distribution with an explanation of all its critical details and nuances. At the succeeding class meetings, you likely get requests for a copy of the syllabus from students who either missed the first class meeting or misplaced the original copy distributed. Such requests not only become increasingly annoying as the term unfolds but also shift your focus from more critical issues that you need to communicate to all students. In addition, there are times between class meetings when you want to clarify wording that appears on the syllabus, to ensure that the potential for the student grapevine to misinterpret your intentions is minimized.

One proactive way to organize class instruction is to leverage the technology at your disposal and create a course Web page. On this page you can not only post your syllabus but also highlight important dates, such as test days, project due dates, fieldwork days, and so on. Posting your syllabus on your Web page ensures that the students will always have a copy of it conveniently available—rather than being dependent on the hard copy distributed in class that is now in their car, somewhere in their book bag, or elsewhere. You can also add links to clarify sections of the syllabus and provide specific instructions for assignments. Explicit information about how papers are to be formatted, how fieldwork or laboratory assignments are to be completed, how to prepare for class presentations, what rubrics will be used to guide your evaluation—all of this and more can go on your Web page. You may even provide study guides for the readings that you assign. Other links on your Web page might lead to supplementary material, such as a tutorial that will help students with specific, course-related information. All of these can be created on an "as needed" basis and then readily accessed by your students.

Many colleges and universities now have support resources for faculty who wish to post their own Web pages. But even if such support is not available, you can easily find programs available to help you develop and post your Web page on your institution's server. And if the college or university server is not available to you, you can find a host of options through one of the commercial Internet service providers. (One word of caution—be very clear from the beginning on your institution's Web page policy. Most institutions have strict guidelines for all Web pages that are either housed on their servers or linked to the institution in some other way (e.g., "distributed" as part of a course). It is much easier for all if you meet the guidelines up front rather than having to go back later and fix glitches. The policy should be available through your institution's webmaster or office of communications.

In addition to getting help from your campus technology staff, consider asking some of your students for some "reverse mentoring." Many students are quite proficient at Web design and may be able to help you identify appropriate sites with which to link your Web page. Once your page is up and running, you might create an assignment that encourages your Web-surfing students to find and evaluate links for the class, either as a part of their regular assignments or as extra credit. You can then review these sites, continually upgrade your page, and plan your course for the following term.

Support from your administrators for your Web page development is critical for very practical reasons (not the least of which is the time it takes to create a Web page). Contemporary administrators will probably offer strong support, but you should still be prepared to provide a rationale to help gain their backing. That rationale could include some or all of the following (depending on what the listener needs to hear):

- Today's students expect 24/7/365 access to a full range of course resources.
- Students like to be able to sneak a peek at the course syllabus before actually registering for the course.
- Well-designed Web pages can serve as marketing tools for professors, departments, and institutions.
- Making the syllabus and its accompanying print materials available online can reduce the department's budget for paper and reproduction costs.
- In a school that charges student technology fees, students expect those fees to be used to make their lives easier; Web-supported courses make their lives easier.
- Improved communications with students would seem to improve the retention and completion rates of your course.
- Faculty Web pages' potential to foster more time-sensitive communications with students will likely reduce the number of complaints administrators receive about the inaccessibility of the faculty.

Even as we head farther into the new millennium, there remains a very significant "digital divide" between the "haves" and "have nots," which results in some students coming to college with extensive computer experience and others whose families and schools had no budget for computers. You must be careful not to assume that all students are comfortable going online or surfing the Net, because they are not. Consider holding an after-class session for all interested students at a campus computer lab. Or offer to help students in your office should they need assistance. Since fewer and fewer students each year will be unfamiliar with the technology, this is not an overwhelming time commitment on your part—and it will pay dividends for all.

Nearly all colleges and universities provide Internet access for students through computer laboratories, and it is imperative that your students know the locations, hours, guidelines, and restrictions of these labs. If warranted, include this information on the hard copy of your syllabus, on a label students can attach to a notebook, or on a card t they can keep in their wallet or backpack.

Except for those who teach Web-based courses in which there is no face-to-face interaction, most professors with course Web pages continue to provide students with a hard copy of certain key information on the first day of class. Others have one complete copy of their syllabus accessible through the school library or the department files. You may eventually teach a course in which students do not require access to paper copies of a syllabus, but for the foreseeable future, be aware that the hard-copy handout is an expectation and a source of security for some students.

Faculty members who have created and used their own Web pages usually believe there is no turning back. Once you experience the array of possibilities it offers for enhancing communications, convenience, and accountability to your students, the option becomes not only intriguing and attractive but also highly preferable to the low-tech or nontech alternatives.

Fostering Richer Learning Relationships with Students through Technology

Mindful of the high-tech/high-touch paradox, we are nonetheless convinced that the effective use of common technologies can provide more opportunities than obstacles for fostering richer learning relationships with students. Strategies with especially strong potential are ongoing use of targeted e-mail messages to students, use of courseware programs, distribution lists, and listservs. We will discuss each of these in this section.

Targeted E-Mail

In Chapter 5, we suggested the strategic use of e-mail to increase student retention throughout the term. We suggested that the first message of the term should be delivered to students' personal e-mail accounts within a day or so of the initial class meeting. That message should carry a friendly tone to support your classroom-expressed desire to foster a community of learners within your course—a community that shares freely of its resources and insights. That first e-mail may also summarize some of the informal feedback you received from students as they departed the class meeting and could perhaps clarify issues regarding the syllabus. You could also use that e-mail to remind the students of key issues that may have gotten buried in the rush of the first week of class.

There is, of course, no absolute number of e-mail messages to send to your class, but we recommend approximately one per week, sent at a regular time. This message can be used to:

- Reinforce a few key ideas from the previous week's class.
- Build anticipation for the upcoming week's topics.
- Remind students of special arrangements they need to be making.
- Provide learning tips or study helps.
- Offer answers to the whole group—even though the questions may only have been asked by a few students.
- Clarify difficult passages in the text by offering a variant explanation or sources for other views.
- Commend the class (sincerely) on something that went particularly well.
- Pass along positive anecdotes that have been shared by class members who have attained some success with a study method, means of accessing data, or some other pertinent experiences.
- Stay connected!

This last reason is widely reported by students as being of key importance. Regardless of whether you are teaching small or large classes, it is difficult to connect face to face with all the students in the class each and every week. E-mail can let students know that you are thinking about their learning and provides encouragement for them to think about their learning as well.

In addition to your weekly e-mail messages to your students, you can target key retention mileposts. Just prior to the first examination or submission of the first major assignment, you can send a message with some study or research tips, rhetorical questions that focus attention, or evaluation rubrics. Prior to the midterm meeting, your e-mail might summarize the progress students have already made in the course and sketch out a vision for the rest of the term. As the term draws to a close, some tips for time management and multitasking might be in order.

The following list of tips for employing e-mail in your course is a compilation from David G. Brown (2001), Greg Kearsley (2000), and Kerry Hannon (2001):

- In class, give students directions for how to create an e-mail group so that they can do so with their study group or another small project group.
- Direct them to your first group e-mail message they should access within the first day of class.
- In your syllabus and first class announcement, state that you expect each student to check e-mail messages at least once a day.
- Agree on the use of one or more short, special subject lines in e-mail messages so that course e-mail will be clearly distinguished from other e-mail.
- Use e-mail for general and good news only. Deliver bad news face-to-face, in private.
- Tell students that you expect all e-mail communications to be civil (i.e., they should avoid sarcasm, flaming, and the use of ALL CAPS). They should also be sensitive to the different ways in which their fellow students might perceive the content of an e-mail.
- Use e-mail for managing the flow of your course and to distribute materials and updates.
- In small classes, send specific, personal notes to those who might need extra encouragement.
- At the end of class sessions, encourage students to e-mail you about unclear issues.
- At the end of difficult sessions, send a group message that summarizes and clarifies details.
- Consider allowing students to submit drafts of work by e-mail. You can comment on these drafts using any of a number of software functions.
- Encourage students to e-mail each other.
- Consider requiring each student to e-mail you once per week.
- Check your e-mail messages every day, and a second time the evening before major assignments are due or an exam is to be given.

- When responding to an e-mail, include the entire message you received, relevant parts of it, or a simple summary of what you are responding to.
- When responding to an e-mail, note whether it is necessary to respond to an entire group to whom the e-mail was addressed or only to the sender, saving others from excessive mailbox clutter.
- If you refer to a specific Web site in your e-mail message, include a link to it.

One extra caution: Install and regularly update reliable virus protection software, and ask your students to do the same. New viruses and worms are reported frequently, and while some are merely annoyances, others are capable of shutting down the networks of large institutions. No longer can faculty or students claim ignorance when they have exposed someone else to a virus. There are several common and widely respected virus protection software packages available. You can set them to check DAILY (and, yes, we are shouting) for upgrades. Students should do the same.

Courseware Applications for E-Mail, Distribution Lists, Listservs

Most e-mail programs have sorting provisions. If you have this option, be sure to establish a unique location for student inquiries and comments. That way, you do not have to sort through all of your e-mail messages to address the concerns of your students. If your college or university has licenses for WebCT or Blackboard, you can use the internal e-mail application to confine your students to the specific Web sites for your courses where you are using these applications. These applications allow students to post to open forums or privately to you. They also allow you to set up group discussions and follow threaded conversations. Both WebCT and Blackboard are primarily asynchronous, meaning students can access them at any time and are not confined to a specific time slot to communicate with their classmates. However, both applications also allow you to set up "live" (synchronous) chat rooms, in which participants are all logged on at the same time.

If you do not have access to WebCT, Blackboard, or any of the other courseware programs, it is prudent to set up a distribution list for each of your classes so that you can get messages to them quickly. Also consider setting up a listserv for each class. A listserv differs from a distribution list in that a distribution list is for one-way communication from you to your students, and a listserv allows anyone who is registered on the listserv to initiate a communication. The listserv is great for making announcements, asking students to react to some relevant event that just occurred in your community, or asking for help on something. Explore the e-mail options you have at your institution and see what you can arrange so you have a focused means of using technology to communicate with the students in your classes.

Enhancing Instructional Presentations

Clearly one of the major advantages of technology is its ability to help instructors deliver instruction in a professional manner that accommodates multiple perceptual modalities. We will explore a few of the technological advances in the following sections.

Overhead Projection

In today's classrooms, some form of overhead projection is nearly as common as the chalkboard or the whiteboard. Two widely used forms of projection are the familiar overhead projector, which uses transparencies, and the newer document camera, which allows you to project from printed pages. Both tools have many advantages over the traditional board on the front wall.

The first, and perhaps most important, advantage is that you never have to turn your back to the students. This allows you to monitor reactions and gives you a degree of control over the behavior of your students—still a consideration in many classes. Overhead projection allows you to record students' ideas on the transparency or document being projected, while still watching for responses and questions. More students get to participate this way because so often when the professor's back is turned to the class, the ideas that get recorded are the ones "shouted out" by the more outgoing students.

The second advantage is that you can prepare transparencies or documents ahead of time. Using your computer to do so enables you to enhance your documents with color and use large fonts so that everyone in the room can see the print. With transparent overlays (which can be used on either the overhead projector or the document camera), you can demonstrate stages in a life cycle of a plant or steps in solving a problem, include pictures or cartoons that emphasize points in your lecture, illustrate statistics on graphs and charts, which will improve the comprehension of your students, and so much more

A final benefit of using overhead projection, specifically the document camera, is that you can project items besides plain-text documents. Photographs, insects, experiments, rocks, children's books—all can be projected with ease. It is truly fabulous technology because it brings the learning experience closer to all the students instead of just the brave few who sit in the front of the room.

Often the effectiveness of this tool is diminished because teachers do not use it properly, so like all technologies, how you use overhead projection is important. Here are some very basic rules to help you get full use from overhead projection:

- Be sure that the print on prepared transparencies and documents is large enough for all students to see regardless of where they sit in your classroom.
- Keep the amount of print to a minimum. The transparency or document should be used to highlight points, not to give full-text information to the students.
- Writing on transparencies requires practice. You want to be certain that what you write is legible and evenly spaced for easy reading by your students.
- When using the overhead, face the class. Do not put a transparency or document on the overhead, then turn around and read the projection to your students. Keep your eyes focused on the transparency or document on the bed of the projector, pointing to items of interest with your finger or a pen. You do not need to see what is projected behind you; it is exactly what you have in front of you.

Presentation Software

Several presentation software packages are available for you to use, but perhaps the most popular and readily accessible program to date is PowerPoint. Presentation software offers support for your lectures, as we discussed in Chapter 7. The decision to use presentation software, like all other strategic decisions about your teaching, should be based on what you want your students to learn and then thinking about how best to ensure that learning. We believe that, in many instances, presentation software allows you to teach more content and to teach it more effectively than you can do otherwise. Here's why:

- When you use a program such as PowerPoint to create the visuals to support your lecture, you have several options. These include printing the slides as handouts for the students as well as making them available on your Web page for the students to print and bring to class. When you make bulleted points on your slides, the students do not have to spend time copying information you want everyone to have; instead, they can find and add supplemental information, write down clarifications made in the class, and so on. Note, however, that younger and/or unsophisticated students may think that a handout *is* the lecture, so be sure to help them know what *else* they need to be writing.
- Preparing excellent presentation slides for a class causes you to think through your course material carefully. This process increases your focus on important content, thereby increasing students' focus as well.
- As we have discussed earlier, presenting information in more than one way is important because of students' diverse learning styles. When you use PowerPoint or other presentation software, you are supporting your oral presentation with a visual component. Even if you only have words on your slides, this increases the learning potential for some students. If you have

more than words, then you can really make a positive impact on what students learn and retain from a class. Just as graphing calculators have made a world of difference in students' understanding of and willingness to tackle difficult concepts, so too can visual presentations bring concepts to life.

Countless Web sites, books, and articles provide suggestions for effective use of presentation software, but the following points address some basics:

- If you use a template, be sure it is uncluttered and provides adequate contrast between the print and the background on the slide. You want the print to stand out so that all students can read it regardless of where they sit in your classroom.
- If you want to have your statements or data "fly" onto the screen, make sure that you keep the direction uniform throughout the presentation.
- Use sound to accompany the words or symbols only if it is directly related. Otherwise the sound is distracting.
- If you mark points already discussed by changing or fading the text colors, be consistent with your technique throughout the presentation.
- Like overhead transparencies, the slides should highlight main points, not convey the entire message. "Bullet" information and keep statements concise.
- Be sure you use a font size large enough for everyone to read.
- Use no more than three fonts in a presentation.
- Do not become dependent on your presentation software to carry your lessons. Technology should strategically support your lesson.
- Have a Plan B. Although software and hardware glitches are less frequent than they once were, they do happen. Think about what you will do if the computer crashes or does not recognize the software you are using. Some faculty members choose to make backup transparencies or paper copies of each slide that can be displayed using overhead projection equipment. Alternatively, if you have chosen to provide your students with handouts, you can proceed with aplomb.
- Developing a good media presentation takes a great deal of time, generally more than you might imagine. Therefore, to begin with, choose only one lecture or one topic that you think could most benefit from presentation software-enhanced support. Then proceed to another one that is in need. It is not realistic to think that you can start with the first class of the semester and work through week to week until all class meetings have a PowerPoint component—nor is it necessary that every lecture incorporate PowerPoint. Remember, you are being strategic about your course planning and your use of technology.

Smart Boards

Some colleges and universities have invested large sums in "smart boards"—interactive whiteboards that serve as an enlarged monitor for a computer to which they are connected. The most advanced enable you to write on the whiteboard with special pens and then send the captured information to the computer so that it can be stored and/or printed out. While these devices may or may not remain popular, the technology is a harbinger of devices you can expect to see installed in many campus classrooms.

Course Management Software

In recent years, the market for course management systems—sometimes called courseware—has exploded. Providing electronic grade books, class rosters, course outlines, assignments, and quizzes, the growing array of competing products includes WebCT, Blackboard, Course Compass, and others (Olsen, 2001). But even if you do not have specific grade book software, you can use spreadsheets to record and calculate your grades. In a spreadsheet, you can make provisions to weigh various projects, quizzes, tests, or presentations. If you are using a mastery learning technique in your classroom in which you allow students to retake quizzes or exams several times until they get a "mastery score," you can set up your spreadsheet to count only the highest score in calculating the student's grade for the class. Spreadsheets provide a great deal of flexibility for use in recording and calculating grades for your classes.

As we discuss in Chapter 10, good test construction takes an enormous amount of time. If you are using a textbook that has an accompanying test bank of multiple-choice items, then selecting items from the test bank poses no major problem. If you are not using such a text, you can establish your own database for test items by using various software programs. As you write items for a test, you input them into a database. Eventually, you can accumulate a rather extensive database from which you can select questions for future tests. Your database can include short-answer and essay questions as well as multiple-choice items. As you grade the tests, you can do an item analysis to determine which questions worked best, and which were least effective and adjust your database accordingly. If you continue to teach that class but change the reading materials, you may still have a viable group of questions. Spending the time to create a database of questions is well worth your efforts.

Leveraging the Learning Resources of the Internet

Many of today's students are entering our colleges and universities with much experience in using various technologies. Don Tapscott (1998) refers to these students as the "Net Generation." Unlike radio, television, or film, the computer and the Internet provide active engaged time, not passive. The Internet opens the world to most students; there are no geographic boundaries or time constraints for communication. Most technology advocates also claim that the Internet knows no race, color, age, or ethnicity, thus persons are more likely to engage in communication to learn and share since the medium has greater neutrality than other media previously used in educational settings.

The Net Generation uses technology more easily and frequently than the older generations. Its members are at ease with technology and certainly not fearful of using it; rather, they embrace it with vigor. Members of the Net Generation are navigators in a new world of learning. They may question traditional practices and institutions, and they have a tool, the Internet, to help them challenge current ideas and thoughts. According to Tapscott (1998), the Net Generation "is more knowledgeable than any previous generation and they care deeply about social issues. They believe strongly in individual rights . . . [particularly] rights to information" (p. 9). They are going to challenge and question ideas and concepts and will be able to provide data to support those challenges. The concern you must have, as the teacher, is to channel their curiosity, social justice ideas, and independence in positive ways.

There are literally thousands of Web sites that can enhance your instruction. As previously indicated, you can link your class Web page to sites that can enrich class conversation. If you do not use a class Web page, you may still direct the students to various sites by giving them a supplementary reading list that includes Web sites and their respective URLs. Some interactive Web sites can be used as either acceleration or remediation opportunities for your students. Some sites are designed to engage students in problem-solving activities and/or reflective-thinking strategies, opportunities you might not have time for in your face-to-face meetings.

Using the Internet can enhance your instruction immeasurably, but it is initially terribly time-consuming on your part. You must locate and evaluate the sites and think about how you will incorporate that information into your teaching. As noted earlier, you might engage your students in the search for appropriate sites—a worthwhile learning experience for them. By linking and de-linking sites on your Web page or supplementary reading list, you can indicate how much Web access you deem appropriate for your students.

Evaluating Web sites for possible inclusion in your course is also time-consuming. There are a number of Web-site evaluation instruments available on the Internet for your use. You might again ask your students to locate and evaluate using one of these instruments and then determine from their evaluation whether or not you would want to include that site as part of the resources for your class.

The Internet certainly contains volumes of information—some of which is useful, some that is not. If students are going to use the Internet for gathering data, they need to know how to evaluate the information they retrieve. College librarians can usually provide an orientation for students on how to effectively use browsers and delineate searches to return the most relevant information they need for their purposes. The librarians can also help the students learn how to evaluate the Web sites. As mentioned, there are instruments available to assess the quality of Web sites. One simple device is the Credibility, Accuracy, Reasonableness, and Support (CARS) checklist, which is summarized in the following table (Harris, 1997). For research papers or other assignments in which students are required to cite sources, many faculty members find that it helps to have students actually explain how they determined a site was worthy of being included in their reference list.

Credibility	trustworthy source, author's credentials, evidence of quality control, known or respected authority, organizational support. Goal: an authoritative source, a source that supplies some good evidence that allows you to trust it.
Accuracy	up-to-date, factual, detailed, exact, comprehensive audience and purpose reflect intentions of completeness and accuracy. Goal: a source that is correct today (not yesterday), a source that gives the whole truth.
Reasonableness	fair, balanced, objective, reasoned, no conflict of interest, absence of fallacies or slanted tone. Goal: a source that engages the subject thoughtfully and reasonably, concerned with the truth.
Support	listed sources, contact information, available corroboration, claims supported, documentation supplied. Goal: a source that provides convincing evidence for the claims made, a source you can triangulate (find at least two other sources that support it).

Through the Internet, students have access to many libraries scattered around the world, including the U.S. Library of Congress and most university libraries. Databases that were previously difficult to access are now readily available to students (e.g., local, state, and federal demographic and economic statistics; NASA's database indicating current and future projects). Using the Internet, students can view the collections of some of the world's finest museums—the Smithsonian, the National Art Gallery, the British Museum, and so on. The sources for information are endless, and they provide a timeliness that heretofore has not been available to students.

Students can access professional expertise via the Internet—television networks, national professional associations, universities, corporations, and government agencies have Web sites. Frequently, they will announce that a particular celebrity, author, politician, pundit, or scholar will be available to "chat" with an "audience" at a given time. In addition, many of these recognized names maintain their own Web sites or at least make their e-mail addresses available to the general public. Several students in our classes have contacted authors of the textbooks they were using and were impressed to be able to ask them questions related to the content presented in the books. Most of the authors were very accommodating.

The audio and video possibilities available through the Internet are staggering in terms of their potential to involve and excite your students. Students can hear or see real-time legislative debates, speeches, or other notable events using streaming video. Even if their home computers do not have the capability that will allow them to do so, your campus computers should. In addition, many speeches and interviews have been stored, to be accessed by anyone, anytime, using the tools of the Internet. There is no need to haul in tape recorders, record players, or other ancient means to let students listen to political speeches given twenty, forty, or sixty years ago. You (or they) need only find the Web sites that have stored these speeches, then point, click, and listen.

Organizing and Processing Information

Computer technology not only allows professors to be more efficient in organizing and processing information but also allows students to be so. Some of this technology is nearly omnipresent, but we will mention its benefits here, with a few caveats.

Word processing is the most widely used application of computer technology in schools, colleges, and universities (Ravitz, Wong, and Becker, 1999). As you know, word processing programs allow you to input, store, retrieve, format, edit, and print text and some graphics, as well as put information into outlines or tables and integrate graphics from other sources. The beauty of word processing is that it enables students to submit initial drafts, receive specific feedback quickly, and develop rewrites while the content is still fresh in their minds. Cut-and-paste, delete, insert, grammar check, and spell check features all make revisions easy. By manipulating the text and incorporating graphics, students can produce professional-looking documents.

However, students must sometimes be cautioned against substituting stunning appearance for quality text. Another caution relates to the ease with which students can cut and paste other people's work into their document. The growing concern over plagiarism in college and university classrooms will be discussed in the following section.

Spreadsheet programs allow students to manipulate and interpret numerical data. Storing, interpreting, and querying are relevant tasks in many fields: business, political science, mathematics, engineering, physics, chemistry, sociology, biology, economics, education, and finance, to name a few. The cells on a spreadsheet usually are filled with discrete numbers; however, formulas can be used to calculate which numbers go into a cell. Useful statistical calculations can be derived such as averages (means) and standard deviations. Mathematical data such as the tangent of an angle or the logarithm of a number to base 10 are all possible using a spreadsheet. Most spreadsheet data can also be displayed in chart and graph formats, such as bar graphs, pie charts, and line graphs. Learning to display the information they have collected can help students better understand the data they collected.

Databases are used to organize, store, and search for information. When students do an online search in the library, they are doing so via the databases available to them at the library. Databases organize factual information and allow the student to examine relationships within that database. Many organizations keep membership databases, while businesses may compile product databases. In a typical membership database, the data can be sorted by address, by alphabetical listing, by gender, by age group, or by any other factor that was originally included in the data entered into the database. The National Assessment of Educational Progress (NAEP) database allows a researcher to look at test scores by region of the country, specific state data, ethnic data, age-level data, and so on. The U.S. Census Bureau maintains a large database of census results. As students work on projects in their classes, they can search for databases that can inform their research. Thus, databases are great learning tools.

The net generation is driving some of the trend in higher education toward student-centered versus teacher-centered instruction. Its members want to be actively engaged in their learning rather than passive recipients of a teacher's lecture, and they know that computer technology allows for such engagement. Computer technology can be applied to small-group learning. In fact, group work takes on a different dimension when technology is involved. Some students become the "data collectors" while other students become "data presenters." They find collaboration projects beneficial, for each group member contributes unique skills. Students who are independent learners will often find that working with a computer encourages group participation, even if they participate only through e-mail. Students who are normally quiet in class often come alive in online discussions in chat rooms or by posting ideas on bulletin boards or listservs.

Higher education is also about developing higher-order thinking skills, problem-solving skills, and critical-thinking skills. Technology infusion into your classes can help students develop these skills with ease and assurance. Because the Internet provides an abundance of information, students are immediately engaged in classifying, sorting, and evaluating activities. They get involved in organizing, comparing, and contrasting. Because data can be collected and imported into databases or spreadsheets, students can manipulate, sort, analyze, and draw conclusions about the data. You no longer have to do most of the work to collect and manipulate data—students can do it. Students may be able to provide much more information for you to use in your classes than you can do alone—and the process itself can help them meet their learning goals.

Resist the temptation, however, to view technology as a panacea for quality improvement of instruction. Quality still depends on your ability to develop your class objectives, content, and activities. Technology is a terrific aid to making your ideas work in the classroom. Initially you may be intimidated, particularly if most of your students have an edge on you with respect to their fluency in technology; but most students are patient and will help you learn. This is, after all, the Net Generation.

Dealing with Technology-Facilitated Plagiarism

As you evaluate your students' papers and projects, you will undoubtedly come across some work that makes you wonder whether it was plagiarized. For all the positive opportunities that have been afforded by the Internet, one downside is the ease with which students can obtain information and pass it off as their own. There are scores of sites on the Web where students can obtain anything from well-designed essays to full-blown research papers. Students can also use the Web to purchase papers from commercial paper mills, get translations of papers from foreign sites, participate in paper swaps, and cut and paste all manner of text. Even the traditional fraternity/sorority files or other paper-sharing mechanisms operating on most college campuses are now online.

According to Robert Harris (2001), there are several reasons why students cheat. First, many students simply do not understand what plagiarism is. They may have been copying material for reports ever since elementary school without being taught that such copying is unethical or even illegal. Second, some students are sloppy about their note taking—when doing their research, they neglect to distinguish their notes from paraphrased data or from direct quotes. Consequently, when they write their paper, they cannot make a distinction between their own ideas and those of their sources. Third, stress and competition affect students' decisions. To someone balancing work, school, and parenting, the easy availability of prewritten papers or projects can be too tempting. And, since most students do not get caught, many feel the risk is worth it. Another factor that encourages cheating is self-defense. Students who see other students getting good grades through cheating believe that to survive in a competitive situation they also need to cheat. Sadly, the fifth factor is really a societal one. Students routinely see politicians, athletes, businesspeople, professionals, entertainment figures, educators, and artists cheating in a variety of ways and not getting punished for their behavior. The perception that cheating is an acceptable practice in contemporary society is hard to combat in the academic arena. The final reason is one you can work to combat: Students cheat because they believe they can get away with it. They know that some professors never really read the assignments that are turned in. Although most professors do check student work thoroughly, desperate students are willing to take their chances with cheating and hoping they will not get caught.

There are several clues you can look for which would indicate that a student may have plagiarized, likely using some form of computer technology:

- The quality of the work does not match that of the student's previous work.
- The language used in the paper is not typical of the student's work.
- The references and citations are not done consistently throughout the paper or are not done according to your guidelines. Many students who copy do not pay attention to bibliographic references and mix together those they have found regardless of style.
- The paper lacks references or citations altogether.
- The paper has inconsistent flow and voice or lacks logical argument. Generally this is a sign of a cut-and-paste job.
- The bibliographic references or the dates quoted in the paper are not current.
- There are anomalies in content. For example, a giveaway sentence would be "The legislation is expected to pass in 2001."
- The content is familiar to you. One of the authors of this book had a student turn in a paper with the author's work embedded (without citation) within it.

While these indicators of plagiarism are fairly common, be aware that the evolution of more sophisticated software and students' technology skills requires your continuing vigilance.

There are several strategies you can employ to make plagiarism less likely to occur in your courses, many of which relate directly to effective planning, clarity of objectives, and specificity of requirements.

- Regularly ask yourself why your students would plagiarize. Perhaps they do not value the opportunity of learning, or perhaps they are working too many hours at outside jobs and allow themselves to get trapped by easy "solutions." Avoid fostering a "gotcha" paradigm (Howard, 2001).
- Be specific with your expectations on all projects, and give students a copy of your scoring rubric. The more particular and distinct your assignments are, the more difficult it will be for students to find a source from which to copy.
- Maintain samples of your students' written work. On the first or second day, give an in-class writing assignment that you can collect and place in a file for possible comparison purposes later. In addition, you can save a copy of an early out-of-class assignment as well, since this is more likely to show students' final draft style than something written somewhat hastily in class is.
- Require students to turn in progress reports for major assignments. Set up dates on which they must identify and submit their topic, their references, an outline of their paper, a rough draft, and so on.
- Ask students to include annotated references. With the ubiquity of online bookstores and library card catalogs, keep in mind this is not a foolproof

tactic. So you might want to spot-check the annotations by going online yourself.

- Require students to submit photocopies or printouts of their resources, particularly journal articles, Web sites, or pages from the books they cited.
- Become familiar with software and online resources that enable you to enter a questionable sentence and conduct a search for a "match" with published work.
- Have students make class presentations to the class followed by a question-and-answer period.
- Require students to sign an integrity oath. This is done routinely at many campuses.
- Invest some class time in defining plagiarism and discussing the consequences of being caught. Review your institution's policy with students so that they take the plagiarism issue seriously.

If you suspect plagiarism, follow through on the situation. Your best tactic is to gather documentary evidence and then to have a conference with the student in which you draw out the critical facts. If you calmly point to the evidence, most students will admit their guilt. Be prepared, however, for some students to refute your accusation, perhaps angrily. If the evidence you have gathered is not yet sufficient, or if the student challenges what you have found, let him or her know that you will continue to pursue the matter and communicate your findings.

If ethical students in the class know you are checking for plagiarism, they will appreciate and sometimes reinforce your efforts with their peers. Honorable students are rightly frustrated by the cheating of others, but perhaps even more so when a professor fails to enforce ethical standards, especially when those standards were noted in the course syllabus.

Where Teaching and Learning with Technology Intersect

Writers today know that by the time their words appear in print they may already be obsolete. We know this is especially true of any that address distance learning. Distance learning is not a new phenomenon. For many years, students who had limited time or lived in remote areas took advantage of distance-learning opportunities in the form of correspondence courses. In some extension divisions at universities, paper/pencil correspondence was the dominant mode of operation. With the advent of the Internet, all of that has changed. Distance learning now is defined as online courses, video-broadcasted courses, or interactive television courses. Although we do not have the time to delve into all aspects of distance learning in this book, be aware that when you as the teacher use the Web to enhance your course and students can use the Web to access your course, you are close to offering an online class.

Fully Web-based classes are becoming very popular and competitive. A look at the ROI (return on investment) of such higher education companies as the Apollo Group, ITT Educational Services, the University of Phoenix Online, and others (*Chronicle of Higher Education* Almanac, 2001) demonstrates this fact clearly. Some universities now offer entire programs via the Web, in spite of the fact that the attrition of students from distance-learning courses is often much higher than for traditionally delivered sections of the same courses. The added access it provides time- and place-challenged students and the cost savings it provides to institutions seem to be strong incentives for the future growth of distance learning. The population growth among college-age citizens coupled with the mushrooming growth of the Internet indicate that, for the foreseeable future, large amounts of investment dollars will flow into distance-learning technology. In addition, many governors and state legislators, as well as their economic development-minded constituents, view distance learning as a viable tool for improving access to higher education and increasing the degree completion rates among citizens who reside in remote areas or who travel widely as a function of their work. Various stakeholders expect distance learning to increase the productivity of publicly funded systems and to expand the economic base of their respective states.

Thus, colleges and universities can expect to see companies developing more increasingly student- and professor-friendly software programs and customer support systems for distance learning. You would do well to follow this growth and to continually look for ways to integrate related strategies into your instruction. Be aware as well that, with their mandates for inclusion, many state legislatures, as well as additional funding sources, are creating incentives for you to add technology to your kit of teaching tools. However, in doing so you will probably not be limited to delivering instruction by distance learning only. Realizing that some students' learning styles, technology skills, or other factors make them unlikely to succeed in distance-learning-only education, many institutions are experimenting with various forms of "blended" or "hybrid" courses that provide many of the conveniences of distance learning while maintaining the high-touch aspect of traditional teaching.

Although many see value in this mode of program delivery, Web-based instruction should not be entered into lightly. Serious consideration should be given to what is gained and what is lost by this form of course delivery. A major concern for university administrators is the retention rate for online classes. Data are not very plentiful, but indications are that student retention is problematic. If students become disenfranchised on the Web, it is much more difficult for professors to encourage them, since they have never met, than to support students in a traditional class where there has been at least at a modicum of eye contact. Also, faculty members are usually clued in faster about potential dropouts in face-to-face situations than in a Web-based class, where students can "hide" from the professor and thus delay intervention.

Faculty members who choose to deliver their courses fully on the Web need extensive planning time to rethink, restructure, and redesign their courses and then to develop the Web site and the activities. Without some type of program management, such as WebCT or Blackboard, course design and management becomes much more challenging. All of this means that online teaching is far more time-consuming and time-intensive than traditional teaching methods. And those who venture into video broadcasting or interactive television teaching have to think in entirely new ways. Teaching to students who are seen on a small screen, or not at all, is very challenging, to say the least.

We mention distance learning here because it employs many of the technology tools for both teaching and learning we discussed earlier in this chapter. However, if you choose to go this route, you will need to learn much more than we can share in this book. We simply warn you to be prepared for an entirely new way of thinking about how and what you teach and be prepared to spend considerable time rethinking your courses in whatever medium you choose to use for distance-learning activity. In this area, as in all areas of your teaching, it is very important for you to recognize that technology is only a tool. It cannot substitute for genuine concern about the complex needs of your students. If you rely too heavily on technology while ignoring the personal touch, you may lose more of your students than is acceptable. In this age of accountability, retention is the critical issue. Therefore, it is imperative that you use technological tools appropriately and remain sensitive to the needs of your students.

Summary of Key Points

- The use of technology can be an asset to both the professor and the learner.
- There is a growing array of ways in which professors can use technology to enhance their course organization, presentation, and assessment.
- Technology provides students with multiple opportunities to enhance learning.
- Technology engages students in their learning and increases their opportunities to develop higher-order thinking skills, including problem-solving and critical-thinking skills.
- Technology can improve your communication with your students markedly.
- Technology has increased student access to material, with both positive outcomes and negative temptations (e.g., cheating).
- Distance learning is a growing area of higher education that holds great potential but also presents many challenges.
- Inappropriate use of technology can dramatically affect the retention rate in your classes, particularly if students see it (and thus you) as impersonal and uncaring.

Through the Professors' Eyes

KIM: Having worked with computers a great deal during my doctoral program, I am really comfortable with the new technologies. This is one area that I know more about than my mentor and many of my colleagues, and I feel good sometimes teaching them new uses of the technology. It helps me feel like I am repaying the effort they have invested in me. I am excited about integrating technology into my courses. I already have e-mail distribution lists set up for each class, so I can easily send students messages that clarify class activities and upcoming assignments. I use e-mail a lot, and my students know they can always get a response quickly through e-mail. I have set up chat rooms for my students and learn a lot from "listening" to their conversations. This certainly has helped me to understand better what they are thinking. I have time to decipher their language—that helps me so much. I have separate Web pages for each of my classes and have all the assignments, due dates, exam dates, and so on posted on them. I am considering using more Web-based options to enhance my classes and perhaps develop a fully Web-based class. I know this takes up huge amounts of time but believe it might gain me some notice for what I right now am best able to contribute to my department. Most of my better students and I are in similar places with respect to technology, and using it so much gains me respect in their eyes.

PAT: I thought I knew everything there is to know about teaching, but the new advances in technology surely have posed additional challenges for me. While certainly no technology guru, I am beginning to see how the technology can help me achieve more learning effectiveness, which is the name of the game in this new age of accountability. I fought the technology initially, believing it detracted from the quality of learning, but now I am a strong advocate of its incorporation into teaching. Participating in several workshops on technology use and getting trained to be an online teacher convinced me that there are some definite advantages to using technology to teach and to learn. The key is appropriate use. We must be careful not to throw out the "high touch" with the adoption of more "high tech." In fact, we need to be very careful to incorporate elements of interpersonal savvy into instructional technology.

For each of my classes, I have established Web pages that post all of my course syllabi. My class schedules, reading lists, assignments with full instruction on how to complete them, and their due dates are all posted. Examples of the types of papers I expect are also available for the students to peruse, as are examples of outstanding projects submitted by students in past terms. I now accept assignments through e-mail attachments and have even designed a reduced-seat-time class, which my students really like. Taking care of the high-touch element, I still need to meet my students face-to-face. Through a focus group setting, I have asked my students to help me decide what content should be delivered "live" and what content can be developed through

Web-based activities. They appreciate, and really grow from, being involved in these decisions. The technology has created more flexibility with schedules, but it is also very time-consuming if you do it right. Clearly, the investment has been worth it up to this point!

DALE: Now we are talking about important changes in teaching. I just learned WebCT and am really impressed with its classroom management strategies. I can communicate to my entire class or to just one student. I can post exams and quizzes, have them graded immediately as the students take them, and have the scores posted on the individual student's progress sheets—this is great! I am also establishing Web pages for my class where the students can get all the information they need to know and I don't have to worry about what to do if someone misses class—I post my lectures there as well. I even agreed to teach a large class (rather than two smaller ones) because I can use the technology to handle the paperwork. Now I will have more time to work on my own research and publication agenda. I got myself a graduate assistant, and he really manages my class. He answers the e-mails, since most of them are requests for routine clarification of assignments or grades. He forwards the especially challenging ones to me, but they represent a very small ratio of those received. I have even thought about enhancing my classes with some of my research findings and data from the Internet. This technology has made a big impact on the ways I think about my teaching.

Tips for Thriving

As technology continues its proliferation within higher education, it will become increasingly critical that those facilitating technology-enhanced instruction, especially distance learning, sensitize themselves to the psychological and emotional needs of students. Said another way, professors must be consistently mindful of the high-tech/high-touch paradox. Those most successful at employing technology will be able to view their strategies through the eyes of those with whom they are interfacing at a distance.

An interesting example comes to mind. One of the authors of this book has a colleague who is currently enrolled in a graduate-level course in statistics, delivered via the Internet. A sharp person with some degree of experience in statistical concepts, the colleague has been appalled by the terseness of the course facilitator's communications. Frequent technical difficulties prevent the students from receiving communications as intended, and the result is that the students do not understand the professor's policies or procedures. (Not surprisingly, this professor is known for retention problems in traditionally taught courses.) Is it not simply common sense to ease into a distance-learning environment, ensuring that all of the students are on board with policies and procedures before moving down the road together?

In contrast, a team of physics professors at the U.S. Air Force Academy, Indiana University/Purdue University at Indianapolis, and Davidson College have collaborated to develop what they call just-in-time teaching (JiTT). JiTT employs the World Wide Web to deliver multimedia curricular materials and to manage communications between faculty and students, while emphasizing personal teacher–student and student–student interactions in the classroom. By increasing interactivity and offering rapid responses to students' problems, the strategy increases students' engagement with material often regarded as of secondary importance. The professors firmly believe their strategies can be employed in courses that are taken largely to satisfy requirements, and those taken by part-time students (Novak, Patterson, Gavin, and Christian, 1999).

SUGGESTED READINGS

Brown, D. (2001). "The Power of E-Mail." *Syllabus: New Directions in Education Technology* 24, no. 12 (July), p. 26.

Grabe, M., and C. Grabe. (2001). *Integrating Technology for Meaningful Learning*, 3rd ed. Boston: Houghton-Mifflin.

Hannon, K. (2001). "Using E-Mail to Communicate with Students." *ASEE Prism: Exploring the Future of Engineering Education.* 10, no. 6 (February), pp. 34–35.

The Jossey-Bass Reader on Technology and Learning (2000). San Francisco: Jossey-Bass.

Katz, R. N., et al. (1999). *Dancing with the Devil: Information Technology and the New Competition in Higher Education.* San Francisco: Jossey-Bass.

Kearsley, G. (2000). *Online Education: Learning and Teaching in Cyberspace.* Belmont, CA: Wadsworth.

Ravitz, J., Y. Wong, and H. Becker. (1999). *Teaching, Learning and Technology National Survey.* www.crito.uci.edu/tlc.

Sanders, W. B. (2001). *Creating Learning-Centered Courses for the World Wide Web.* Boston: Allyn & Bacon.

Tapscott, D. (1998). *Growing Up Digital: The Rise of the Net Generation.* New York: McGraw-Hill.

10 Managing the Examination Process

FOCUS QUESTIONS

- What are the characteristics of an effective examination?
- How is an effective examination constructed?
- What are the best procedures for administering an examination?
- What follow-up activities are essential to the administration of an examination?

For most professors and students, no activity is more daunting than evaluating student learning. Everyone reading this book can probably cite horror stories about college testing experiences—from both the test-taking and test-giving perspectives.

One of this book's authors had a professor who told students exactly how many lines in a blue book constituted an adequate answer to an essay question. If students exceeded the prescribed length, the professor would cross out the excessive words. Students who answered in the allotted number of lines received full credit, while those who wrote shorter or longer answers received no more than half credit. The professor's argument was that a student who knew the material could synthesize it in the allotted space—end of explanation. No consideration was given to the size or style of students' handwriting or to any other factors. Lines simply equaled lines. Another author recalls being asked on a final examination to identify the writer of the textbook for the course. The professor had not mentioned the name during the course, and the writer was not known to have made any significant contributions to the discipline. The only purpose of that question seemed to be to round out the total number of items on the exam, making scores easier for the professor to calculate. And since nearly everyone missed the question, the overall results approximated the bell-shaped curve that the professor believed documented the rigor of his course.

While most professors have not created snafus of such magnitude, almost all have at one time or another created a test item that upset a student. With today's emphasis on accountability, however, a faulty test can provide public relations fodder for those seeking to build a case against professors as narrow-minded nitpickers who are more invested in finding the flaws in, rather than fostering the success of, their students.

As you approach developing your exams in an increasingly accountable manner, try to keep in mind not only your stated learning objectives but also the varied perspectives of those, besides yourself, who have a stake in your exam—the students enrolled across different sections of the course; professors who teach other courses from which, or to which, your students matriculate; and your institutional leaders. Recall the valuable strategy of developing your exams in the early stages of your instruction, then allowing the exam to help guide your management of the material.

All stakeholders rightly expect your test items to accurately reflect the content and logic articulated in the course textbook and in other instructional materials you have used in class. A significant disconnect between the texts and the exam will contribute to confusion and frustration, stymie learning, and foster ill will among students and other stakeholders. Increasingly time-conscious students expect an exam that provides a fair opportunity to demonstrate their knowledge of material in which they have invested precious hours studying. When their expectations are not met, today's students are typically not shy about expressing their concerns on end-of-course evaluations, whose content is fed back in a communications loop to those with the authority to evaluate your effectiveness.

Although both students and instructors typically associate one overriding type of decision with examinations—grade determination—tests have at least two other important uses as well. First, tests should help students themselves assess their progress toward achieving their overall educational goals. Second, exams should help professors make better instructional decisions, such as how much class time and which instructional resources to dedicate to teaching particular concepts. With so much riding on the results, the exam items you develop must be grounded in sound pedagogical principles and must take a perspective sensitive toward students.

Qualities of an Effective Examination

Traditionally, experts in educational testing have emphasized the importance of three attributes of an effective examination:

1. *Reliability* refers to the consistency of students' scores. A very important concept for those who are concerned about accountability issues, reliability comes in two forms. First, if a test does not produce consistent results at different testing times with the same group of students, then it is not a reliable measure of student learning. This form of reliability is referred to as *stability*. Second, some professors typically design two or more versions of a test to be administered to multiple sections of a class or to be used as makeup tests. If you do this, you need to be certain that the different versions are equivalent, so that students should not be able to score better on one version than another. The term used to describe this type of consistency is *alternate form reliability*. This term is most often associated with high-stakes or standardized tests.

2. *Validity* is focused on the *inferences* educators make from test scores about student achievement or status in class. High scores lead to one type of judgment, low scores another. Validity, then, "hinges on the accuracy of our inferences about students' status with respect to an assessment" (Popham, 1999, p. 43). As a professor, you need to be extremely conscious of judging students according to their performance on a test. Even a well-designed test will lead to invalid inferences if it is given to an inappropriate group of students. Do not use the same test each semester without considering the nature of your students and the content you addressed. In an age of accountability, you need to be certain that you are making valid inferences about your students. Thus, you need to be conscious of how well your tests *measure the content* that was taught. Validity is a filter through which professors seek to answer the question "Does the test reflect the content and skills emphasized in the process of teaching the course?"

3. *Absence of assessment bias* refers to a test's score flowing primarily from students' mastery of course learning objectives rather than from the idiosyncrasies of the developer of the test items. In other words, is the test free of bias? Test items worded as if they were fact, when they are actually the opinion of the test item developer, *lack objectivity*. Some test items can *offend the examinees*. Angry, upset, or frustrated students cannot be expected to do their best—their scores are probably not an accurate reflection of their mastery of the concepts addressed on the exam. With the increase of diversity in college courses, the use of unbiased language in exams has become critical. Nonnative speakers of English may not understand colloquialisms or slang, for example. Many English words are open to multiple interpretations, so test items must be written as unambiguously as possible.

While these three general test properties—reliability, validity, and absence of assessment bias—should undergird your development of test items, you should also recognize the following principles:

- An effective examination should be a learning experience, as well as an evaluative one. It should serve as a thorough review that enables students to deepen their mastery of the concepts included and to perform more effectively throughout the remainder of the course.

- Each examination should be a win/win proposition for students and the professor, not a battle of wits. Effective test items are clear, concise, and subject to limited interpretation.
- An effective test item should evaluate the understanding of the most critical concepts rather than the rote memorization of trivial factual data.
- An effective test differentiates levels of mastery by addressing different levels of Bloom's taxonomy. Including a mix of questions will help you understand which students are developing *grounded* rather than *surface-level* knowledge.
- An effective examination will have no significant surprises for the well-prepared student.
- A well-developed examination will reflect class time spent on all significant ideas and concepts taught. No student should leave an exam thinking its contents did not measure key ideas that were perceived as highly relevant or that too many items were focused on a narrow range of concepts.

James Popham (1999) has developed five general item-writing commandments that apply to any type of test you develop:

- Thou shall not provide opaque directions to students regarding how to respond to your assessment instruments.
- Thou shall not employ ambiguous statements in your assessment items.
- Thou shall not provide students with unintentional clues regarding appropriate responses.
- Thou shall not employ complex syntax in your assessment items.
- Thou shall not use vocabulary that is more advanced than required. (p. 112)

Typically, introductory college and university courses—and the textbooks adopted for them—focus on students' achieving learning objectives at the *knowledge*, *comprehension*, and *application* levels. Subsequent courses within a curriculum, and their textbooks, tend to focus on a middle range of Bloom's taxonomy, while capstone courses, and their textbooks, typically focus on the high end of the range.

The various test formats lend themselves to evaluating student learning at different levels of Bloom's taxonomy. Introductory courses typically employ *selected response* test items (true/false, multiple-choice, and matching). The terms *selected response test* and *objective test* are often used as synonyms for *forced-choice test*. These issues will be addressed more fully as the chapter progresses, but it is most important to recognize the need to make sure that the majority of questions in your test bank are at the level the course and its textbook predictably address. Among students' greatest test frustrations is to be *taught* at Bloom's knowledge and comprehension levels and then to be *tested* at the application and analysis levels, or higher. That is not only unfair and demotivating to students but also inherently ineffective in achieving teaching and learning objectives.

Developing Effective Selected Response Items

Unseasoned professors often wonder about the best format for their tests. What is "best," however, depends on the level at which instruction took place, the nature and complexity of the learning objectives, the preexisting level of typical students' knowledge and experience, and other factors. Selective response items provide ease of scoring and quick turnaround, providing timely feedback to students, which fosters rapid advancement up the levels of Bloom's taxonomy. The major types of selective response items will be addressed in the following subsections.

True/False Items

On the surface, true/false items seem to be easy for the instructor to develop and employ in a test. However, to make true/false questions even the least bit challenging, the instructor must be creative without employing tactics that students might regard as tricky or deceptive. Most faculty members want to avoid causing heated discussions when scored exams are returned and reviewed in class. Being known as a professor who includes tricky questions would set up an undesirable adversarial relationship with students. Also, regardless of how well or how poorly they are written, true/false items give students a 50 percent chance of success—even without reading the question. Although they are not as effective in most college course environments as other types of test items, true/false questions lend themselves to evaluating the lower levels of Bloom's taxonomy. They can work quite well for evaluating knowledge of definitions, comprehension of the characteristics of key entities (especially when those characteristics are quantifiable), and applications of terminology (e.g., x is an effective example of y). In evaluating at the upper end of Bloom's taxonomy, true/false items typically require greater complexity, and therefore phrasing them in a way that is easy for students to decipher is especially challenging.

   In summary, the following tips can help you develop effective true/false questions:

- Focus them at Bloom's levels of knowledge, comprehension, or application.
- Keep their wording concise, focused on a single issue, and free of unnecessary detail.
- Use quantifiable terms—that is, word and concepts than can be measured precisely.
- Construct true items so that they are completely true, false items so that they are totally false.

- If *no*, *not*, or some other negative word is used, italicize or underline it.
- Avoid using the words *never* and *always*, which usually render an item false.
- For each examination, employ true questions and false questions in roughly equal numbers.

Matching Items

After the basic true/false format, most test developers would consider the matching format the next most sophisticated of forced-choice test items. Most commonly, matching exercises employ two vertical lists, one in which items are numbered, the other in which items are lettered. The student is typically expected to write the correct letter in a blank beside each number. One set of items is a definition or description; the other set is a term or name to be defined. Since the matching format does not easily lend itself to machine scoring, it has become nearly obsolete for large classes. Some authors and publishers no longer use this format for questions in their test banks. However, well-written matching items can be more challenging and effective than true/false items for evaluating students' mastery of vocabulary words or basic definitions of key concepts. Like true/false items, matching items fit Bloom's knowledge, comprehension, and application levels and are not effective for more-sophisticated levels of learning.

The following tips should be followed in developing effective matching items:

- Focus them at Bloom's knowledge, comprehension, or application levels.
- Ensure that directions are very clearly stated.
- Position the descriptors (defining phrases or sentences) in the left-hand column, and designate them with numbers.
- Position the terms or names in the right column, and use letters to designate them.
- Develop an easily recognizable theme common to all items in the matching exercise.
- Alphabetize the terms/names in the right column to help students locate them.
- Make sure that none of the definitions could match two terms.
- Develop extra names/terms for the right-hand column that do not match any descriptor in the left-hand column, thus avoiding a situation where a student automatically misses two questions by answering one incorrectly.
- Avoid using "clangers," which are clues that facilitate guessing a correct answer.

Completion Items

Completion items, sometimes called fill-in or short-answer questions, share a number of features with matching items. The key difference is that the student calls to mind a word or phrase and then enters it in a blank within a statement or sentence, in the process making it complete and accurate. Some professors employ a hybrid format—between matching and total recall items—in which they provide a list of terms at the beginning of a testing exercise or enter them on the board prior to the examination. Students are then directed to select their answers from the list provided.

In addition to most of the tips in the preceding matching section, the following apply to completion items:

- Provide sufficient and precise details in the sentence so that there is only one correct answer.
- Eliminate unnecessary detail that might serve as a barrier to students' achieving a clear focus on the issue to be decided.
- Avoid using phrases verbatim from the text, unless it is your goal to evaluate students' recall of a famous passage.
- Avoid giving clues—i.e., clangers—in the sentence, such as "The rather bald and plump moviemaker who directed *The Birds*, *Psycho*, and *North by Northwest* was _____."
- Place the blank to be completed either first or last in the sentence, in order to focus the student's decision-making effectively.

Multiple-Choice Items

With increasingly larger class sizes and stakeholders' demands that professors turn around test results more quickly, multiple-choice items have become the favorite testing format for most U.S. college instructors today. These items not only are relatively easy to develop but also lend themselves to being machine-scored and analyzed. When properly constructed, multiple-choice items can be made valid, reliable, and unbiased in situations that call for knowledge, comprehension, application, and even limited analysis.

The following are tips for creating effective multiple-choice items:

- Ensure that correct answers are facts, rather than opinions, unless you clearly indicate which famous person or recognized body held the opinion.
- Arrange the question so that the "stem" (opening statement) includes all necessary qualifiers and that the response options are relatively brief.
- Ensure that both the correct response and distractors are approximately the same length, with similar amounts of detail and levels of complexity.
- Avoid clangers, such as having only one option whose verb agrees with the subject in the stem, or having only one response begin with a vowel when the last word of the stem is *an*.
- Ensure that none of the distractors could be considered correct by someone truly knowledgeable in the field.
- Omit nonfunctional words and trivial facts from both the stems and the options.

- Avoid negative phrasing in the stem. For example, rather than "Which of the following is *not*," use "All of the following are true, *except.*"
- While limited use of options such as "Both *a* and *b* are correct," "None of the above," or "All of the above" might contribute to the effectiveness of a test, be careful that such questions are not disproportionately reflected in your inventory of questions for each chapter. Too often, "All of the above" is the correct answer.
- Avoid response options that overlap or include each other. For example, "Less than 25 percent" is included in "Less than 50 percent."
- Whenever possible, use situations to which students can easily relate as the focus for application and analysis questions, thus encouraging immediate clarity and longer-term retention.

Although the task of incorporating all of the above advice into the development of your test items might seem a little overwhelming, you likely enter this activity more experienced, and better equipped, than you might recognize. Because of time constraints, you might be tempted to employ a *test bank* provided by the publisher of your adopted textbook. While many such resources are quite good, others are extremely poor. Review closely all items before including them in your exam. Some test bank items are perfectly acceptable as written, others may need some editing, whereas some may be unusable because they are irrelevant, invalid, or inconsistent. Ultimately it is your exam, not the textbook publisher's, so invest the time to do it right. In the long run, you and your students will be glad you did.

Developing Effective Essay Test Items

While selected response test items clearly are convenient to score, many stakeholders in higher education, both external and internal, claim that their overuse has contributed to a marked decline in the writing and critical-thinking abilities of college graduates. Their concerns have led to a resurgence of essay items on exams, including those administered in introductory-level courses. Essay writing is widely accepted as a factor in the development of higher-level thinking, since it encompasses Bloom's application, analysis, synthesis, and evaluation levels. More specifically, essay questions are useful in helping students:

- Establish connections between theoretical principles and real-world situations.
- Compare and/or contrast two or more approaches to an issue.
- Explain the range of factors that contribute to a particular situation.
- Integrate information from several sources to explain a particular situation.
- Propose and defend a grounded solution to a problem.
- Evaluate the quality or appropriateness of a product, a process, or an action.

Besides requiring a great deal of time, scoring essay questions holds several other challenges for professors. First, students often have been conditioned to equate "quantity of words" to "quality of response"—a perception that unfortunately has been reinforced in some classrooms. Second, essay question responses require psychic energy to score. Finally, scored essays may contribute to uncomfortable dialogue between professors and disagreeable students when results are shared. Rubrics are well recognized for their ability to focus student thinking, while increasing objectivity and reducing time in scoring. The rubric might be as simple as the following:

Opening: Provide clear introduction/ restatement of the key issue	2 pts. possible
Body: Provide sufficient, correct detail and logical reasoning	5 pts. possible
Conclusion: Provide effective summary and application	3 pts. possible
TOTAL POINTS POSSIBLE	10

In summary, the following tips can help you develop effective essay items:

- Include clear parameters within the directions and/or the essay question itself so that students will not be tempted to write unfocused or unnecessarily long responses.
- Provide precisely identified elements to which you expect students to respond.
- Avoid starting an essay question with *how*, *why*, or *what*. Instead, use a descriptive verb such as *explain* or *describe*.
- Provide students with a scoring rubric that will be used to guide your evaluation.

Facilitating Student Success

Effective, accountable professors and their students both want to be successful in the examination process. There are proven steps that you can take to increase the probability of such win/win outcomes. First, students should not enter a testing situation without knowing what to expect. Your students deserve to know in advance exactly what content is going to be assessed and the types of items you will include on the test. The best way to provide this information is to provide a review session at the class meeting prior to the examination. How you conduct the review will depend on the nature and experience of your students. If your examination will solely comprise selected response items, you might provide students with sample questions. Knowing how you construct multiple-choice distractors, phrase true/false items, or structure matching items can help them avoid confusion and anxiety during the test. Consider showing them samples from a previously administered examination, having them work in small groups to answer the questions, and then reviewing the answers as a class. Students need to be reassured that questions will not be tricky and that they will be relevant to the content that has been addressed. For the first examination in your course especially, you might provide a study guide that lists the most important ideas on which the examination will be based. The key is to assure students that the examination will be a fair assessment of your expectations of the students' learning.

In addition to reviewing content and exam formats, you might also want to review your test administration procedures. The following are some suggestions:

- Identify the supplies the students should bring (e.g., Scantron sheets, blue books, pens/pencils).
- Explain any special seating arrangements you intend to employ on examination day and why you will institute them.
- Explain the schedule to be followed for the exam. Tell students when the test will begin and end and whether class will resume after the administration of the examination. The latter would be particularly important for classes that only meet once a week for an extended period of time.
- Explain when and how students can expect to receive their scores.
- Reiterate the penalties for missing the examination and review makeup procedures if applicable.

Administering the Examination

When the examination is to be administered, arrive early and have all the materials ready for distribution as soon as the class is assembled. Arrange the seating, and check the lighting and temperature of the room. Provide a special seating area near the door for students who might arrive late. Proofread your examination one last time and correct any errors on your key. Greet students as they enter the room, and try to orchestrate a comfortable atmosphere. Avoid joking about the difficulty or simplicity of the examination.

When the class is fully assembled, ask whether anyone has any specific questions regarding the procedures. Keep responses brief. Have students clear their desks of all items except the materials necessary for taking the examination. Identify where they should place their completed examinations and answer sheets, and remind them what time the class will resume if that is an option. Distribute the examination and bring to their attention any errors you found while proofreading it, both orally and by writing the correct construction on the board. Remind them of the time allocation for the examination and wish them good luck.

Although you may have brought your own work to do while the students are taking the examination, do not get so involved in it that you lose sight of what is going on with the examination. A few minutes into the test, circulate the room quietly—it is imperative that the students recognize your attention to their behavior during the examination. Respond quickly to raised hands, wandering eyes, or puzzled looks. Since it serves to discount the importance of the test and your standing in students' eyes, do not make a habit of having someone else proctor your examinations. Also, watching your students take an examination can be very revealing. Observing their comfort level or frustration with the examination's content and approach can help you the next time you prepare and administer an examination.

Dealing with Student Cheating

According to several recent reports, cheating among college students is becoming more widespread (McCabe and Drinan, 1999). While the majority of dishonesty takes the form of plagiarism (as discussed in Chapter 9), cheating on examinations is also a concern. Most professors want to believe that the care they have taken in constructing their examinations should preclude any cheating. The reality, however, is that some students continue to peek at other students' papers, while others use crib sheets and other methods of cheating during examinations. Technology, larger classes, machine-scored answer sheets, and the risk-taking mind-set of many students have evoked brazen methods of cheating, including:

- Storing potential answers on calculators, microcassette recorders, and other electronic devices.
- Recording answers on a duplicate Scantron answer sheet that they then give to a friend as they leave a classroom.
- Having another student take their exam for them.
- Accusing the instructor of losing an examination they never submitted.
- Using nonverbal cues, not readily recognizable by the instructor, to indicate correct choices (e.g., rubbing the nose indicates answer *a*; scratching the head means answer *b*.)

Students who perceive that their peers are cheating and getting away with it often lack the self-discipline to resist cheating themselves. They may also be reluctant to alert the professor to the cheating of other students, for fear that they will be identified as snitches. Clearly, the best strategy to minimize cheating is to be proactive in its prevention. Disbursing students throughout the classroom, monitoring the materials on students' desks, and moving throughout the room all stifle cheating during the exam. More important, however, are establishing a trusting relationship between you and your students, designing tests perceived as fair, and preparing students adequately.

If a student does come forward and indicates that cheating occurred during the examination, take the complaint seriously. Carefully analyze the answers on the test, and look for patterns in grades (e.g., a failing student abruptly scores very high). If you can identify an individual as likely having cheated, ask him or her to see you privately, and ask them some nonthreatening questions, like what they are doing differently to account for their success. Unless you have absolute evidence, however, you should never accuse a student of cheating. The best you can do in this case is to put the student on notice through your behavior. The next time a test is administered, be sure the suspected cheater is more isolated within the classroom and observe him or her carefully.

Scoring Examinations

Earlier in this chapter, you were given some guidelines for scoring answers. Traditionally, professors constructed scoring answer keys that could be positioned next to the exam to highlight erroneous responses, which were then marked by hand. Through technology, however, this task has been simplified. Among the makers of scoring machines and specially designed answer sheets, the most familiar is the Scantron Corporation. For a given exam, Scantron machines are programmed by inserting a correctly marked answer sheet. As each student's answer sheet is fed through, the machine marks incorrect responses and prints the total number of correct responses. Machines of the most recent technology will also provide item analyses—that is, they can calculate the number of times each question was missed, mean scores, medians, ranges, and other descriptive analyses.

Machine scoring can save you time—which you can then invest in making your test items more reliable, valid, and bias-free. If the item analysis indicates the vast majority of students missed an item, you might consider dropping that item from the number of scored items. If other items do not indicate quality or level of learning (i.e., everyone got them right), you might consider restructuring those items the next time you employ the exam.

Reviewing Results of Examinations

In today's accountability environment, students expect quick feedback on their examinations. Although using selected response items can help you provide it, be sure to budget sufficient time to score the more grounded essay items, especially if you have large classes. Nevertheless, you should make every attempt to return examination results to the students by the next class.

To foster grounded learning in your students, you must review scored examinations. Try to ensure that any makeup tests are given prior to the session at which the examination results will be reviewed, so that those students can participate in the review as well. The most effective way to review a selected response examination is to first distribute the test itself and discuss the correct responses before returning the answer sheets to students. This encourages students to better understand the concepts addressed by the test questions rather than focus on the questions they missed. If your item analysis identified questions you have decided to delete, explain your rationale in terms of a question's ineffective construction, not the fact that too many students missed it. Then explain how you recalculated scores. This tactic and your refusal to curve the exam scores—our practice explained in Chapter 6—will demonstrate your fairness and reinforce your high standards.

After all questions are reviewed, write the scores on the board in descending order and provide the calculated average score in the class. Only then should you distribute the students' answer sheets. They can then look at their test scores, compare their results to those of the class as a whole, and analyze the questions they missed. Giving the students ample information about the test results typically prevents anyone from becoming unruly during the review. Solicit questions, but do not engage in arguments over particular test questions. Invite any especially distressed students to stay after class, and encourage others to come to your office later to talk about their specific test results. Quick attention may not only alleviate students' frustration but also mitigate what might be an irrational decision to drop the class. Remember, many of your students are trying to balance school with other obligations, so they may need some time to accept the poor results of a test. Keeping the door open to conversation is very important to helping students properly assess and manage their progress.

Reviewing the results of essay items during class time is a little more difficult, but scoring rubrics can help objectify the discussion and reduce students' emotionality. You might also provide examples of high-quality responses, so that students understand your expectations on subsequent exams. Again, inviting students to your office is likely to be useful, especially for those whose writing skills might benefit from further coaching.

Our entire society increasingly relies on examinations to sort out those who have mastered skills and concepts from those who need further development. The strategy you employ in managing examinations in your classes will serve to provide a lasting statement about your integrity as a learning facilitator. Commit yourself to continually improving your abilities in this critical area.

Summary of Key Points

- Examinations contribute to the students' overall perceptions of the professor.
- Examinations measure not only student learning but effective teaching as well.
- Construct drafts of examinations as you plan your instruction.
- Ensure that your examinations are reliable, valid, and unbiased.
- Test items should reflect a variety of levels of Bloom's taxonomy and emphasize the levels as presented in class.

- Popham's commandments for constructing good test items include giving clear directions, avoiding ambiguity, not giving clues to answers, keeping syntax simple, and using appropriate vocabulary.
- Tests should be constructed to make judicious use of selected response items and essay items.
- Prepare your students for your examinations by keeping them informed of your expectations and providing appropriate review time.
- Administer your examinations in an organized way yourself, rather than through a proctor.
- Analyze the results before returning the examinations to your students. Be prepared to explain any anomalies to them and what your plans are to accommodate those anomalies.
- Return examinations promptly—preferably at the next class meeting—and review results in a systematic manner.
- Demonstrate sensitivity to student anxiety before, during, and after exams.

Through the Professors' Eyes

DALE: Since I got interested in the new course design and management software my college purchased, I converted all of my examinations and quizzes so that they can be delivered on the Web. Since we don't even have to meet on those days, I gain a much more flexible schedule. My students take the tests it is automatically scored, and grades are posted by my graduate assistant. This technology surely has simplified my life. I can even design my tests to present the questions randomly, so that I have several forms of one test. This means that makeup exams are really easy to give. I can't seem to get the conversation with Orwin Luke out of my system. Is he ill? Has his family life disintegrated? He was undoubtedly the most scholarly and wise person in that department, and he had to fight his own occasional battles to maintain the integrity of the program. I think I owe him a callback, and maybe a lunch. I wonder if he's going to the conference this spring?

PAT: I've always struggled with exams. I'm not convinced that all students perform well on exams, but I think they are important. I use primarily multiple-choice items, but now I include at least one essay item on each exam. While essays are time-consuming to score, the use of scoring rubrics helps a great deal. Rubrics also improve the quality of student writing, because they allow students to better organize their thoughts and approach their written responses from a more grounded perspective. I have noticed a major decline in the quality of items in the test banks accompanying the textbooks we have adopted, and so I have reverted to designing my own test items. That takes a good amount of time. But I want to get my students to operate at higher cognitive levels, so I guess the time is well spent. I am creating my own test bank of questions.

KIM: Like many international students, my secondary and early college work required writing responses to very comprehensive essay examinations. I never saw multiple-choice and true/false tests until I came to this country. I am struggling to learn how to construct good test items, because my students expect multiple-choice questions. The test banks that come with the books I adopted do not seem to focus on what is most important, and I don't find them very helpful. My students need to understand concepts and applications, not just facts. I try to get them to do that on essay exams, but they really have a hard time writing them. My mentor is helping me and has encouraged me to teach my students how to study for my exams by providing study guides and scoring rubrics for essay questions. I wonder sometimes if that is considered cheating. I want to be certain that my students not only achieve good grades in my class but also really learn what they need to know to successfully continue the sequence of classes. I don't want to cause my students any difficulty in the future.

Tips for Thriving

Since the first examination is such a critical milepost in retaining students throughout the entire term, go the extra mile to give students every chance of success on it. Depending on the level of your course, the nature of your students, the difficulty of the subject matter and other factors, you might want to (1) host extra study sessions, (2) post mock questions to your course Web page, (3) agree to stand by your computer to respond to e-mail questions the evening before the exam, and (4) place old exams in binders and make them available through the reserve room of the campus library. Fostering the best results on the first exam is a win/win strategy paradigm for you and your students.

SUGGESTED READINGS

Angelo, T,. and K. P. Cross. (1993). *Classsroom Assessment Techniques: A Handbook for College Teachers*, 2nd ed. San Francisco: Jossey-Bass.

Bloom. B. S., ed. (1956). *Taxonomy of Learning Objectives: Cognitive Domain*. New York: David McKay.

Cranton, P. (1989). *Planning Instruction for Adult Learners*. Toronto, Canada: Wall and Emerson.

Hativa, N. (2000). *Teaching for Effective Learning in Higher Education*. Dordrecht, Netherlands: Kluwer Academic Press.

Macmillan, J. (1997). *Classroom Assessment: Principles and Practice for Effective Instruction*. Boston: Allyn & Bacon.

Popham, W. J. (1999). *Classroom Assessment: What Teachers Need to Know*, 2nd ed. Boston: Allyn & Bacon.

APPENDIX 10.1

Analyzing Selected Response Exam Items

Directions: For each of the following potential exam questions, explain why it would be inappropriate for inclusion on an exam. (Discuss items 7 through 16—the Matching section—as a whole.)

True/False

____ 1. The climate of Georgia is *humid* and *subtropical*.

____ 2. The "father of American education," John Dewey taught for many years at the University of Minnesota.

____ 3. The two elements that make up CO_2 are carbon and oxygen.

____ 4. Washington, D.C. has always been the capital of the United States.

____ 5. When he gave his *"Ich bin ein Berliner"* speech, John F. Kennedy was not in Germany for the first time.

____ 6. The U.S. Supreme Court hears only cases whose decisions have been appealed from lower courts.

Matching

____ 7. Dwight D. Eisenhower
____ 8. Joseph McCarthy
____ 9. Harry S. Truman
____ 10. Sandra Day O'Connor
____ 11. J. Edgar Hoover
____ 12. Franklin Delano Roosevelt
____ 13. Admiral Hyman Rickover
____ 14. Madeline Murray O'Hare
____ 15. Robert Dole
____ 16. Medgar Evers

a. A state senator
b. Wrote books used in American schools
c. President of Columbia University
d. World War II hero
e. Critic of prayer in school
f. Civil rights activist
g. Critic of progressive education
h. Authorized use of atomic bomb
i. A zealot anti-Communist
j. President of the United States during World War II

Completion

17. Winston Churchill was _____.
18. During World War II, George C. Patton, the _____, was the first militarist to use _____ during wartime.
19. During World War II, Iosif Dzhugashvili led _____.

Multiple Choice

20. Which of the following is not true of an effective course syllabus?
    a. It serves as a contract between the instructor and the student.
    b. It includes a "tentative schedule" that the instructor should expect to change.
    c. It provides answers to most questions students are likely to have about the class.
    d. It is especially clear on the issues of grading and attendance.
    e. None of the above.

21. During the first class meeting,
    a. distribute your syllabus, but don't review it until the second meeting.
    b. the classroom and your handouts should create a positive visual impression.
    c. wait ten minutes before starting to allow latecomers to arrive.
    d. take about fifteen minutes to review your professional and personal background.
    e. be sure to tell the students if the class was assigned to you on short notice.

22. Which of the following is the most important reason to conduct an icebreaker?
    a. To break down barriers between students who are likely to be reserved.
    b. To give students a chance to have fun as a balance against "heavy stuff."
    c. To provide students a chance to satisfy their need to fit into a new group.
    d. To foster a positive learning atmosphere.
    e. To encourage students to begin relationships that might launch study groups.

23. Which of the following is true of "learning domains"?
    a. The *psychomotor* domain refers to the thought processes.
    b. The *effective* domain refers to attitudes and appreciation of artistic work.
    c. The *cognitive* domain refers to physical skills and dexterity.
    d. All of the above are true.
    e. None of the above are true.

24. Which of the following provides the correct sequence of Bloom's taxonomy?
    a. application, analysis, knowledge, comprehension, evaluation, synthesis
    b. knowledge, comprehension, analysis, application, synthesis, evaluation
    c. analysis, knowledge, comprehension, application, evaluation, synthesis
    d. knowledge, comprehension, application, analysis, synthesis, evaluation
    e. comprehension, knowledge, analysis, application, evaluation, synthesis

25. When a college or university professor is urged by instructional leaders to employ cooperative learning practices within his or her classroom:
    a. Students work in small groups to process information or solve problems.
    b. Groups work best when members are alike in age, gender, and ethnicity.

c. Students should work with the same group of students throughout the term.

d. Groups should include no more than five students so that everyone can contribute.

e. Both *a* and *d* are correct

Essay

26. How will reading this book help you be a better facilitator of learning?
27. What did Jesus mean when he said, "Blessed are the meek, for they will inherit the earth"?

Key:

1. Which Georgia—the state in the United States or the former Soviet republic that is now an independent nation? Reword to: "Using the Koppen classification system, most of the southern U.S. state of Georgia has a humid, subtropical climate." Or, include a section heading or similar element that indicates the geographic range of the question.

2. Two thoughts are included, one arguably true, the other false. Reword to: "The renowned American educator John Dewey taught over thirty years at the University of Minnesota." (The answer would be false; Dewey taught at the University of Chicago.)

3. The stem contains a clanger—CO_2. It would be difficult to make this a valid true/false question; a completion or multiple-choice item would work better.

4. The words *always* or *never* should not be used in a true/false question, because doing so makes the answer disproportionately false. Reword to: "Washington, D.C., has been the capital of the United States since the country's founding." (The answer would be false; Philadelphia and New York City were each once the capital.)

5. The word *not* should be underlined or italicized. We would ask, however, what knowledge the question is designed to elicit. Do you want students to recall that JFK had visited Germany as a journalist just prior to World War II? Or that he did in fact make the speech mentioned? Or that the speech was made in Germany?

6. As it reads, the question is *nearly always* true. However, the seldom-used *writ of certiorari* empowers the Supreme Court to recall cases for review whose decisions have not been appealed. This item should be reworded so that it does not appear to be a trick question—for example: "The vast majority of cases heard by the U.S. Supreme Court are ones that have been appealed from lower courts." (True.)

The matching exercise illustrates an array of problems. First, the names should be positioned in the right-hand column and alphabetized for easy identification. Several extra, yet logical, choices should be added to the mix so that students who make one inaccurate match will not be locked into making a second mistake. The phrases used to describe the activities of the individuals listed are not of equal quality, in that some refer to major activities and others refer to trivia. For example, Dwight D. Eisenhower is far better known for his military accomplishments and his role as president of the United States than for his presidency of Columbia University. Likewise, J. Edgar Hoover's role as director of the FBI is much more significant than his authoring a social studies textbook used in American schools. There is also a problem in that several descriptors fit several names. There are four persons on the list who were U.S. senators, two presidents who served during World War II, several World War II heroes, and at least three persons who could be described as staunch anti-Communists. Clearly, there are questionable matches on the list. (As given, the "correct" answers would be 7c, 8i, 9h, 10a, 11b, 12j, 13g, 14e, 15d, 16f.)

17. Insufficient detail is provided in the stem for students to determine what is requested about Winston Churchill. While Churchill was prime minister of Britain from 1940 to 1945 and again from 1950 to 1955, he was also a well-known author, a leader against Germany during the Battle of Britain, and a British statesman. Any of these answers could be considered correct or incorrect, depending upon the professor's whim.

18. In this question, any of several descriptors could be used in the first blank— general, commander, leader of the Third Army, leader of the African Campaign. The use of the article *the* before the blank would indicate that the answer should be a phrase, but only one blank is given, which suggests that the answer should be a single word. The second blank is very ambiguous. The desired word is *tanks*, but any of a large number of words would seem to make sense.

19. This question is focusing on relatively trivial information. Unless students knew that Iosif Dzhugashvili is the transliterated name of the person we know as Joseph Stalin, they would have no clue as to what to provide in the blank. Furthermore, the question is structured for many different responses. The teacher may have been looking specifically for "the Soviet Union," "the USSR," or "Russia," but without more context, students could put any number of answers.

20. While *b* is the "correct" answer, students must employ some convoluted logic to arrive at that choice. Especially troublesome is the relationship between the stem's use of the word *not*, and choice *e*, "None of the above." The stem of the question should be rephrased to read "All of the following are true of an effective course syllabus, except:" and by making choice *e* a true statement.

21. The stem lacks a phrase that would focus the respondent's search for a correct answer. A better stem would be: "During the first class meeting, an effective instructor should:" In addition, the correct answer to the ineffectively

written stem is *b*. Notice that it is the only option that begins with a word other than a verb, providing the respondent with a "clanging" clue to the correct answer.

22. The correct answer to this question is a matter of opinion—different people could see different reasons as the "most important." Any of the answers could conceivably be correct.

23. The definitions of choices *a* and *c* are reversed, and thus both are incorrect. Choice *b* looks correct on the surface, but the word *effective* should actually be *affective*, making the "correct" answer *e*. This item would be interpreted as mean-spirited by anyone answering it. "All of the above" and "None of the above" are clearly space takers.

24. Did you look back in the book to find the correct answer? Whether this question is effective depends largely on the level at which the course is delivered and perhaps the textbook from which it is taken. If it is an introductory course, choice *b* is probably too similar to the correct answer *d*. If the question is for an advanced course in educational psychology, the question is probably okay, although one could make the case that an essay item would work better than a multiple-choice item for such a key concept.

25. The stem has too much unnecessary detail. Reword stem to: "Which of the following is correct about the effective use of cooperative learning?"

26. This question needs boundaries so that respondents can tailor their response appropriately. Reword to: "Identify and explain three reasons why higher education is shifting from teaching-centered to learning-centered instruction," or "Compare and contrast five student-driven learning methods."

27. Theologians have written volumes on this question. The stem needs boundaries so that respondents can give focused responses.

APPENDIX 10.2

Essay Question Exercise

Directions for students: Score the two responses to the question below, using the criteria provided.

Question: Explain what you learned about yourself from completing the Decision Style Inventory. Address your typical problem orientation, information orientation, management style, and organizational preference. Also tell how your weaknesses are likely to appear to others.

Scoring Criteria:		A	B
Opening: provide context and overview	2 points	__	__
Body: provide sufficient, correct detail	5 points	__	__
Conclusion: make application to your management career	3 points	__	__
Total possible	10 points	__	__

Response A

The Decision Style Inventory was very useful. It identified me as having a "behavioral" style. I like people and make decisions that tend to make others happy. I support people, because they need that in order to stay motivated and continue to learn. I prefer to work in companies that demonstrate the same concern for others that I have. As I start my management career, I will become the kind of manager that others will always want to follow.

Response B

The Decision Style Inventory is a tool to help us better understand how we typically go about making decisions, how our decisions are likely to be perceived by others, and the types of organizations in which we are most likely to be successful. Completing the inventory identified my dominant decision-making style as "behavioral."

I tend to make decisions that stress the human aspects. I gather information by having empathy toward others and by listening and reading others' body language effectively, and I tend to see things in right-or-wrong terms. My management style is supportive, encourages team building, and avoids conflicts. I prefer to work in environments that are well designed to support members of the team, like having open-door policies. Some people are likely to see me as overly sensitive and unable to make hard decisions, such as disciplining wrongdoers.

While being a behavioral decision maker can be very effective at times, I will also need to demonstrate an understanding of the financial and technical aspects of getting the job done. It seems few top managers have my style and may well regard me as a pushover unless I can develop these other skills.

11 Alternative Methods of Assessing Student Learning

FOCUS QUESTIONS

- Why should you invest the extra effort required of authentic assessment?
- What kinds of learning lend themselves to being assessed in alternative formats?
- What are the advantages of portfolio assessment?

Assessment should promote learning, not simply measure it.
—Grant Wiggins

You probably remember at least one time when you came out of an exam thinking some of the following: "I knew so much more than what this test is going to show!" "Why didn't the professor ask me about _____ in depth, instead of asking for so much trivial information?" "This test only covers about 10 percent of what we've done but it's going to count for 50 percent of my grade! That's crazy!" "This exam wasn't fair! I know a lot but I couldn't show it because of the way the test was set up." "The professor keeps talking about critical thinking skills, but then tests us with true/false and multiple-choice questions. That makes a lot of sense. Not!" These sentiments are still being expressed on campuses across the country, but there is a growing perspective that addresses many of these concerns: the alternative assessment movement. This movement is not limited to higher education by any means; many K–12 educators are exploring alternative ways to determine what students have learned. At every level, though, the idea is to seek ways of assessing students that, in the words of Grant Wiggins (1993), promote learning rather than just measuring it.

In Chapter 10, we focused on helping you understand and develop the standard forms of assessing student learning—written examinations. Although both selected response and essay tests are valuable tools for any professor, the reality is that much of what we should do in our courses is not an effective match to these forms of assessment. This is especially true in advanced courses within our curricula, designed to address the higher levels of Bloom's taxonomy. Since the quality movement began to affect the business community significantly in the late 1980s, an increasing number of leaders in higher education have come to view traditional testing as disconnected from the ultimate goal of education, that is, to prepare students for real life (Huba and Freed, 2000). In real life, they say, graduates are seldom expected to take paper-and-pencil tests and are instead expected to identify real problems and orchestrate multidimensional projects designed to solve those problems nearly every day of their lives.

Higher education, consequently, has experienced a mushrooming interest in developing more genuine and effective ways of assessing student learning. Advocates of alternative assessment, sometimes called "authentic" or "genuine" assessment, believe that we should focus on student learning rather than on teaching. Recall from Chapter 8 the paradigm of constructivist learning: rather than passively receiving knowledge from their professors, students make sense of new material by linking it with knowledge they already possess. Said another way, students "construct" new knowledge on their existing foundations. Advocates of alternative assessment speak of introductory courses developing a "scaffold" upon which more advanced learning is built; they also speak of the need to link courses so that students avoid both gaps and excessive overlaps in their knowledge structure. All students, they say, should be encouraged to demonstrate their learning frequently, through a variety of authentic means in either real or realistic (simulated) settings. Alternative assessment attempts to place learning within a systems context, in which courses in a curriculum dovetail smoothly with each other—as perspective students often see (and appreciate) more readily than do professors invested in developing and refining a single course or two.

To demonstrate the importance of the concepts presented in this chapter, we present you the following exercise, in which we ask you to actively take part rather than just reading the words.

1. Think about there being two kinds of knowledge, "declarative" and "procedural." Declarative knowledge can be thought of as information and usually involves component parts, that is, facts, concepts, ideas, and principles that we want students to know. It is the kind of knowledge that students can declare (hence the word *declarative*). A student might be able to declare names and dates pertinent to a period of time being studied in history, or be able to declare definitions of words related to a course of study in biology, or in an economics course be able to declare five reasons why the gross national product (GNP) has declined.

Thinking of the discipline you teach, write, in the box below, some examples of declarative knowledge that you want your students to know.

2. The second type of knowledge (for our purposes) is procedural knowledge, which can be defined as skills, strategies, and processes that students need to know *how to do*. Generally, procedural knowledge involves procedures that students must perform or execute (hence the term *procedural*). Examples of procedural knowledge would include being able to write a persuasive paragraph, solve for x, use HTML to code a Web site, and so forth. Again, thinking of your discipline, use the following box to identify some examples of procedural knowledge that you want your students to possess.

3. In the first column of the table below, list three or four of the classes you teach. Fill in the percentage of declarative knowledge you want your students to learn in column 2, and then write the percentage of procedural knowledge you want your students to learn in column 3. The two percentages should add up to 100 percent. Just ballpark it—this is not a scientific determination; it is for illustrative purposes only.

Course Number/ Name	% Declarative Knowledge	% Procedural Knowledge	Assessment Ratio (Declarative:Procedural)

Now look at the last column in the chart. Think about the assessment you do in each class. What is the percentage of declarative knowledge assessed versus the percentage of procedural knowledge assessed? Write this is as a ratio.

4. Obviously, we do not know what you found, but we will tell you what professors in our workshops have found—a major mismatch. For example, it is not uncommon for a professor in a lower-division undergraduate course to state that his declarative percentage is 70 percent and his procedural percentage is 30 percent, but that his assessment ratio is 100:0. An upper-division professor might list her intended declarative knowledge as 40 percent and procedural knowledge as 60 percent—and then find that her assessment ratio is 90:10.

Traditional paper-and-pencil objective tests are often quite appropriate for measuring students' learning of declarative knowledge—and should be used for that purpose. However, if you, like most professors, are teaching to help students learn procedural knowledge as well as declarative, then you know the frustration of trying to measure this on a selected response test. It is extremely difficult to accomplish.

Incorporating alternative assessment into your courses achieves the following objectives:

- Allows you to measure the student learning relative to some of your objectives, particularly procedural ones, that are not measurable through traditional paper-and-pencil examinations.

- Provides students alternative—often better—means to examine their own learning.
- Helps students see connections between what they are learning and real-world applications.
- Fosters creative thinking and collaborative learning.
- Increases the likelihood that the learning will be retained longer because the performance was done in context.
- Encourages self-reflection and self-evaluation.

So, what alternatives do you have? There are many, but the ones we feature in this chapter are performance assessment, oral presentations, writing assignments, portfolio assessment, and individual learning agreements.

Performance Assessment

In an age of accountability, across all disciplines and fields, being able to "perform" is a major predictor of success. Professors working to prepare students for the knowledge age would do well to measure—and, most important, provide genuine, specific, and timely feedback on—their performances. Performance assessment can be generally defined as "an activity in which students construct responses, create products, or perform demonstrations to provide evidence of their knowledge and skills" (Hibbard et al., 1996, p. 277). Be aware, however, that constructing responses, creating products, or making demonstrations alone does not constitute performance assessment. Only when you build in an assessment tool and a feedback process do you have an alternative form of assessment.

There is no limit to what you might use as a focus for performance assessment—you are limited only by your discipline and your imagination. Students can write, draw, act, create, interview, dance, propose, prepare, build, evaluate, exhibit, and so on. Performance may also include providing assistance to a person or group in the community (i.e., service learning, which we discussed in Chapter 8). Projects we have seen include a videotaped orientation program for new employees in a human resource management course, a mock education summit with presentations by various stakeholders in a curriculum development course, and a costumed, choreographed skit in a leadership course. In each case, the students attained high level of content mastery because of their voluntary investment of creative energies in a synergized effort with others.

When designing a performance assessment, you should ask yourself the following questions:

- What do I want students to know and be able to do? (Look at your objectives and choose the ones you cannot measure using a traditional examination.)
- How will I know if they know and can do these things? (List the behaviors, the indicators, and/or the skills that you want to be able to see in their performances.

- Can I design an assessment for a real-world situation, or will I need to set up a mock situation? (Can advertising students design an ad campaign for a nonprofit organization, or do you need to set up a fake company? Can engineering students build and patent an invention, or do you need to have them build a model of an existing invention?)
- What are the standards by which I will judge the students' performance? (List the various levels and criteria by which you will evaluate the students' work. What will be considered superior performance? Satisfactory performance? Unsatisfactory performance? The more specific you can make this, the better the work you will receive from students and the easier it will be for you to grade.)
- What weight will I give each of the criteria? (Will the *content* of a writing assignment be worth more than the *conventions?* The design specs worth more than the actual object? The number of people interviewed worth more than the depth of the interviews?)

Once you have thought through these questions, you can design the assessment instrument. Most important is to create a meaningful context for the assessment task—one that is based on the real experiences, issues, concerns, or problems that students face now or will face in the future. Walvoord and Anderson (1998) recommend the use of the acronym AMPS when writing your assessment:

- A = Audience. (Who are the students to keep in mind as they do the work? Children? Corporate executives? Out-of-work single parents?)
- M = Main point and purpose. (What is the reason for having students do this particular assessment task? Your main point may be defined in one sentence or a whole paragraph.)
- P = Pattern and procedures. (What processes, steps, or parts do students need to include as they work through the assessment task? You want to be quite explicit on this portion. Do not assume that students know what you want. Tell them what you want and you are much more likely to get it.)
- S = Standards and criteria. (Write a description of the ultimate product. Let students know how you are going to evaluate their work and at what level.)

James Popham (1999) identifies several factors to consider when determining which tasks you intend to use as performance assessment tasks:

- *Generalizability*. Will the performance on this task be applicable to other tasks?
- *Authenticity*. Is the task similar to what students might encounter in the real world, rather than just a "classroom" task?
- *Multiple foci*. Does the task measure more than one instructional objective?
- *Teachability*. Will the students increase their proficiency in completing the task as a result of the teacher's instruction?

- *Fairness.* Does the task avoid bias based on student characteristics such as race, gender, socioeconomic level, or age?
- *Feasibility.* Can the task be reasonably accomplished with respect to time, cost, space, and/or equipment?
- *Scorability.* Will the task elicit student responses that are measurable?
- *Significance of the skill to be assessed.* Is the skill worth spending the time required for adequate performance assessment? (pp. 165–166)

An alternative form of assessment requires alternative modes of evaluation. Chapter 8 introduced the concept of rubrics as evaluative tools for student presentations. A rubric, you will recall, is a scoring device that lists the criteria on which an activity will be evaluated. An effective rubric distinguishes between unsatisfactory, satisfactory, and excellent quality. The criteria on the rubric should address both content and presentation skills. Recall also that you must *share* your rubric with your students before they engage in their projects. Many professors find that it is valuable to have the students grade themselves using the rubric prior to turning in their work. Mature students' self-assessment is often quite close to the professor's assessment; less mature students are not as clear on how they are performing relative to a standard.

Rubrics work best when they are appropriate for the task, easy to understand, and focused on the most important aspects of the project. When students understand your expectations, they can strive for quality rather than spending time second-guessing what you want. With a rubric they can constantly evaluate their progress toward the known goal as they prepare their work.

From a more practical viewpoint, having your criteria clearly delineated in a rubric will usually prevent students from questioning their grades. Also, the rubric will help you focus your energy during scoring, fostering greater consistency of grading across projects and reducing total scoring time. While developing an effective rubric requires an initial investment of time, you can leverage that investment by creating a template upon which subsequent rubrics can be built. The consistency you gain, the time you save, and the trust you build with your students all will make you more than glad you made the effort to design the rubric.

Oral Presentations

Perhaps one of the most wasted opportunities in higher education is the area of student oral presentations. Living it every day, we understand the inherent benefits of preparing a convincing argument, presenting it to others, and responding to their questions and signals. As a means of alternative assessment, oral presentations allow students to master an array of other life skills that seemingly can be mastered through no other vehicle. Many professors do require students to make presentations, but, unfortunately, they provide such muddled expectations of student performance that they set their students up for failure. Some students will thrive in spite of their professors' poor handling of the process; many others, however, will become so unnerved that they will literally become sick. How can you make sure that you do not waste the opportunity to help students be successful?

First, explain to students that they already do oral presentations every single day of their lives—presentations that are called by such innocuous names as conversations, discussions, and interviews. Second, to help students deliver a solo performance in front of the entire class, you can stair-step them to that point rather than tripping and shoving them into what they often perceive as a lake filled with alligators. For the first step, start small, by having students interview a single other student and then report the results, while seated, to the rest of the class. Move up to panel discussions, in which each student is expected to present a specifically selected portion of a broader topic. Continue upward by having students deliver an extemporaneous thirty-second response to a course topic drawn from a hat or shoebox. Finally, if you have provided ample verbal feedback (not just numerical scores) throughout the preliminary activities and have given students a clear rubric well in advance, they can reach the high point of giving a short presentation in front of the class. Even those few experienced high school debate team members you may have who are capable of delivering a moving presentation on the first day of class will benefit from the preliminary activities.

Many students may think that oral presentations should be limited to speech classes, but the reality is that being well prepared to make presentations to other individuals is a necessity in today's society. This applies to health care professionals, salespeople, administrators, training officers, managers, and on and on. To leave your students unprepared would be to shirk your responsibility as an educator. With the development of students' speaking skills, as you well know, come their growth in self-esteem, poise, and leadership. Appendix 11.1 provides a very basic rubric for guiding the planning of a presentation, delivering an effective presentation, and providing useful feedback. Think about using it to guide your development of a rubric that is a tighter fit with your students' learning objectives.

Writing Assignments

One group of stakeholders increasingly significant in higher education is the employers of students, both before and after their graduation. Employers who reimburse students for their educational expenses and/or invest large amount to recruit the most capable graduates expect their employees to be able to write position papers, reports, e-mail messages, and an array of other documents that communicate complex situations succinctly and accurately. One of employers' greatest criticisms of recent years has been that student writing skills have declined. Professors in fields other than the humanities often say, "Teaching students to write is the job of the composition instructors, not ours." The composition instructors say, "We do the best we can, but many students come to us with base-level writing skills far below what they need to be." With the challenges that elementary and secondary schools now face, students entering college in the foreseeable future are not likely to exhibit writing skills any better than those of the past decade. It is not possible for composition instructors to turn our students into acceptable writers after just two or three required composition classes.

Over the past few years, a movement called *writing across the curriculum* has sought to take hold in higher education. Research in this area promises to help professors outside English departments attack the problem of poor student writing skills. In short, writing across the curriculum aims to have professors in all fields integrate more writing opportunities into their courses. In Chapter 10, we emphasized the inclusion of essay items on course examinations. This would be a start, but all professors must give additional writing assignments if students are to master the writing skills employers and other stakeholders expect.

As with oral presentations, you can build your students' writing skills step by step. "One-minute papers," in which students respond to one or two questions at the end of a class session, are recommended strongly by Robert Boice (2000) and others. Such brief writing assignments:

- Require students to reflect critically on content to which they have been exposed during the class session, perhaps synthesizing it with another concept.
- Prompt students to pay closer attention and pose more pertinent questions.
- Provide prompt feedback to the professor on the comprehension level of students.

Journaling is another way to engage students in writing/thinking activities. Most teachers who utilize this technique have students keep journals in which they assess what they learned after each class meeting and explain how that learning can be applied to other areas they are studying, or describe any confusion they have about something presented in class. Journaling allows students to examine, reflect on, criticize, identify, and interpret material from lectures, presentations, and readings. In the process, students practice their writing skills in an authentic, nonthreatening way. Journals can be deemed for students' eyes only, or you may wish to occasionally interact with the students' journals, providing feedback, raising questions, commenting on their ideas. If this is your process, you need to be careful not to judge the students' reactions to what they are learning but to understand their feelings and interpretations. Journaling between the student and the professor can be very revealing and meaningful in helping you to understand your students, but we must warn you that this is a very time-consuming activity if done properly and thoughtfully by both the student and the professor.

Journaling is employed by Wilbert McKeachie (2001) and many others to:

- Stimulate students to focus on course content outside the classroom.
- Encourage students to link course content with their interests.
- Address issues as they arise with students.

Another way of helping students to develop their knowledge/process base is to divide major writing assignments into smaller segments. You might ask the student to submit portions of extensive papers to you, then score each segment as a component of the overall grade of the entire assignment. This process enables you to provide feedback to your students in a timely and meaningful manner. Students can then make adjustments to improve the quality of their work. At each juncture, a rubric should be provided in advance to focus student efforts and establish a framework for providing more meaningful feedback that enables students to improve their future efforts. Fostering better student writing grounds critical thinking skills—the mission of all in higher education.

Portfolio Assessment

The use of portfolios in higher education is not a new phenomenon—at least in some fields. Having students create portfolios to present their ideas and accomplishments to prospective clients or employers has been standard practice for art departments, journalism schools, marketing programs, and the like for decades. These portfolios are a means of demonstrating the quality and range of work produced by the student, just as a working artist's or an advertising executive's portfolio showcases the quality and range of work he or she has produced.

In other fields, however, the use of portfolios is much more recent. As educators in academe have realized that the portfolio concept is not just for artistic work, they have come to use various types of portfolios as assessment tools in many areas of the curriculum. Portfolios can provide a professor with a body of student work that shows growth in performance, illustrates a range of quality, or demonstrates achievement of specific skills. Three basic forms of portfolios in use in higher education are working portfolios, showcase portfolios, and assessment portfolios.

Working Portfolios

Working portfolios are designed to be ongoing interchanges between you and your students. Based on specific learning objectives, they serve as "holding tanks" for student work. By frequently examining their working portfolio, you can diagnose students' strengths and weaknesses and provide guidance for the students in how to improve or perfect their work. Working portfolios can also show you what you might need to emphasize in your teaching. Term papers or research projects are ideal candidates for inclusion in a working portfolio.

However, the main audience for the working portfolio is the student. With feedback from you, students can develop their reflective skills and learn to be self-evaluative by working on the projects within the portfolio. The substance of a working portfolio is specific content related to course learning objectives. As students complete their projects, they can move some of the pieces from the working portfolio to a showcase portfolio, discussed below.

Working portfolios allow for iterative processes of instruction. That is, students complete an assignment, get feedback from you, make alterations, and resubmit the assignment for your input. This cycle can be repeated as often as necessary within your given time constraints. Ideally, each cycle increases the students' learning and their perceptions of their learning, both of which are important. Students usually view this iterative process as much more personalized than grades on a test or general statements made during a class about writing skills, grammatical errors, paper organizations, and so on.

As you might imagine, going over working portfolios with students is a time-consuming process, and this must be taken into account prior to implementing this form of alternative assessment. We recommend that you use the working portfolio first with a very small class or with a subset of a class who wants to explore this level of interaction and feedback. As with so many instructional techniques, this one will become easier as you gain experience with it.

Showcase Portfolios

Compiling a showcase portfolio is an especially rewarding experience for students involved in ongoing creative work. Including their best work in a showcase portfolio enables students to define who they are in terms of their culture, learning, experiences, and beliefs. Showcase portfolios can be used in just one class or an entire program. The latter case allows students to have a collection of their best work developed over several months or years. A program showcase portfolio can serve as a culminating activity for the program in lieu of, or in addition to, comprehensive examinations.

The audience for showcase portfolios includes the student, the faculty, and potential employers. The content may include projects created in class as well as projects done outside of the classroom environment, maybe for a part-time job or a volunteer experience. The main advantage of a showcase portfolio is that the students can select their best work from a variety of experiences to demonstrate their skills and learning.

In addition to sharing showcase portfolios with potential employers, you can, with students' permission, display them to potential donors, prospective students and their families, or accrediting agencies. In imagining how to demonstrate what students in a program have learned, contrast the impact of displaying a showcase portfolio to that of displaying student test scores. We know you can see the difference.

Assessment Portfolios

A third type of portfolio is the assessment portfolio. The primary purpose of an assessment portfolio is to document what the student learned during the course. Items in an assessment portfolio must be designed to help the student manifest learning related to specific course objectives defined in the syllabus. Assessment portfolios can be used to demonstrate mastery of both skills and content. The specific audience for the assessment portfolio is the teacher. The items in the portfolio must show that the student has achieved the intended learning outcomes of the class. An assessment portfolio can include lab activities, notes taken in class, artwork, drafts, book reviews, audio/video productions, or whatever else the teacher and student together feel serves to document learning of the course objectives.

The following three steps need to be followed when using assessment portfolios:

1. Identify what forms of procedural knowledge will be assessed through the portfolio process.
2. Design assessment tasks for the identified learning objectives.
3. Identify the criteria for each assessment task.

As with all types of assessment in the strategic classroom, students need to know the target, that is, they need to know what your standards are and how their work will be measured against those standards.

General Suggestions Regarding Portfolios

James Popham (1999) suggests five steps necessary to assure quality portfolio assessment:

1. Recognize that students own their portfolios; that is, the material in the portfolios belongs to the students and is not merely "stuff" to be graded by you.
2. Help students determine what should be included in the various types of portfolios, and clarify which type is being used, why, and how it will be used.
3. Select the criteria by which you and your students will judge the quality of the products within the portfolios.
4. Require students to continually evaluate their own products. One of the values of portfolio assessment is student self-reflection.
5. Schedule portfolio conferences with your students in which you can provide feedback on both the products and the self-assessments by the students.

Through portfolio assessment, students gain a more positive perception of themselves as learners, as individuals, and ultimately as professionals, ready for the world of work. As you examine individual portfolios, you get a more complete picture of your students as persons who are unique and who have lives beyond the classroom.

Another important benefit of portfolio assessment is that, since they are participants in their own assessment, your students *share* in the responsibility for their learning. In this age of accountability, this shared practice is a must. In the long run, as students assume more of the responsibility for their own learning, you will have more time and energy to devote to other aspects of your instruction. Therefore, portfolio assessment can be a win/win situation for both you and your students.

Some of your students will have had experience with developing portfolios, but for others it will be a brand-new experience. They will grow through the discomfort, but too much discomfort is counterproductive. Therefore, provide adequate explanation and support for students as they embark on this contemporary form of assessment.

Portfolio assessment is labor-intensive and time-consuming, so you may want to start on a small scale. Once you become comfortable with the process, you can expand your portfolio activities. It is much better to grow with the process than to start on a large scale, become frustrated, and then vow never to try it again. It is too valuable an assessment tool to avoid.

Portfolios are one of the types of authentic assessment that do not just measure learning but also promote it. This is true for the college classroom, but you are also preparing students for the world they will live in after college. Wright and his colleagues (1999) posit that professors and students are entering the age of "'portfolio careers,'" in which continuing employment depends on the evidence that we provide of our wide range of skills, understanding, and qualities" (p. 89). It behooves us all to prepare our students to live in this age.

Individual Learning Agreements

In Chapters 2 and 3, we addressed learning styles and generational influences that affect the capabilities of students within a given course section. If your ultimate goal is to maximize student learning, you should probably offer structured learning opportunities for doing so within each class you teach. One of the authors of this book has successfully implemented Individual Learning Agreements as an assessment tool that contrasts with the "contract grading" approach that many professors have employed by for years. Contract grading typically focuses on the quantity of work to be performed by students (e.g., reading a certain number of books or journal articles, writing a certain number of reviews) without measuring learning achievement (McKeachie, 2001). In contrast, Individual Learning Agreements provide options for achieving specific course learning objectives consistent with students' unique learning strengths and interests.

An Individual Learning Agreement (a sample of which appears in Appendix 11.2) requires linkage with one or more objectives for the course syllabus, and then places the responsibility for proposing a suitable product on the student. Because students are empowered to use their own creativity, the energy they invest in the project will typically exceed that which they would apply to traditional textbook reading assignments and professor-constructed exams. The Individual Learning Agreement approach emphasizes the "win/win or no deal paradigm" of Stephen Covey (1989). Attuned to this approach, students are encouraged to look for opportunities that not only satisfy a portion of their course grade, but also provide potential benefits for their employer and their own career development, the interests of an organization to which they belong, the status of a relationship within their lives, and/or other such areas of their lives. The "no deal" aspect of the paradigm requires the student and professor to arrive at a final agreement on the project through a set of proposals and counterproposals. While it might seem that this process could become somewhat convoluted, it rarely does. The energy students invest in the proposal process typically pays off in high-quality learning.

While the Individual Learning Agreement is usually designed to assess only a portion of a particular traditional or distance-learning class, it might be expanded to address the full range of learning objectives, through a directed independent study. The instructor should build in multiple opportunities for feedback to the student throughout the independent study, with the number of sessions dependent on the array of objectives and related factors of complexity. Individual Learning Agreements offer a significant opportunity to demonstrate accountability to a wide variety of stakeholders in the success of a particular student.

Summary of Key Points

- Alternative assessment supports and reinforces student-directed learning.
- Alternative assessment is a strong bridge between schooling and real-world application.
- There are three major categories of alternative assessment: performance assessment, portfolio assessment, and Individual Learning Agreements.
- Genuine learning is achieved when students have choices in the development of assignments and the evaluations of those assignments.
- Portfolios can serve three different purposes: working, showcase, and assessment.
- Rubrics are good tools to evaluate alternative assessment strategies.

Through the Professors' Eyes

KIM: In my culture, nearly all classes had only a midterm and a final examination, so I never thought much about using any other way to measure my students' learning. Some of these ideas are very intriguing, and I particularly like the portfolio concept. I could easily incorporate working and display portfolios into my teaching. I think they not only would help my students reflect on their work but also would help me understand my students better. I could see their progression throughout each class and have a final project where they turn in their best work. I like that. I think the portfolios will be very manageable for me, much more than some of the other ideas for genuine assessment about which I have heard. While others might have potential, I am not sure how to incorporate them into my class right now.

PAT: Even before we started discussing what are today called individual learning styles, I was a strong advocate of multiple methods of learning and assessment. I have used group work, projects, and independent study. I've designed effective rubrics for these activities as well, so scoring these nontraditional activities is nothing really new to me. Approaching retirement, I am especially intrigued with the idea of service learning. Its new popularity conjures up memories of the early days of the Peace Corps under President Kennedy and the efforts many of us made in my college days to improve our society. I am going to explore ways to incorporate service learning projects into one of my classes, with an eye toward making it an option in all. I need to figure out how to monitor and evaluate activities so that they have integrity and achieve genuine learning objectives. Maybe I'll ask my students to help me design monitoring and assessment procedures. This could be fun!

DALE: Up to now, I've been a traditionalist in terms of testing, but I'm beginning to see some potential for using some of this alternative assessment stuff. I have a few students I've been working with on a special project, and they provide high-quality help with my research. Reflecting back on that phone call from Orwin Luke, I still remember his saying, "Dale, it's about their learning, not your teaching." Many of these students demonstrate learning at a much higher level on Bloom's taxonomy through the research and the oral quizzing I give them than they do by performing at a 95 percent level on some multiple-choice/short-answer exam. The Covey workshop at the beginning of the term used the phrase "win/win or no deal"—a great paradigm to bring to this issue. Come to think of it, one of the sessions I accidentally attended last year at our national conference was about the benefits of undergraduate research experiences. The presenter said there is even some NSF funding earmarked for this kind of project. I need to track down that paper, look at the NSF Web site, and really formulate some specific strategies for getting even more valuable help, while giving my students learning opportunities through my research. I know this won't work for all the students, but there are a few in every class I teach who could really benefit from this kind of opportunity. Orwin Luke would suggest I look especially closely at the potential for some minority students to participate—and he's right that this could be especially rewarding and good exposure for them.

Tips for Thriving

In *Millennials Rising: The Next Great Generation* (2000), Neil Howe and William Strauss express great optimism about the most recent generation of students to enter college. Members of this generation, they say, will embrace strong values and thrive on giving back to their communities. Concurrently, the United States has failed to solve many of its problems to the satisfaction of those who remain marginalized by poverty, racism, homophobia, and the like. Professors in nearly any college course have a great opportunity to embrace service learning in a successful way. John Dewey (1916) viewed education as the most critical vehicle for the advancement of empowered citizens within democratic society. Why not research the needs in your area, connect with a community service organization that is doing really good work, and develop some opportunities for synergism that make a difference?

SUGGESTED READINGS

Angelo, T. A., and K. P. Cross. (1993). *Classroom Assessment Techniques: A Handbook for College Teachers, 2nd ed.* San Francisco: Jossey-Bass.

Brookhart, S. M. (1999). *The Art and Science of Classroom Assessment: The Missing Part of the Pedagogy.* ASHE-ERIC Higher Education Report 27, no. 1. Washington, DC: The George Washington University, Graduate School of Education and Human Development.

Carnegie, D. (1962). *The Quick and Easy Way to Effective Speaking.* New York: Pocket Books.

Huba, M. E., and J. E. Freed. (2000). *Learner-Centered Assessment on College Campuses: Shifting the Focus from Teaching to Learning.* Boston: Allyn & Bacon.

Walvoord, B. E., and V. J. Anderson. (1998). *Effective Grading: A Tool for Learning and Assessment.* San Francisco: Jossey-Bass.

APPENDIX 11.1

Oral Presentation Rubric Model

Student _____

Key dimensions of audience:
Goal of the presentation:

Opening   *(__ points possible)*   ***Earned:***
Effectively gain audience attention? How?
Establish common ground with audience? How?
Topic framed effectively? How?

Body of presentation   *(__ points possible)*   ***Earned:***
Logical points developed to support goal of presentation?
Presentation remain focused on goal?
Presentation follow a logical sequence?
Sufficient evidence provided to support goal?

Closing   *(__ points possible)*   ***Earned:***
Essential points summarized?
Audience asked to take a specific action?

Vocal qualities   *(__ points possible)*   ***Earned:***
Volume?   Rate?
Tone?   Vocal variety?
Articulation?   Energy?

Nonverbal qualities   *(__ points possible)*   ***Earned:***
Facial expression?   Eye contact?
Posture?   Gestures?
Use of notes?   Appropriate props, visual aids?

Additional comments:

APPENDIX 11.2

Learning Agreement Proposal

Student _____

In satisfaction of the required project weighted at 20 percent of the final course grade in MAN 2021, during the Fall 20— term, I propose the following project that satisfies learning objectives(s), of the course syllabus:

Product to be delivered (e.g., videotape, written plan):

Approximate length:

Resources upon which the development of this project will rely:

Detailed outline of project:

Due date of final project:

_____   _____
Student   Date submitted

_____   I have reviewed and approve the project with conditions noted above, with the understanding that the student will schedule a progress meeting for the week(s) of _____, by returning a photocopy of this proposal.

_____   I will accept the following counterproposal:

_____   _____
Merriam B. McAllister, Ph.D.   Date approved

12 Bringing Your Course to an Effective Conclusion

FOCUS QUESTIONS

- How do you maintain enthusiasm as the term draws to a close?
- How do you energize a class that seems to be losing its momentum?
- How do you manage the critical questions related to final student grades?
- What end-of-term procedures can you improve?

People usually fail when they are on the brink of success. So give them as much care to the end as to the beginning; then there will be no failure.

—Lao Tzu

As discussed at the outset of the book, a growing number of stakeholders in higher education are emphasizing the need for colleges and universities to retain students throughout each course and on through completion of their degrees to employment and/or acceptance into higher levels of education. College graduates tend to lead far more productive lives than those who fall by the wayside. In the process, graduates contribute more significantly than noncompleters to the prestige of their institutions and to the leadership and economic well-being of their communities. Education's stakeholders are coming to recognize that the success of individual students can be traced to individual classrooms, led by individual professors (Moxley, Nojor-Durack, and Dumbrigue, 2001).

Even if you have been careful to manage effectively the key mileposts within your class—the first meeting, the first examination, and the midterm meeting—toward the end you will most likely experience some loss of momentum. Given your and your students' multiple responsibilities outside the classroom, along with all the tasks, assessments, and projects related to the course, it is no wonder that mental fatigue starts to creep in. Your students need extra attention and support to ensure powerful sessions near the end of the semester. Blaming students for slacking off only tends to alienate them. Instead, work to remain on common ground with students, bring them in as problem solvers, and offer regular encouragement. This chapter will help you deal with issues that frequently arise as you seek to lead the class to the finish line.

Energizing Your Class as You Approach the End

As you enter the last few weeks of the term, it is common for some students to demonstrate telltale signs of fatigue. These include:

- Expressing frustration over the collective demands of their professors.
- Arriving late to or not showing up at all for class sessions.
- Submitting assignments late and/or below acceptable standards.
- Exhibiting a lack of mental engagement and/or participation in class discussions.
- Demonstrating a decline in spontaneity and sense of humor.

As in personal or work relationships, the key to solving this situation is proactive, positive communication. Assuming you have done most of the things previously recommended in the book, you are reasonably well positioned to achieve success if you will simply make it a point to talk with students.

If the problem is widespread, you might want to talk to the entire class at the beginning of a session. Otherwise, you will probably achieve better results in addressing students individually, before or after class. Be careful to use a constructive approach and a nonjudgmental tone of voice. Negative statements might create a self-fulfilling prophecy.

Straightforwardly share your concerns, identify some of the behaviors you have observed, and then provide students the opportunity to respond. They may tell you how much they enjoy the course and your instruction but then describe the challenges they are experiencing. Demonstrate clearly again that you believe in win/win relationships, and remind them of the goals you and they established as you began the course together. Reinforce their commitment to those goals, and confirm your determination to orchestrate a valuable learning experience for them. At the same time, let them know you are especially energized and will exceed their expectations if they will agree to finish the course strongly. If you are so inclined, share a motivational story, or video clip, relative to the positive rewards that accrued to someone who overcame challenges to see a goal through to its conclusion (Duffy and Jones, 1995).

After the midpoint of the term, it is not uncommon for one or more students to stop coming to class altogether. Initially, you may want to just write these students off as having lost their commitment, but try to remember that they probably became overwhelmed by the multiple demands on their time. We suggest you telephone such students at home to encourage them to return and finish the course. Be prepared to hear a wide variety of excuses and comments, from the trivial to the serious. Listen genuinely and try to understand the students' perspectives. Quitting may be a model or pattern in their lives. Be willing to offer some specific type of relief, such as an extra tutoring session or an extension on an assignment, as well as some level of extra performance you would expect in return. Follow up with an e-mail message to reassure the student of the sincerity of your concern. Offering a lifeline to students demonstrates a level of concern, perhaps unexpected, to which many will respond in a very positive way.

In your closing class sessions, use responsive teaching techniques to energize the course:

- Adapt the learning environment by taking the class to a new meeting environment—outside under a tree, to the student union, or someplace else that lends itself to rich communications.
- Shorten the length of lecture segments.
- Employ more cooperative learning activities, engaging students in the application of concepts addressed earlier in the course.
- Use appropriate audiovisual materials and action-based activities, which engage the minds of students.
- Schedule an upbeat guest speaker who will tie together several key concepts of the course, emphasizing the analysis, synthesis, and evaluation steps of Bloom's taxonomy.
- Provide positive, timely, and specific feedback to students collectively and individually, as often as possible.

Note: The energy that you invest will counteract any drain you would feel at the end of the course if you do nothing. Doing nothing intensifies the psychological drain on you that could last a long while.

One of the best ways to assess the energy in your classrooms—throughout the semester, but particularly at the key retention mileposts—is to consider the four energy quadrants and their characteristics shown in Figure 12.1.

High positive energy is present when both you and the students are in a state of upbeat, active involvement. Anyone who walks into a classroom that is in the high positive energy quadrant knows it—the overall feeling is "Wow! There is great stuff happening here." Students in this quadrant are intensely involved in a lab exercise, a small-group project, or experiential learning. The instructor strategically plans for this quadrant, although there are those rare serendipitous occasions when high positive energy emerges seemingly on its own.

High Positive	High Negative
• Lots of involvement • Lots of productive interaction • Purposeful movement • Lots of learning	• Sarcasm • Frenetic movement for no reason • Anger and resentment • Little desired learning
Low Positive	Low Negative
• Little movement or active involvement • Pondering and introspection • Focused energy • Learning can occur	• No energy • No movement • No thinking • No learning

FIGURE 12.1   Classroom Energy Quadrants

Low positive energy is present when the students and the instructor are engaged in thinking, working, reflecting, listening, observing, and the like. Observers who come into a classroom that is in the low positive energy quadrant may say, "Hmmmm, these students are 'into' what's happening here. This professor has really drawn them into the learning experience." The strategic professor plans for periods of low positive energy that allow students to reflect on the learning, to listen carefully to a musical piece or a literary selection, to work intently with a partner on finding an answer, and so on. Low positive energy must be managed carefully, as we will discuss.

Low negative energy is likely to show up at midsemester and/or at the end of the semester. It generally appears when students are exhausted from staying up late working on projects, studying for tests, or working at outside jobs that leave them little time for rest. Professors who sense that students are in the low negative energy quadrant must take action, because to leave students in this place ensures that there will be no learning. The strategic professor might elect to have students stand and do quick stretches or even sing and exercise to "Head, Shoulders, Knees, and Toes." Getting students to move and laugh helps bring up the energy level. Knowing that students tend to fall into this quadrant during certain times of the term, the strategic professor will plan for learning experiences that inspire more energy and movement than usual. It is essential to use change-ups, as discussed in Chapter 7, during periods of low negative energy.

The last quadrant, which can appear at any time but which is to be guarded against at all costs, is the high negative energy quadrant. In this quadrant, students are mad, frustrated, and contentious; it is not a pretty sight. This quadrant can rear its ugly head in the following situations: (1) a project or an exam is returned and the overall grades were far lower than students expected; (2) a cohort of students has just received bad news from another class; (3) some type of bad news has just been delivered to a large group of students (e.g., a program has been discontinued, a key class has been eliminated, a new class has been added to the requirements). The best direction for a professor to take when a class is in the high negative energy quadrant is *out*. Get the students out of that quadrant as quickly as possible, because teaching and learning cannot occur here. One technique is to ask students to write a complaint on a piece of paper, crumple it up, and throw it at the professor. The sight of a classful of paper wads being thrown at the professor is enough to make almost everyone laugh—and to break the tension—which is the point. Another strategy is to give students each an envelope, ask them to write their concerns on a piece of paper and seal it inside, and then take up the envelopes telling students you will return them at the end of class. Assure them that their concerns will still be there, but that you need them to focus on what you are trying to teach them at this juncture. If you have established a proactive working relationship with your students, these sorts of techniques will work to refocus them on the task at hand—learning the content of the course.

Although some would read the description of the high positive energy quadrant and think, "That's what I want all the time," it quickly becomes apparent that neither the professor nor the students can maintain high positive energy throughout a whole class period and certainly not throughout an entire term—it would be too exhausting. Therefore, it is best to plan for periods of high positive energy interspersed with periods of low positive energy. Picture in your mind's eye undulating waves of high positive energy, low positive energy, high positive energy, low positive energy and you will get the desired rhythm. Early in the semester, when students' energy is fairly high anyway, it is possible to spend long periods of time in low positive energy. Later in the semester, however, it is best to plan for fairly short periods of low positive energy along with fairly short periods of high positive energy.

If you embrace the concept of energy quadrants and are strategic in your management of these quadrants, you and your students will benefit from productive teaching and learning situations.

Supporting Your Students' Time and Project Management Skills

Having retained your students so far, you should be proactive in fostering their completion of the course. As the term winds down, students are likely to find themselves overloaded with more than they can manage. (Professors do, too, but that is the topic of another book.) Teaching your students basic time and project management skills will serve them not only in your course but also in other courses and throughout their lives. Here is one activity for guiding your students to a productive course conclusion:

1. Ask students to bring their calendars or planners to class one day, along with copies of their various course syllabi. Tell them that you are going to help them be more successful and less stressed as they complete the semester.

2. On that particular day, have each student make a master list of every single project that still needs to be completed before the end of the semester. The list may include daily assignments, tests, lab reports, and papers. Some students may experience minor (or major) panic when they see everything written down, but assure them that the first step to getting the projects completed is to understand them more completely, in context.

3. Next, have them look through the list and determine the order in which the projects are due. They can just put a 1 next to the first one that is due, a 2 next to the second one, and so forth. At this time, there is no need to rewrite the list in order. Suggest, however, that they later redo their list on their own computers so that they can manipulate the projects easily—they can move the first one to the top, deleting it as it is completed, and so on.

4. Once each student has determined the order of the due dates, they need to look at the first project and list all of the tasks that constitute it. For example, if they have a paper due, they should write down the steps of choosing a topic, gathering research materials, and so on. Encourage them to break the project into small, bite-size pieces—the smaller the better, actually.

5. Lastly, have them schedule work on the individual tasks. Tell students that just as they schedule time for appointments (haircuts, visits to the doctor, etc.), they must also schedule time for the tasks they have listed. They should look at their calendar for the following week and make sure that every single "appointment" is scheduled in—classes, work, sleep, group meetings, whatever. Then they need to schedule their project tasks in the hours between the appointments. Tell them to schedule the first task of the first project first, the second task of the first project second, and . . . you get the idea.

There is no magic bullet for time management, but the process outlined above does give students a handle on what might otherwise be overwhelming at the end of a semester. If they can get in the habit of listing all their projects, breaking the projects down into manageable pieces, scheduling the first ones first and the last ones last, and then started to work straight through their list and calendar, they will be amazed by their accomplishments and motivated to continue. One can hope that this motivation then carries them into future terms in which they manage their time well, right from the beginning.

Determining Final Course Grades

One of the thorniest challenges facing contemporary college and university instructors is the awarding of final course grades. On the one hand, most instructors seek to establish and maintain a standard of true excellence for their courses, to motivate students to produce their best work, and to demonstrate traditional values to their colleagues. On the other hand, they know that students feel enormous pressure to get high grades. These pressures may come from family members, employers (many of whom offer tuition reimbursement, but only if above average grades are received), coaches who want students to maintain eligibility, or organizations that grant scholarships. Meanwhile, institutional leaders concerned about maintaining enrollments may, tacitly or explicitly, promote a "recruit, retain, and satisfy" mind-set that puts pressure on some professors to award higher grades.

In recent years, grade inflation has permeated American higher education. External stakeholders perceive that they had to work harder to make a good grade than today's students do. While some college and university administrators have sought to curtail grade inflation, others have turned a blind eye, believing it has at least a short-term positive impact on the retention of students. Many who study the situation agree that grade inflation is most prevalent at highly selective private colleges, although grades at public universities and less-selective institutions have risen also (Gose, 1997). Still, some professors bring to their teaching the grading standards they experienced as students, sometimes decades earlier. Against all of the factors in this contemporary context, it is critical for you to analyze your grading practices and impose a strategy that is in the best interests of students.

At many institutions, professors receive mixed messages about determining final course grades. A college may have a formal, written statement of academic freedom that says a professor is free, within reasonable parameters, to deliver instruction and assign grades according to his or her personal standards. Yet at the same time it, may monitor final course grades. Instructors who assign a disproportionate number of low and/or high grades may be required to fill out a "grade justification" form on which they explain how they arrived at the range of scores within each class section. Instructors new to an institution would do well to investigate, understand, and adhere to the formal grading protocols of their institutions.

In addition, each institution, and often each department within the institution, has an informal grading system based on historical precedent, the philosophy of its leaders, the nature of the student body, and the philosophy of competing institutions to which students might transfer. Expectations of parents and other stakeholder groups can contribute to this system. Whatever the pressures they feel from this system, professors must take the high road to maintain long-term integrity. The new professor might consider soliciting input on grading from a variety of sources. Ethical dilemmas might require significant dialogue and personal reflection.

After developing a full understanding of your institution's formal and informal practices, you must deal with the dynamics of your students in each particular class section. Many younger students were conditioned in high school to expect ample opportunities for extra credit, curving of grades, and in general receiving higher grades then they might deserve. They may object to receiving low grades yet may not invest the energy required to attain higher ones. It is your legitimate role to consistently explain your performance standards. Older students may take more responsibility for their grades and will often exert a great deal of effort to achieve one more point on a test or project.

In summary, your personal discretion has been historically recognized and you are ultimately the standard setter for each course you teach. The key to managing final course grades lies in being consistent in your practices while remaining focused on the best long-term interests of your students and the communities to which they will advance.

Conducting Effective Closing Class Meetings

Nearly as much as the first class meeting, the final session or two can determine the success of your course. The final exam and the course evaluations will reinforce each student's sense of personal achievement, attitude toward you, and valuation of the total learning experience. If you started your class with a bang, you do not want to end it with a fizzle.

With so much riding on the outcome, it is critical to effectively manage each aspect of the closing class meetings. Be sure to:

- Prepare in advance an agenda of items you should address prior to the final examination and course evaluation.
- Create a professional image within the classroom—students should see clean chalkboards, appropriately arranged desks, and orderly materials.
- Reduce the predictable tension of exam-taking by greeting students by name as they enter the classroom; be relaxed, but also be careful not to discount the importance of the exam.
- Thank students for their effort and reassure them that the energy they invested in the course will pay off—be as specific as possible about the likely payoffs.
- Review key items from your agenda, such as the status of projects and papers students may have submitted and when/how examination scores will be available.
- Encourage students' progress toward their educational goals by identifying the next logical course they should take within the curriculum. Be specific about course numbers, dates, times, and instructors.

- Identify the next course you expect to be teaching for the institution and encourage students to enroll.
- Outline the procedures for the course evaluation (your institution may require you to leave the room as students complete these—be sure to follow the set policy).
- Ask for last-minute questions prior to distributing the final exam.
- Specify the procedures for submitting the exam, along with directions for picking up graded assignments.
- Avoid saying much more—students are usually anxious about the final exam and want to get on with it.
- Say a warm good-bye to each student as he or she leaves. If you can do so without disturbing any remaining test-takers, share some bit of personalized, positive feedback about a well-done project or contribution to the class, and wish the student well in future courses and beyond (Lyons, Kysilka, and Pawlas, et al. 1999).

Students vividly remember teachers who go the extra mile to ensure they learned not only the subject matter but also the context into which that subject matter fits. By managing the last moments of the course effectively, you increase the likelihood that your students will be encouraged to pursue their educational goals even more passionately than before they enrolled in your course.

Once you have graded all assignments and final examinations, consider sending an e-mail to all students in each course section. Your message might:

- Summarize the major accomplishments of the class in its entirety.
- Remind students of the logical courses for them to take next, as well as those that you will be teaching the following term.
- Invite them to continue to regard you as a mentor and to tell you, in person or through e-mail, about their challenges and progress.
- Wish them well in their future endeavors.

In the days following the conclusion of the course, do not be surprised if your more engaged students seek you out—via telephone or e-mail or in person, to bring to closure their feelings about their experience with your course. Maintain a professional stance, but be assured that most efforts of students are genuine. Such encounters are among the most gratifying within the overall teaching experience, and they go a long way to helping you build a following that helps you achieve improved enrollments in future course sections.

Submitting End-of-Term Reports

By the end of the term, your institution or department will have given a final grade roll and most likely some standard report forms. Plan accordingly to submit these materials on time. If any procedures are unclear, consult the faculty hand-book, an office manager or secretary, or your instructional leader well in advance of the deadline.

A word about confidentiality: Professors in the past commonly posted the names and final course grades on their office doors, or some other accessible area. The Federal Educational Rights and Privacy Act (FERPA) sometimes referred to as the Buckley Amendment, requires professors to maintain the privacy of infor-mation related to students, including grades (http://www.cpsr.org/cpsr/privacy/ssn/ferpa.buckley.html). Grades and other such information should be shared only with the student and with those at your institution with a *legitimate* need to know. Parents, employers, and fellow faculty members probably do not have such a legitimate need—make sure you know both your institution's poli-cies and the law. Be understanding, but be firm and professional in dealing with requests for confidential information about individual students.

Summary of Key Points

- Look for telltale signs of the loss of student momentum.
- Expect to invest class time into energizing students' progress toward the conclusion of your course.
- Remind students of the learning objectives you established together early in the course.
- Telephone or e-mail students who stop coming to class.
- Calculate and monitor students' overall grades throughout the course.
- Become familiar with your department's and your institution's formal and informal policies regarding grade distribution.
- Carefully plan and conduct the closing two meetings of the class.
- Submit end-of-term reports on time.
- Consistently maintain the confidentiality of students' grades and related information.

Through the Professors' Eyes

PAT: One of my new duties for this academic year was serving on the Student Retention Committee. We've met three times so far this term, and it has been interesting! A solid block of traditional (that's a euphemism for *older*) full pro-fessors was very resistant to serving—and displayed their resistance at the first meeting. Our new dean clearly recognized that these folks, in spite of their predictable resistance, were opinion leaders who would need to be won over in order to get a majority of the total faculty on board with the committee mission. Another full professor—interestingly enough from the math depart-ment—and I both saw that this service could make us miserable if we didn't practice sound emotional intelligence. We realized that these folks would be won over only if we could provide some proven, easy-to-use techniques that could improve their retention success. We focused on managing the first exam/major project milepost, which occurred, for most, between the first and second meetings of our committee. Besides the two of us, three of the newer professors had some practical, proven ideas. It worked! The veterans attended the second meeting really energized and much more open to ideas that can improve retention rates without sacrificing quality or integrity. The math prof and I had gotten together prior to yesterday's meeting with a second-year assistant professor from business; the three of us outlined some tips for managing the closing of the term, with an eye toward retaining students in courses that normally have low enrollment. Focused primarily on energizing the class when students are running on empty, the full profs left the meeting talking openly about sharing the strategies with their departmental colleagues. It's been a neat experience!

DALE: I don't know of many professors who really like awarding grades. They are a necessary evil. Students e-mail you now, the day after the final exam, expecting you to relay their grades. I guess it's not so surprising given their addiction to fast food, instant cash at the ATM, and all, so I'm not going to let it irritate me anymore. Once grades are given, students start to complain, though, and that still bugs me. It's as if they couldn't predetermine their grades. My test results pretty much reflect the bell curve, so there shouldn't be many surprises with respect to grades. I do have a dilemma, though. Now that I have committed to inviting some students to work with me on my research, I'm not sure how to adjust the grades to reflect this activity. I am a little embarrassed that I didn't think this through before asking them to help me. The quality of the work is not the same for each participant, but they learn a whole lot more than the rest of the students in class. I'll have to think about this—it could really screw up my bell curve grading.

KIM: I have probably assessed my class too much this term, but I also kept trying to have them stay aware of how much progress they were making. My paradigm of learning requires students to take responsibility for their individual learning, and therefore regular personal assessment of progress is critical. My mentor kept telling me that I have too many graded assignments, but I want to be sure that my grades adequately reflect what my students learn. I do not want my colleagues to say that I am too easy or too hard, or that my students are not learning what they should be learning. I have hundreds of grades and am overwhelmed with trying to make sense of what I have. But I am accountable for my students' learning, and I need to be sure of my evaluations. For next term, I need to give more thought to how and what I assess and do a better job of weighing the importance of the assignments. I want do the right thing. Now if I can just calculate all of these grades!

Tips for Thriving

We are convinced that our former students remember disproportionately the first thing we said to each individually and the closing statement we made as they left our class. Therefore, prior to your final class meeting, jot down one or two positive experiences or thoughts about each student (using your class roll as a guide). As individual students gather their belongings and bring you their final exam, check your notes, approach them, and warmly shake hands. Deliver the essence of your thoughts in a sincere, positive way. Some students may make smart remarks or express disdain, but keep your own comments positive. If possible, walk them to the door and wish them well. Your sense of professionalism will likely make a lasting impression and contribute to your gaining a reputation that any successful professor would prefer to have circulating the campus.

Often those in education, at all levels, celebrate the completion of a term with a social occasion of some sort. You should support such events and attend them, albeit briefly, when appropriate. However, as we noted earlier in this book, be leery about participating in any function whose activities might jeopardize your position (e.g., those at which alcohol is served). Seek to move end-of-course celebrations to places or times that can include everyone—most students will appreciate your integrity.

SUGGESTED READINGS

Duffy, D. K., and J. W. Jones. (1995). *Teaching within the Rhythms of the Semester.* San Francisco: Jossey-Bass.

Gose, B. (1997). "Efforts to Curb Grade Inflation Get an F from Many Critics." *Chronicle of Higher Education* 43, no. 46 (July 25).

Moxley, D., A. Najor-Durack, and C. Dumbrigue. (2001). *Keeping Students in Higher Education.* London: Kogan Page.

13 Evaluating the Effectiveness of Your Teaching

FOCUS QUESTIONS

- Why should you evaluate your performance informally throughout your courses?
- How can you effectively solicit meaningful feedback from students and colleagues?
- How should you manage the common procedures for end-of-term evaluation?
- Why should you cycle feedback into your continuously developing teaching style?

Teaching without learning is just talking.
—Thomas Angelo and K. Patricia Cross

Throughout this book, we have sought to reinforce the point that each professor's commitment to excellence is the most important key to improving an institution's accountability. Such excellence requires careful planning, a thorough understanding of today's students, creativity, a willingness to try new teaching and learning methods, and consistently communicated high expectations. It also requires, as this chapter will address, continuous evaluation. Some professors may feel threatened by the call for increased accountability, but most will realize that the opportunities it presents are far more numerous and of significantly greater impact than leaving action plans in others' hands.

The expanding array of stakeholders in our higher education system—focused on a global society and marketplace—has become increasingly concerned about effective, lifelong learning. As the business community has embraced a "quality movement," various governmental entities and regional accrediting associations have mandated more genuine measurements of the output of higher education. Colleges and universities must—sometimes over the objections of academic traditionalists—be prepared to convincingly document the learning of their graduates. This emphasis has an impact on every professor—new or veteran, full-time or adjunct. Readers of this book are likely to be the opinion leaders for fostering its growth.

In any field of endeavor, a critical characteristic of those dedicated to long-term success is their commitment to continuous self-improvement. Virtually all institutions of higher education employ formal instructor evaluation procedures. But because they work independently, professors must "own" the process of ongoing data collection, analysis, and the response. They improve their teaching by continually focusing on which concepts or skills are most essential for students, regularly assessing student progress, and identifying ways to more effectively facilitate student learning. Waiting passively for the end-of-term student evaluations or classroom observation by an instructional leader is quite risky. In nearly every case, employing proactive measures early in the term could have uncovered and corrected ineffective practices and negative student perceptions.

The literature of education differentiates formative from summative evaluation. For professors, *formative evaluation* provides immediate feedback while the course is still in progress and allows them to change their performance to increase effectiveness. Typically, formative evaluation methods are "unofficial"— that is, they are not recorded, made public, or used in promotion and tenure decisions. Conversely, *summative evaluation* takes place toward the end of a course and thus gives professors no opportunity to improve performance within that particular course. Summative results are recorded and made known to appropriate officials for use in official decision making. As originally conceived, the course evaluations that students completed were intended to be *formative* in nature. However, in recent years, they have become increasingly official. Some are even posted or circulated on campus or appear on one of the growing number of Web sites that respond to the consumer orientation of many students (Vargas, 2001).

Conducting Informal Student Evaluations

Most people are of two minds about being evaluated. They want feedback to affirm their efficacy and show them how to strengthen their performance, but they also fear bad news. Those who have previously been disappointed by feedback and those who are new to a particular endeavor usually are the ones most resistant to being evaluated. Thus, veteran professors who have read students' derogatory comments sometimes find it easy to discount the entire process. Some even say that students are incapable of providing meaningful feedback. New professors, who often perceive great risk in asking for help from any stakeholder, are equally reluctant to solicit feedback. Paradoxically, they are the ones who might benefit the most from being evaluated because their teaching styles are still under development. On the opposite side, students completing evaluations are often reluctant to provide meaningful evaluative data for fear of being penalized in future dealings with the professor. Therefore always make this exercise optional and anonymous and you will find participation usually quite high.

Evaluation in your classroom should be a natural, informal, ongoing component of your regular practices. Most students will respond very positively to being asked to provide feedback on your teaching, so consider adding this tactic to your practices. Even a good thing can be overdone, however, so think carefully about how often to conduct such informal evaluations. Some professors seek feedback at every class meeting—a practice that many students might regard as intruding on their goodwill or a sign of the professor's insecurity. There are several key mileposts during the term, however, when evaluation is especially valuable and a natural fit with the rhythm of the course. These include:

- At the end of the first class meeting.
- At the end of the third week of class.
- At the time of, or immediately after, the first examination or submission of first project.
- At midterm.
- Several weeks prior to the end of the term, when a formal process will shortly follow (Lyons, Kysilka, and Pawlas, 1999).

Gathering data at these times will enable you to discover problems prior to their becoming too difficult to overcome. Furthermore, it will encourage students to give you additional individualized feedback on a regular basis and will reduce the chances that a student will harbor a complaint until the formal, end-of-the-term evaluation—on which it would otherwise appear as an unpleasant surprise. In the following paragraphs, we will look more closely at each of the evaluation points suggested above.

The suggestions for conducting an effective first class meeting in Chapter 5 were also meant to foster an environment in which students feel very comfortable providing useful feedback. Some additional ways to garner feedback at the end of the first class meeting include the following:

1. Ask students to respond to the following four stems:
   - I came expecting . . .
   - I got . . .
   - I am looking forward to . . .
   - I am hoping . . .
   You can imagine the wealth of information and insight that you will gather from the students! You are likely to feel affirmed and alerted—both of which are important as you make early adjustments.
2. Give students an index card and ask them to write down a question they wish you had answered in the first class meeting or a point that is still "muddy" to them (Angelo and Cross, 1993).

3. Put a "so far" graph on a piece of chart paper on the wall. Just before the end of class, give students colored adhesive dots and ask them to put their dots at the appropriate places on the graph. Mark off six to ten categories: "I love this class," "I am anxious about keeping up with the workload," "I am nervous about the content," "I think I already know most of this stuff," and the like. Since students are doing this as they leave, you can be attending to business at the front of the room and just gather the chart paper when everyone has finished.

After the first three weeks of class, your students will have gotten a better sense of the class and what it will entail. They will have had an opportunity to see you in action, and they will have begun to know you and your expectations. They also will have seen how the class typically flows, so their feedback at this point can be much more directed and specific than it was after the first class meeting. The following are some ideas you might use at this point:

1. *Thumbs up/thumbs down.* List aspects of the course that students will have experienced so far (e.g., small-group work, homework problem sets, guest speakers, lectures, textbook, readings). Ask students to give each of the aspects a rating. A thumb up is positive; a thumb down is negative. You can compare and contrast the responses that you get and gain an overall sense from the class about what is going well and what is not going so well. You can always come back to the class for clarification if ratings were mixed.

2. *A mock evaluation.* Ask students the actual questions (or at least a few of the ones that you are most concerned about) that will appear on the end-of-term formal evaluation. Tell them that you are working to make this the best class possible and that their feedback is critical to your being able to accomplish your goal. Provide some instruction on the kinds of responses that are helpful.

3. *Learning logs.* Learning logs are full- or half-size sheets of paper with one question at the top. We use questions such as "What do you think the professor of this class believes about teaching and learning? How do you know?" and "What is the most surprising thing you have learned so far this semester? Explain." Immediately after students complete the learning log, the professor collects them to read for the feedback provided. In some cases, you may write comments on them before returning them to students, but most often, you are keeping them for the information provided and they are not returned to students.

Another natural milepost for seeking evaluation from students is either the session during which the first examination is administered or the first major assignment is submitted. The evaluation can be conducted during that class meeting or the one following, when the graded items are returned. The former will tend to provide better feedback on the nature of the assignment, while the latter will yield more information on your grading procedures, so identify your objective clearly before conducting the exercise. Employing the same anonymous index card procedure used at the end of the first class meeting, write several items on the board, such as the following:

- What was your biggest challenge in completing this assignment [preparing for this exam]?
- What would you do differently on this assignment [test] if you could?
- Which resource (library, fellow student, other teacher) did you most rely on for help?
- How, without being shorter or easier, would you make the assignment [test] even more worthwhile?

You may get some creative excuses for what turned out to be less-than-exemplary work, but as with the first informal evaluation, you probably will be surprised by the quality and quantity of feedback that this activity elicits. Having asked students for their feedback, you are obligated to do something with it, such as responding to their comments in an e-mail summary or opening the following class meeting with summary feedback and an opportunity for questions. While resisting the fleeting temptation to lower your standards, you might want to consider implementing some of the suggestions when you assign the next project or as you clarify expectations for the following examination.

The next convenient milepost for eliciting informal feedback is at midterm. By that point, students likely will have completed several out-of-class assignments, one or more tests and/or quizzes, and several in-class activities. Having established a precedent through the first two informal evaluations, you are likely to sense that students are increasingly comfortable sharing their deeper feelings. Employing a similar procedure as before, ask students to respond to several of the following:

- How do you feel about the learning environment created within the class?
- What have you most benefited from in the course to this point? Why?
- What could have been left out, and what could be added or modified? Why?
- How would you assess your own efforts to this point?
- On a scale of 1 (poor) to 10 (outstanding), what score would you now give the course? Why?

These questions should elicit your most detailed and deeply grounded responses to date, providing you with meaningful data upon which to base changes in class procedures for the remainder of the term or for the next time you teach the course. Again, you should respond in some way to demonstrate your commitment to the concept of continuous improvement. You should also expect some critical comments by this point—which can be interpreted as much a strength (your students are being honest with you) as a weakness. Resist the urge to strike back at the class over such comments or to single out a person who might have made them. Protect the integrity of the process by demonstrating a constructive attitude.

Stephen Brookfield (1995) suggests using a method called the Critical Incident Questionnaire (CIQ). You can ask the following questions at most any point in the term, from beginning to end. Brookfield suggests compiling the answers and sharing them with the class, in addition to using them for your own personal use.

1. At what moment in the class this week [term] did you feel most engaged with what was happening?
2. At what moment in the class this week [term] did you feel most distanced from what was happening?
3. What action that anyone (teacher or student) took in class this week [term] did you find most affirming and helpful?
4. What action that anyone (teacher or student) took in class this week [term] did you find most puzzling or confusing?
5. What about the class this week [term] surprised you most?

In addition to these periodic feedback sessions, we have found it useful to solicit conversational feedback from key students throughout the term. The results of your first exam, coupled with volunteered student feedback, will help you identify those who are most invested in the course's outcome and most able to provide you effective feedback on your teaching performance. (In most classes, several students will fit these criteria providing breadth of perspective that reduces the chances of making changes based on too small a sample.) Several times during the middle of the term, ask this group to stay at the end of class and help you assess your teaching strategies—that is, what worked for them. Those teaching especially large classes have sometimes formalized this process somewhat by instituting "teaching circles," similar to focus groups used in business, comprising diverse student volunteers who meet with the professor, or graduate teaching assistant, at several junctures throughout the term.

Gathering feedback informally throughout the term will enable you to produce an ever richer learning experience for the overwhelming majority of your students and will make teaching more rewarding for you. In addition, it will likely reduce the amount of negative feedback you would have otherwise received on the formal, end-of-the-term student evaluation so important to your career success.

Arranging Informal Assessments by Colleagues

Another extremely valuable activity that you might employ is to invite an experienced instructor with whom you have developed rapport—perhaps your mentor or peer—to attend your class, observe your teaching, and give you feedback.

While you might ask your colleague to use a form such as the one in Appendix 13.2, or the official one from your department or institution, be aware that some colleagues will resist such a degree of formality and would prefer to give you general written or verbal feedback.

Note that there is significant risk in this process unless you are absolutely comfortable with the person observing your teaching and that person, likewise, is comfortable playing this role. If the person you chose declines—for perfectly understandable reasons—resist applying pressure of any kind. The simple fact that you invited him or her to participate in the process might plant a seed that will bear fruit at some later time. Note too that an informal assessment may be especially useful when there is a formal process in place that you must satisfy later—your colleague's observation can serve as a trial run. Therefore arrange it far enough in advance so that you have time to make changes based upon its feedback (Chism, 1999).

Videotaping a Classroom Presentation

Having gathered data from students and perhaps a peer, you have no doubt begun to identify several significant tendencies in your teaching style. As a way of confirming these initial findings and/or gaining additional insights, you should consider viewing yourself in action—that is, on video. If your institution has a teaching and learning center or other faculty development entity (discussed in more detail in Chapter 14), you would be wise to find out whether its staff can assist you in this.

If you decide to videotape yourself, we would make several recommendations. First, be aware that the tape may well give you more information than you can digest. You might therefore want to approach this type of self-assessment incrementally by first audiorecording a session. An audiotape presents a narrower set of data—you can focus on your vocal style, your timing, and your ease in making transitions between segments of the class meeting. Reviewing this data first may enable you to focus more objectively on a video recording of your teaching.

For your videotaping session, you will need to recruit a camera operator in advance. We suggest you find a person somewhat familiar to your students but not a member of the class. A colleague from your department or a former student would be two possibilities. Tell your students about the videotaping at least one class session in advance. Orchestrate it as a learning opportunity for them by explaining that you are dedicated to continually improving your teaching, just as you hope they will be when they enter their profession. If students who normally sit in the front row are uncomfortable about being in the video, allow them to change seats. At the same time, you do want to have some student faces in your tape, so invite others to move up for the occasion. Prepare the camera in advance of the class meeting, and check that the lighting, sound, and framing will give you the finished product you need. To minimize the impact on your students, you will not want to make more than one video during a given course, so make sure you get it right the first time.

You will probably want to view the finished video by yourself, at least the first time through. We suggest that you use the self-assessment form in Appendix 13.1 to maximize your objectivity—and minimize the emotionality—of your review. Regardless of your perceptions, congratulate yourself on your courage in conducting an activity that many would not attempt—it says a great deal about your professional dedication. Keep the videotape and review it later, perhaps with the input of a colleague or mentor. After you have reflected on this first effort, consider conducting a second videotaping session, in a different class.

Gathering the Official Ratings

At nearly every college and university, it has become common practice to ask students to evaluate instructor and course effectiveness at the conclusion of each term. Many professors dread this experience and make their negative opinions on the issue known to their peers and sometimes even to students. Remember, however, that your earlier efforts at informal evaluation—student input, peer review, self-assessment by audio- and videotape—have provided you a significant edge.

Although admittedly imperfect, the practice of conducting student evaluations is likely to take on even more significance in an age of increased accountability. Institutional leaders rely on the results, so to openly fault the process can set up some unhealthy psychological dynamics in the classroom or between you and the administration. As stated earlier, the process especially affects contract renewal decisions for new professors. Therefore, we encourage you to view student evaluation in its most positive light—an opportunity to gain feedback that will enable you to improve the quality of your instruction in succeeding courses.

Most official student rating processes employ some type of standardized form, unique to a particular instructional unit or to the institution as a whole. The form typically contains a series of statements such as the following:

- The instructor was knowledgeable in the subject area.
- The instructor was well prepared for each class meeting.
- The instructor presented the material in a clearly understandable manner.
- The course examinations and other evaluative measures fairly and accurately measured students' mastery of the course material.
- The methods of instruction were effective and appropriate for this course.
- The instructor used class time wisely, including starting and ending on time.

Accompanying these is, typically, a Likert scale, which consists of *strongly agree* through *strongly disagree*, or some similar system, to which numerical values can be applied. Such a system enables the calculation of an overall score and allows instructional leaders to make a variety of comparisons. Most forms also include several open-ended questions that enable students to provide comments on a wide range of issues. Since the results of student evaluation are so critical, you would be very wise to obtain a copy of the form used in your teaching situation well in advance of its administration date (Scriven, 1995).

To protect the anonymity of students and validity of results, most colleges and universities have developed their own procedures for administering student evaluations. These typically include:

- The scheduling of the activity at the close of the term.
- The administration of the evaluation, and transport of forms, by someone other than the instructor (an administrator, a peer teacher, or student).
- The instructor's leaving the classroom during the administration of the evaluation.
- The availability of the completed forms for the professor to review only after the submission of end-of-term reports or after a specific date.

Many administrators view taking liberties with these procedures, even unintentionally, as a breach of ethical standards. Therefore make sure you know exactly what to do before administering your first official evaluation.

To achieve the goal of improving your teaching effectiveness, you must manage the ratings process carefully. First, give students sufficient time to complete the form thoughtfully. Scheduling the evaluation as the last activity of a given class meeting or immediately before a timed final exam is likely to reduce the quality of student input. Introduce the activity professionally, and emphasize its value. Finally, review the evaluation forms as soon as possible while the issues they raise are still fresh in your mind (Hilt, 2001).

You may be surprised the first few times you read the official evaluations. Students will sometimes rate your performance below what you believe it should be, or they may write comments that are blatantly unfair and perhaps not even true. This is one of the reasons it makes sense to help students understand which kinds of comments are appropriate and which are not. Help them understand that negative statements should be delivered in the spirit of being helpful. Mean-spirited statements make it difficult for the professor to sort out his or her reaction to being attacked from any legitimate complaints or concerns (Weimer, 1990).

Another troubling aspect you may find is that different students' comments are in direct conflict with each other. One student may praise your anecdotes as good ways of emphasizing points while another may criticize them as tangential and irrelevant. There is no way to guarantee that all students will perceive your class the same way. You need to remember this fact as you review your evaluations. Your efforts to informally gather evaluative data throughout the term will likely prevent the type of significant negative feedback that sometimes overwhelms the new professor.

No one likes to be judged. However, the formalization of student voices in the instructional process creates a positive dynamic that, when fully understood and appropriately managed, provides you the most effective and consistent source of data on which to improve your instruction (Marincovich, 1999).

Preparing for Formal Observation/ Evaluation by a Discipline Leader

Although less common than end-of-term student evaluations, many colleges and universities conduct formal observations of professors' teaching as a standard practice. The timing and other factors affecting such observations make it a less than perfect practice as well. As in the case of student evaluations, the rewards of observations are maximized through a constructive perspective on their potential and sound management practices.

First, you must thoroughly understand the process employed in your teaching situation. Gather answers to as many of the following questions as possible:

- Who conducts the observation? Does the observer prefer to be introduced to the students or treated as a fly on the wall?
- Are the observations scheduled in advance, or are they spontaneous?
- Do you have any say about which particular class meeting will be observed? For example, can you give the observer a list of classes when examinations or other activities that would create an inappropriate atmosphere are scheduled?
- Is a form used to guide the observation? If so, is a copy available for you to review in advance? (A copy of a typical observation form is found in Appendix 13.2.)
- What are the unwritten factors that contribute to the unique perspective of the person most likely to observe your teaching?
- How do the observation results factor into later decisions that affect you?
- Is a follow-up meeting with an instructional leader standard? How is it scheduled?

Besides helping you develop a grounded strategy for achieving success in the observation, knowing the answers to these and related questions will likely reduce the anxiety you may experience during this situation. In addition, your chances of success will have been markedly improved by employing the informal methods of evaluation suggested earlier in this chapter.

Regardless of the combination of methods your institution uses to evaluate teaching performance, it is critical to demonstrate to instructional leaders that you are continuously improving your classroom performance. Even if you are not required to do so, seek a brief appointment to discuss results of formal procedures. If you are able to speak with your instructional leader, listen carefully to his or her counsel. In a professional manner, express your responses to the formal evaluation procedures and to feedback gathered through the informal methods you used. Highlight some of the changes you intend to incorporate into future courses you might be assigned. Keep the session brief and focused, with the goal of simply reinforcing your commitment to excellence.

Conducting a Self-Assessment

The professor who regularly engages in systematic self-evaluation will unquestionably derive greater reward (and/or potentially less damage) from his or her institution's formal methods of evaluation. Regular self-evaluation is especially important early in your career as you seek to develop insights and skills to improve your continually evolving teaching style.

One method for providing structure to an ongoing system of self-evaluation is to keep a journal—handwritten or electronic—in which you reflect on your teaching experiences. Regularly invest fifteen or twenty introspective minutes following each class meeting to process and write down the techniques and activities that drew a positive response from students. Word processing software is especially convenient and effective in helping you get the words just right—and for making sure you can read what you have written later on. Focus especially on the strategies and events in class that you feel could be improved. Focus also on the key student retention mileposts that we have emphasized throughout this book. Putting your thoughts into words and editing them to reflect your precise ideas and emotions enables you to develop more effective habits and build confidence in your teaching performance.

We suggest that you invest additional self-evaluation time at the midpoint of your course, much the same way a business conducts an audit or an institution conducts a self-study as a component of the accreditation process. As noted earlier, Appendix 13.1 is an instrument for guiding a self-assessment. Depending on your discipline, institution, or other circumstances, you might want to modify the instrument to more effectively achieve your goals. The key is to begin your self-assessment early in the course and to synthesize your findings with informal input from students and peers to develop a valid assessment of your strengths and needs at any particular point (Chism, 1999).

As you strive to help students master your course material, regularly query yourself using the following questions:

- Am I open to new ways of seeing issues, or do I have all of my answers already?
- Am I trying new things, or am I limited by old approaches?
- Do I inspire my students or stultify them?
- Do I validate others and myself, or do I disparage?
- Do I actively seek challenges, or am I comfortable with the status quo?
- Am I tenacious, or do I give in or give up?

- Am I described as enthusiastic or bland?
- Do I regularly demonstrate that I am a learner as well as a teacher?
- Am I setting new goals or wishing things would be different?

Consider asking yourself these questions at least once each term. Write out your answers and keep them for future reference. Decide whether you need to change direction or just stay on course (Fink, 1995).

Summary of Key Points

- Conduct informal student evaluations at least at these mileposts: the end of the first class meeting, following the first examination or major assignment, and at midterm.
- Informal student evaluations provide you significant data upon which to build your teaching style.
- Informal evaluations reduce potential problems that would otherwise show up in the formal end-of-term evaluation.
- Ask open-ended questions likely to solicit grounded responses.
- Involve peer instructors or your mentor in observing and evaluating your teaching.
- Early in the term, obtain copies of the student evaluation form and observation criteria form from your instructional leader.
- Follow guidelines precisely when administering formal student evaluations.
- Maintain a journal to self-evaluate your early teaching experiences.

Through the Professors' Eyes

PAT: I always get reasonably good evaluations on the student rating forms, but those university-wide forms are not very informative, particularly if you are trying to improve your teaching. I'm looking for ways to maximize my results, especially since I am using more instructional technology. I think I'll use another focus group to help me sort out the impact of the technology on my teaching. I have also been mentoring a new assistant professor this term, and he has been observing many of my class sessions. I'm going to ask him to lunch so that we can talk solely about our teaching—nothing else. I learned some interesting tricks from him that will help me keep the flow of students' papers straight—he marks his grade book and the paper itself when students submit them—so he knows who completed the work on time. I never thought about doing that and have gotten into discussions with students about missing papers.

DALE: I dislike the student rating process—it's really just a popularity contest. But those evaluations are one component of the promotion criteria, and I at least need to have decent student evaluations or else. I've decided to use additional feedback mechanisms to supplement the college forms. I've asked the students working with me on my research to provide structured feedback on their experiences. I also included an opportunity for my other students to submit comments via the Web. The comments can be posted anonymously. I hope I won't regret this move. With the exception of tenure and promotion, no one really pays much attention to student ratings. I know my department chair never looks at the summary sheets for any other than the junior faculty. As long as the students don't go into her office to complain, she doesn't feel the need to review them very closely, with so many other tasks to coordinate.

KIM: I got the feedback from my students, but I am not sure what it means. My students rated me really high in some categories but complained too much about other aspects of my teaching. I tried so hard and I don't feel really good about my evaluations. My mentor is helping me understand my students' comments. He assures me that my overall evaluations are very good. Even though I worked on my speaking so much, some of the students' comments relate to their difficulty in understanding me. Other comments seem to be very positive, like my availability and my use of technology to explain and keep them informed of their individual progress. A few did complain about the amount of assignments I gave, but I had already realized that was an issue that would be addressed for the next term. Some feedback is hard to interpret, and some handwriting is difficult to read. My department chair helped me interpret some of the comments, and he did not seem upset over any of them. My mentor said he had received good feedback "through the grapevine"—whatever that is. I want so to be perfect and to have my students respect me. I am not sure exactly what I can do to improve. I worked very hard.

Tips for Thriving

In recent years, a wide range of professionals, from attorneys to business executives, have markedly improved their job performance by videotaping their preparation efforts. High-achieving professors would do well to follow their example. You can employ this strategy by yourself, but a more effective method might be to do it in concert with another instructor—perhaps your mentor or other veteran professor, or even a new professor colleague. Taping a ten- or fifteen-minute mini-lesson, then debriefing it using the observation evaluation form in Appendix 13.2 would prove to be an especially valuable experience. Critiquing a videotaped session, rather than trying to recall the exact dynamics of a particular class, provides objectivity and is therefore more likely to effect change. Involving another instructor as an informal coach will enable you to gain from his or her experiences and perspective and will reduce the chances of your engaging in self-deprecation.

Finally, reflect on your experiences from the nonacademic world, in which motivated and competent young professionals sometimes see their careers stall in their tracks or even come to a crashing end. Often their downfall is due to a single offhand remark they made at a company function or to an inappropriate tone of voice they used with a client who was unknowingly connected in some mysterious way to an executive of the company. Early in your teaching career, you enter a new fishbowl. Unfortunately, you may at some point be judged by a remark or an action taken out of context by an observer who communicates it through his or her personal filter to a key decision maker. We once knew a promising new professor whose career at one institution was quietly terminated due largely to a derogatory comment made in class about the local public school system. Unknown to the instructor at the time of the remark, the class included the spouse of a prominent system administrator. The course had nothing at all to do with the school system or any other context that would have made the comment appropriate. While professors enjoy the protection of academic freedom, privileges under it are not absolute. People were provided with two ears and only one mouth for a good reason.

SUGGESTED READINGS

Brookfield, S. (1995). *Becoming a Critically Reflective Teacher.* San Francisco: Jossey-Bass.

Fink, L. D. (1995). "Evaluating Your Own Teaching." In P. Seldin, ed., *Improving College Teaching.* Bolton, MA: Anker, pp. 191–204.

Hilt, Douglas. (2001). "What Students Can Teach Professors: Reading between the Lines of Evaluations." *Chronicle of Higher Education.* B24.47, no. 27 (March 16), p. B 24.

Marincovich, M. (1999). "Using Student Feedback to Improve Teaching." In P. Seldin, ed., *Changing Practices in Evaluating Teaching.* Bolton, MA: Anker.

Vargas, J. (2001). "Improving Teaching Performance." In D. Royse, ed., *Teaching Tips for College and University Instructors.* Boston: Allyn & Bacon, pp. 254–280.

Weimer, M. (1990). "What to Do When Somebody Criticizes Your Teaching." In M. Weimer and R. A. Neff, eds., *Teaching College: Collected Readings for the New Instructor.* Madison, WI: Magna, pp. 143–144.

APPENDIX 13.1

Classroom Management Self-Assessment Form

Recognizing that self-assessment is likely to become more deeply internalized than other forms of evaluation, we recommend that you periodically respond to the following questions and contemplate the impact of your answers on your classroom success.

1. How do I typically begin a session of my class?
   Possibilities: By reviewing key points from the previous session? By posing a rhetorical question? By citing a current event or telling a story?
2. How/where do I position myself within the classroom?
   Possibilities: Behind a lectern at the front of the room? Near a student's seating position? Against a table near the front of the room?
3. How do I typically move within the classroom?
   Possibilities: Not at all? Back and forth in front of the room? Around the perimeter?
4. Where are my eyes usually positioned?
   Possibilities: On my notes? On the board? On the back wall? Into students' eyes?
5. How do I facilitate students' visual processing of course material?
   Possibilities: Using PowerPoint or other presentation software? Writing key phrases on the board or on an overhead transparency in advance? As they are spoken? By displaying appropriate props?
6. How do I ask questions of students?
   Possibilities: Ask individual students likely to know the answer? Unlikely to know the answer? To the class as a whole, selecting a random student to respond?
7. How often do I chuckle or smile in class?
   Possibilities: Seldom? When a student initiates something funny? Frequently?
8. How do I respond when students are inattentive?
   Possibilities: Lose my temper? Ignore it and plow on? Pose a nonjudgmental question that engenders focus on the content issue?
9. How do I respond when students express opinions different from those I have expressed?
   Possibilities: Discount their opinions? Ask them to explain themselves so that I can find error in their logic? Orchestrate it into a teaching and learning moment?
10. How do I typically end a class session?
    Possibilities: Abruptly? By summarizing key points? By providing an overview of the following session?

APPENDIX 13.2

Model Teaching Observation Worksheet

Professor: *Date:*   *Room:*

Course Title: *Time:*

Course ID#:   *Number of Students Present:*

Enter objective observations that address each of the following questions:

1. Visual impact created?

2. Devices/techniques used to introduce the lesson?

3. How was student participation elicited?

4. How was professor's expertise demonstrated?

5. Teaching methods used?

6. How did professor contribute energy to the class?

7. Methods of verbal communications?

8. Nonverbal communications?

9. Classroom management techniques?

10. Nature and amount of support materials employed?

11. Comments on factors other than those above?

14 Maintaining Your Edge

FOCUS QUESTIONS

- How can you keep your teaching sharp?
- What are specific steps you can take to set yourself apart from others?
- What difference does it make to students when your teaching is excellent?
- What does it mean to you when your teaching is perceived as excellent?

Being an esteemed professor. Teaching in a discipline that stimulates your mind and brings you recognition. Enjoying the lifestyle and perks of a secure, venerated profession. Putting money away for a retirement that will be stimulating and productive. Working around other intelligent, energetic people. Knowing you have a job that is relatively insulated from the cycles of the economy. Setting your own work schedule. Being allowed—or even encouraged—to pursue your research interests. What a fabulous life!

With so many varied advantages, it is no surprise that college professors want to protect their careers. The call for increasing accountability is a considerable challenge, and the professorship will maintain its prestige and benefits only if its members respond. Life in the academy has changed, will continue to evolve, and will likely never return to the way it used to be, regardless of how much traditionalists resist. Taking a longer view, let us not forget that the root of the word *education* means "to lead out," and professors are obligated to reflect that in their actions.

Those who oppose the accountability movement may talk about intellectual freedom and academic standards, but is not the resistance to change more about protecting turf than it is about ensuring the survival of scholarship? Can college professors claim that their collective mission is more special than that of physicians, journalists, judges, and other professionals—who are likewise being affected by an increasingly accountability-minded populace? The question may only be rhetorical. Professors can still have rewarding lifestyles and careers, but they must either adapt or fade away.

You approach the conclusion of this book with, we hope, a renewed sense of yourself as a facilitator of learning and a refreshed sense of the possibilities for genuinely excellent teaching. We also hope that you have acquired some new insights and implemented some of the strategies we have suggested for improving your skills in recruiting students who might not otherwise enroll in your class sections, retaining those who do enroll, and helping students complete college and enter graduate programs or careers that dovetail with their academic work. Again, stakeholders of your institution and your profession expect no less.

While you have always been evaluated, promoted, and held accountable for your performance in a panoply of roles and responsibilities, you will increasingly be assessed on your ability to foster student learning and measure its outcomes. Research, writing, and other such activities associated with your position no doubt hold great potential for diverting your attention and energy away from teaching, but we hope that as a result of reading this book, you more clearly understand the need to persevere in that role. In this final chapter, we want to suggest ways you can maintain your edge in the challenging and competitive environment in which you work.

Building a Following among Students

Business professionals have long recognized the need for networking, or rain-making, to develop a client base, yet many professors are still reluctant to connect regularly with those outside the academy. Such an inward focus, we believe, is no longer viable. To maintain your edge, you must build a following among present students, prospective students, and those with the ability to direct students your way. If implementing some of this book's recommendations has already helped you improve the quality of your relationships with students, you have taken the first step in this process. Without that quality, additional strategies will be extremely limited in their potential impact.

Reputations are important and get built whether you want them to be or not. To foster the type of reputation you desire and one that genuinely reflects who you are, begin with a self-analysis, such as the one we outlined in Chapter 2. Then consistently manage your teaching activities as suggested in Chapters 4 through 13. If you teach in a behemoth department on a large campus, it may take some time for you to build your reputation. If instead you teach at a medium-sized or small campus, it is remarkable how rapidly you can become known. Negative reputations are built very quickly, whereas positive ones slowly accrue. Bad news always travels fast; students and others love to play "my story can top your story," swapping tales of the most terrible professor they ever had. Your excellent teaching will slowly but surely result in tales that become part of the institution's lore. You can focus on continuing to build your student following by taking some of these positive steps:

- Underpromise and overdeliver. Return graded assignments by the following class meeting whenever possible (which means carefully planning your schedule to allow for grading time soon after assignments are submitted). Tell students that phone calls will be returned within forty-eight hours, but get back to them sooner. Send helpful e-mail messages and include links to useful online resources. Attend your students' performances (theater, sports, music) and congratulate them on their successes.

- Come to class impeccably organized and prepared, belying the stereotype students have, unfortunately, developed of professors. You will immediately distinguish yourself in the students' minds, and they will remember.

- File your completed student profile forms, and refer back to them both during and after the course to refresh your recall of names and faces, identify recruits for new courses you might develop, and so on. Being known as "the professor who remembered my name when she saw me at the supermarket" is a powerful tool for building your student following.

- Become involved, if only in a small way, in some aspect of student life on campus. Choose an area in which you have expertise to share, in which you would like to become more knowledgeable, and/or in which a large number of your students are involved. The possibilities include sports teams, arts organizations, student government, diversity committees, academic support staffs, student chapters of professional associations, and others. Once involved, remain involved for the entire academic year, then evaluate your rewards afterward. Such involvement fosters a broader, deeper knowledge of students, perhaps over generations. Students who have a positive experience often encourage younger siblings and friends to attend the same school and become involved in similar aspects of campus life—so your sphere of influence may very well expand exponentially.

- Become involved in your community, outside the institution. Some professors relate such involvement to their discipline (e.g., a music professor who plays in the local symphony), while for others, involvement might be simply an avocation (e.g., the political science professor who is involved in community theater). As you participate, people learn about you in a rich way. When they hear you speak informally about your teaching, they may begin to refer potential students to you. Over time, if you are perceived as approachable and invested in others' success, your influence will expand.

- Volunteer to speak at meetings of civic and service organizations. Service clubs such as Rotary and Lions would likely jump at the chance to have your expertise presented. They tend to include among their members professionals from an array of fields who generally like to serve as contacts to a large portion of the community. Volunteer for your institution's speaker listing, which is typically sent to service clubs and the local media. If such a listing is not available, contact the clubs in your area individually, letting them know the range of topics you feel comfortable addressing at their meetings.

Although some of these suggestions might lie outside your comfort zone, remember that the zone of discomfort is where the real learning begins. Your reward will come not only from the activities themselves but also from the following you will build. It is not unlike starting an exercise program, which may provide only limited benefits at first but soon shows itself to be making huge contributions to your health. Eventually, you would no more miss your regular exercise session than you would miss eating an elegantly prepared meal or taking part in some other rewarding activity. Once you begin to have students drop by before class to tell you that they have heard good things about you, the parade will become a steady one. Someone in the community may seek you out to tell you about her son, who was one of your students and now recommends your class to his friends.

In formulating a longer-term strategy for developing a following, choose one or two local schools from which your institution draws its students, or perhaps one from which it does not draw but should. Through your campus contacts, identify some of the leading teachers at those schools, and call or e-mail them to see if it would be possible for you to visit in the near future. Spend an entire period in a carefully selected classroom, observing students representative of those you might be seeing shortly in your college classroom. Take the time to ask individual students about their future plans, perceptions of attending college, and the like. What you glean from your observations and interactions will be invaluable as you continually refine your approaches. Close by offering the students your card and encouraging them to contact you when they visit your campus. Few will take you up on your offer, but the invitation itself is far more significant than you might imagine. As you debrief with the teacher before departing, inquire about serving as a judge for a public-speaking contest, a scholarship competition, or some other activity that is a close match with your expertise. Afterward, be sure to send the teacher a handwritten thank-you note.

Since some students will take you up on your invitation to visit your campus, proceed to formulate a plan. Identify people on your campus (e.g., academic and financial aid counselors) upon whom you might draw to provide support. Plan to personally start the visit and then to take the students to meet with your established resources. The time and effort you invest in this activity might not only recruit students for your classes but also increase your standing with your campus colleagues. Such seemingly minor efforts should never be discounted for their ability to contribute an added dimension to your growing reputation.

Developing a following among students is less about popularity than it is about professional respect. As a professor, you hold a position of influence. When people honor that position and do it justice, word gets around, as it should. You must be especially vigilant regarding your teaching reputation. It is the part of your reputation that spreads the fastest around campus and is noted by members of the public, who often are unaware of all the other contributions you make. View yourself as a teaching professor at all times, and be watchful of the messages you are sending. The result will be a professional following based on respect.

Becoming an Advocate for the Marginalized

Much debate has occurred recently concerning some universities' efforts to expand the proportion of minority students among their enrollments. While we will leave that philosophical/political conversation to others, we believe it is critical for all professors to look at this issue through an accountability lens. Among the trends that we see as essential for consideration are:

- Over the next several decades, people of color, foreign-born residents, and children of foreign-born residents are projected to increase both as a proportion of the population of the United States and as a proportion of enrollments of colleges and universities (Howe and Strauss, 2000).
- Addressing the terrorism threat effectively will require us to leverage the foreign language skills and cultural perspectives of our diverse citizenry, and the nurturing of those skills through higher education (Cox, 2001); (Gedda, 2002).
- Only through the delegation of individual responsibility throughout the population—a basic tenet of the overall accountability movement—are we likely to improve the economic and social outlook for marginalized citizens (Banta and Borden, 1994).

While we have seen—and will continue to see—increased institutional initiatives developed to address these issues, the accountability movement will no doubt start to mandate improvements in this arena. As in other aspects of accountability, it will become increasingly incumbent upon individual professors to reach out to marginalized students to ensure their academic and career success within a continually evolving environment.

The vast majority of this new population compromises "first generation" college students. Sandra Rodriguez's research (2002) indicates that success in college allowed first-generation students to radically improve their social and economic tracks. In so doing, they also positively affected the upward mobility of many others by becoming activists who give back to society at a rate far above that of most college graduates. The forces that seem to have life-changing effects on first-generation students are "ascending cross-class identification" and "positive naming"; that is, someone of higher socioeconomic status often shows them the way to become socially, economically, and politically enfranchised. Someone—

often a professor—plays a transforming role in helping these students utilize capabilities that they had not previously realized.

While many readers of this book have played a role in helping marginalized students become more successful, all professors can do an even better job.
Many marginalized students have arrived in our classrooms from environments
that did not value higher education, schools whose resources did not foster their
fullest development, and with little or no advisement that might help them formulate a path to success. Our sensitivity is crucial in recognizing these factors,
mentoring such students, and enabling them to close the gap between their technological and other skills and those of students from more privileged backgrounds,
as early in their college career as possible. This can pay great dividends for their
futures, as well as for our institutions and our personal career success. Marginalized students should be especially encouraged to participate in student organizations and other campus activities that may permit them to close the gap
between their backgrounds and those of students who arrive at college better prepared (Light, 2001). Achieving more accountable outcomes with marginalized
students is a must.

Leveraging Your Institution's Faculty Development Resources

At least partly due to the burgeoning calls for accountability from stakeholders,
an increasing number of colleges and universities have initiated some type of faculty development entity on their campuses, often under the mantle "teaching and
learning center" or a similar title. They range from small, part-time, shoestring-
budget efforts managed by one or more faculty members with a keen interest in
teaching, to large, substantially funded ones managed by a full-time director with
an array of additional staff members. Regardless of the size, these programs are
worth becoming involved in—both as a recipient of and a contributor to their
services. If a faculty development program is available at your campus, investigate it and consider making a commitment to it for at least one year so that you
can experience the wide range of activities it offers.

The first step will be to contact the program—many have Web sites—to
find out what it encompasses. Most teaching and learning centers offer classes
and workshops for professors, which often run the gamut from informal, brown-
bag lunch sessions on a variety of topics to week-long, or even semester-long,
sessions on specific topics related to instruction. You will always learn something
of value to your teaching. Although it requires an investment of time to participate in these activities, there will always be a return on that investment.

After taking part in one or more sessions, volunteer to offer one yourself.
Are your student retention results significantly better than the institution's as a
whole? Why? Others would like to know. Do you have good organizational tips

from which other faculty could benefit? Do your students consistently comment on how difficult, but fair, your tests are? Has another faculty member asked you to review her syllabus because she has heard students comment positively on yours? Have you achieved a high degree of active student participation in your large lecture classes? Think about something you do that others could learn from—and offer to share your skill or knowledge, either in a workshop, during a brown-bag lunch session, or as part of a panel program on good instruction.

Another service of many programs is "instructional consulting," which is:

> a process by which teaching is assessed for formative purposes, that is, for improvement. A consultant visits the classroom of an instructor, collects information about the teaching, and then feeds that back to the instructor with the information that he or she gathered from the visit. . . . Instructional consultation has been found to dramatically improve teaching. . . . Teachers who participate in the instructional consultation process report that the experience is helpful, meaningful, worth their time, and continues to have an effect on their teaching long after they cease contact with the consultant (Brinko and Menges, 1997, p. vii).

This service is always confidential and is worth availing yourself of whether you are a brand-new faculty member, a seasoned veteran, a struggling teacher, or the winner of every teaching award available at your institution. You always grow by having another pair of eyes to help you see what is happening in your courses. And the occasion to talk with someone about what is happening—someone with no vested interest, no ax to grind, and no reason to be there other than to help—is an opportunity you should not pass up.

It is worth noting that by having a faculty consultant observe your class—and introducing the person and explaining why you have asked him or her to visit—you let your students know that you are focused on your instruction and that you want to do the best job possible. Many students are quite surprised by this—and your stature increases in their eyes. After the consultant's initial visit, you might want to record a teaching demonstration or two and debrief it afterward as suggested in Chapter 13.

After working with a faculty consultant, you may want to become trained in instructional consulting yourself. Being of service to another faculty member is valuable, but the real surprise may come from the learning that occurs for you as you consult. That is a benefit that most volunteers do not expect, but it is part of what keeps them in the faculty-consulting cadre.

Another area where you might choose to be involved is being part of a scholarship of teaching and learning (SoTL) group. Such groups—some small, some large—are present on many campuses and are often sponsored by various foundations. SoTL groups provide avenues for reflection, inquiry, and publication related to what is happening in your classroom. There are benefits regardless of whether you are a novice or a longtime faculty member.

Find out if your teaching/learning center has a professional library—sort of a one-stop shop for books, pamphlets, journals, articles, and so on related to teaching at the college level. In addition to checking out the materials, it is often nice to ask someone in the center for recommendations in a particular subject area. Your use of the services of your teaching/learning center will be repaid many times over—both because you can become more efficient at what you do and because your impact on students is multiplied as you become more effective. It is a true win/win situation.

Developing Mutually Beneficial Mentoring Relationships

As much as you may want to keep your own counsel related to your teaching, it is valuable to have at least one trusted colleague with whom you can regularly discuss issues related to instruction. You will have great successes that you will want to share with someone—someone who will understand them. Even though you might have friends or family members who will be happy that you are happy, if they are not professors, they cannot really understand the jubilation you feel when a lesson goes off without a hitch, or when a student who seemed unreachable finally made a connection, or when students become excited about learning a difficult concept. It is at these times that you need to have someone who "gets it."

Likewise, you will have frustrations and disappointments with which non-professors cannot empathize. You need to have someone who knows the anger and, yes, the pain that comes when you are trying to teach and it feels as if no one wants to learn—someone who can offer a supportive, listening ear while you vent, but who can also help you figure out what your next step will be. There are plenty of people who will listen to the venting and join right in, eventually putting all the blame back on the students, but that is not a constructive place to be, nor does it help us stay positive in our outlook and determination to help students learn.

The person who shares your interest in teaching might be in your department or college, across campus, or elsewhere in the country or the world. In this wonderful time of opportunities for around-the-clock communication, it really does not matter where the person is. You can call, write, fax, or e-mail in order to communicate—and that person can respond quickly, if not immediately (Baiocco and DeWaters, 1998).

Just as you fill a variety of roles for other people, you will need colleagues who can fill different roles for you. Certainly you need someone to confer with regarding your research, and that person may also be interested in teaching. The colleague we are talking about in this section, however, is a person who cares more about teaching than about any other aspect of his or her career. You do not necessarily have to adopt this person's views, but you need someone who knows instruction, thinks strategically about teaching, cares about student learning above all else, and seeks constant improvement—even though others may see him or her as the ultimate teacher already. Someone like this will push you to seek excellence in your instruction, to upgrade your skills, to make yourself more accountable for the failures in your classroom, and to celebrate the successes. Colleagues who can serve in this role may make you a little uncomfortable at times because of their passion and zeal for teaching—but they will propel you beyond where you could go on your own, and that is certainly a benefit. Be open to the possibilities of finding such a colleague and, further, of being such a colleague for another person. You may or may not want to formalize the relationship into a true mentoring situation, but doing so is another option.

Becoming increasingly proactive, you would be wise to explore mentoring relationships. *Mentoring* can be defined as the process, formal or informal, in which a knowledgeable and skilled veteran—usually not a direct supervisor—guides a relative novice through the maze of an organization. Thus the *mentee* or *protégé* develops self-confidence and productivity faster and more effectively than he or she could do alone. If you ever had an "aha!" moment evoked by someone who provided you new insight into a challenging situation, were told a story or quote that had long-lasting impact, or were given unexpected positive feedback on an otherwise unnoticed achievement, you have been, to one extent or another, mentored. If you were fortunate enough to have all of those, or similar, experiences provided by the same person, you probably regard that relationship as one of the most significant in your professional life. Mentors provide growth opportunities unavailable anyplace else. Instructional leaders at an increasing number of institutions see mentoring as a critical tool for maximizing the effectiveness of faculty members—particularly new ones—and have developed formalized programs. Although there are a variety of roles that a mentor may serve, for the purpose of this section, we are focusing on a mentoring relationship concentrated on improving instruction by the professor, thereby resulting in increased learning by students.

A successful mentoring relationship must be built on common interests, be nurtured by both parties, and offer mutual benefits. The common benefits to the protégé typically include:

- A grounded orientation to the institution, division, or department.
- Information for developing an enriched perspective of the organization's mission.
- Encouragement at critical times.
- An effective model for accepted organizational behavior.
- Introductions to others, both on and off campus, who might provide insights and support.
- Increased exposure and visibility.
- Support during critical situations.
- Increased self-awareness.

- Feedback on teaching performance without the judgment associated with the formalized work relationship (i.e., supervisor/subordinate).

For the mentor, potential benefits include:

- Developing a dependable crucial support resource.
- Achieving vicariously through the accomplishments of the protégé.
- Being valued as a knowledgeable person.
- Receiving a fresh perspective on key issues.
- Gaining opportunity to repay past debts.
- Developing a replacement when career advancement is sought.

In short, an effective mentoring relationship must provide benefits that are perceived as equitable and significant to both parties. Long-lasting mentoring relationships are built on mutual respect and positive interdependence. Stephen Covey (1989) refers to this as maintaining a positive "emotional bank account" and creating "win/win, or no deal" interactions.

Effective mentors are invested in developing the potential of others. They are open-minded, patient, nonjudgmental, and unselfish. Perhaps most important, they are effective listeners. They understand the need for their institution to invest in its future, and they are comfortable giving the credit for success to the protégé. They understand that the protégé is likely to need help when they themselves are busy, but they are willing to subordinate their own needs at such times. They avoid giving advice and instead simply emphasize their more grounded information and different perspectives on key issues. Mentors realize their role does not include rescuing the protégé from his or her own folly.

Effective protégés reflect many similar characteristics, including being open to constructive feedback (i.e., being a bit thick-skinned), willing to critically examine old beliefs and try new ideas, and able to accept full responsibility for their own success. They view their mentors as resources with whom they must initiate communications and do not expect mentors to rescue them. They regularly demonstrate appreciation.

This being said, we would also encourage you to extend yourself somewhat by not trying to link up with a mentor or a protégé who is just like you—you don't want one or the other of you to be a "Mini Me." Since your goal in fostering the relationship is to grow professionally, you would do well to seek out someone who is quite different from you in age, culture, national origin, perspective, or some other significant way. This means there will be times when the two of you butt heads on issues, but when you work through this confrontation, the result is growth—for both of you.

To manage that growth, develop a written agreement that addresses your individual and mutual needs. A model for your consideration can be found in Appendix 14.1. If you find that model too legalistic, consider an e-mail dialogue that begins with a proposal of conditions of the mentoring relationship. Through the interchange, you can hammer out an agreement with your potential partner that provides the psychological boundaries your relationship is likely to require as it evolves.

Mentoring is only one tool within a comprehensive program of professional development. Research shows that effective mentoring must build upon an existing knowledge base held by the protégé. In other words, the mentor cannot be successful and feel rewarded when mentoring is the only tool being employed by the protégé. Still, it is a powerful tool. The highs and lows of teaching require reflective brainpower. In this case, two heads are better than one (Zachary, 2000).

Developing a Collection of Teaching and Learning Resources

Facing fierce market competition, publishers of textbooks and vendors of other educational materials are providing valuable resources—many online—to support the professors and students who use their products—most free of additional cost. Many of these resources are predicated on contemporary pedagogical research and can contribute much to the professor's effectiveness and students' achievement. Besides using such discipline-specific materials, however, you owe it to yourself and your students to also stay current with teaching methods and strategies—as you are doing by reading and completing the exercises within this book.

Twenty years ago, a professor had to scrounge around to *find* books and articles about college teaching. Today it seems that a new one is published each week, and the choices are excellent. Although there may be a bit of hyperbole in that claim, the truth is that the growing emphasis on good instruction in higher education, not coincidentally related to the growth in the accountability movement, has spawned a proliferation of publications supporting instruction at the college level.

Some of these books are meant to be read cover to cover, whereas most others are designed to allow the busy professor to delve into one chapter or topic at a time. Keep resource materials of interest on a nearby shelf so that if you have a spare moment (waiting for a student to show up for an appointment, standing by on hold during a phone call), and you need a burst of inspiration, or if the answer to a difficult teaching problem is eluding you, you can grab a book or an article to read for ideas. There will be some books that you eventually decide to purchase for your own library, but most college and university libraries are pleased to purchase materials on request. If you have not done so already, let Amazon.com, BarnesandNoble.com, or your local bookstore know that you have an interest in college teaching, and you will be alerted to new books on this topic. The end-of-chapter Suggested Readings sections in this book provide an excellent starting point for your reading list.

As you are likely aware, an increasing array of free teaching and learning information has become available online. Web sites are being launched daily by individual institutions that offer useful information to the continuously developing learning facilitator. As noted in Chapter 9, these resources, as well as listservs of several instruction development organizations, can be accessed through the authors' Web site (www.developfaculty.com).

Participating in Conference Sessions Devoted to Instruction

In response to the accountability movement and related factors, there has been a dramatic increase in the number of local or national conferences focused on sound teaching practices, as well as an increase in sessions at discipline-specific professional conferences devoted to good teaching. Nationally, recognition of the need to improve teaching efficacy is moving through all organizations that serve institutions of higher education. Regardless of whether your field is business, education, engineering, human services, journalism, health sciences, or any of the multitude of others, your professional organization will be sponsoring conferences either partially or completely devoted to improving instruction. Make sure you attend such sessions—and present at one or more of them as well.

Often, in your own classrooms, you may not think you are doing anything particularly innovative. Then, when you go to state, regional, or national conferences to learn new ideas, you may find out that a presenter is talking about something you are already doing—but that others find the idea extraordinarily innovative! You may find yourself saying, "Hmm, well, if these folks liked those ideas, they'd love mine!" Never discount anything you are doing in your classroom thinking it is not such a big deal. If you are getting results, it is a big deal! Share it with others. And, frankly, sometimes it is hard to be a prophet in your own land—that is, your colleagues down the hall may not be interested in your idea, but once you get out of town, you may find it well received. Such positive reception can leave you affirmed and energized. We hope that this situation sounds difficult to resist.

Developing Your Technological Savvy

Throughout this book—especially in Chapter 9—we have emphasized the importance of infusing technology into your instruction, to better engage students in their learning. The key to doing so is becoming as technologically savvy yourself as possible, then staying current. Those professors who have stayed relatively current in technology know even better than the rest of society that they are, in fact, behind—that almost everyone is. The growth in technology's uses, applications, nuances, and challenges has been unfolding faster than anyone could have predicted, and if you are not constantly upgrading your skills in this area, you are at risk of lagging dangerously behind.

Legislators who are asked to increase technology budgets for institutions in their city or state, regents or trustees who are elected by the populace (or appointed by elected politicians) and expected to oversee expenditures at colleges and universities, students who pay technology fees, donors who choose to give money to expand the technology capabilities of campuses, and other stakeholders in higher education expect professors to learn and use the best of what is available. They do not expect to walk by a classroom that is outfitted with a document camera, a high-speed Internet line, and an LCD projector and see the professor standing at the front of the room, reading from lecture notes while students madly attempt to write down the words verbatim.

In order to increase your proficiency in the use of technology to improve student learning, you must take advantage of every means imaginable, including such tactics as searching out training opportunities from your own institution and nearby ones, at retail computer outlets, or at other places that offer them at a time and level that is appropriate for you. Think also about enrolling in an online class (many of which are free) through your own institution or through such entities as Barnesandnobleuniversity.com. Let us repeat: To keep your own competitive edge (and possibly even to keep your job), you must become, and you must stay, technologically savvy. In an age of increasing accountability, you will be glad you did.

Developing a Teaching Portfolio

The concept of the professional portfolio as a tool for student development was discussed thoroughly in Chapter 11. It should not come as a surprise then that portfolios hold great potential for helping you develop your teaching skills. Peter Seldin (1999) defines a teaching portfolio as "a factual description of a professor's teaching strengths and accomplishments, which includes documents and materials that collectively suggest the scope and quality of a professor's teaching performance" (p. 110).

It has become common practice at most institutions for faculty to submit a portfolio as a first step in pursuing promotion. Those who see promotion as the only purpose often will hastily construct a portfolio that not only looks thrown together to members of the Promotion and Tenure Committee but also has little value in other situations. Even if such an event seems in the distant future, you may one day decide to pursue an endowed chair or some other sort of teaching or service award—for which a portfolio would be required. Why risk having to start over to develop a competitive portfolio, when you might update and adapt your portfolio all along? Start to think about setting up and continuing a teaching portfolio that is a systematic collection of materials to document your professional accomplishments, growth, and reflection.

The first step to creating a teaching portfolio is to write out your philosophy of education, as discussed in Chapter 2. Then write out the purpose of your portfolio and the questions you want your portfolio to answer. A single, carefully crafted paragraph usually is enough. Decide whether you are focusing on your growth as a professor in the classroom or whether you want to focus on just one aspect of your teaching—focusing on the area of your greatest strength, for example, will help you figure out why you are so good in one setting or with one kind of student. Or maybe you want to focus on the area that is giving you the most difficulty because you want to ameliorate the situation. When you are using your portfolio to help maintain your edge, focusing both on what you are doing well and what you are struggling with will help answer some questions you have about your teaching.

Next, you need to begin to collect artifacts that demonstrate your philosophy and fit with the purpose of your portfolio. Artifacts might include a course syllabus, a sample of student work, a letter from a colleague who visited your class, comments from student evaluations, and so on. As you select an item, do not just stuff it in the binder or folder but also reflect on it in writing. Why have you chosen this item? What does it say about your teaching? How does it reflect your philosophy? What have you learned as a result of the experience that this item represents? Without the reflection on the artifacts, the portfolio becomes nothing more than a scrapbook—and while scrapbooks have value in some arenas, they will not help you advance in your career or improve your skills.

Creating a teaching portfolio is an ongoing process. Some people devote a whole weekend to start and then continue on a regular basis after that. Others set aside an hour each week to add to their portfolio—making a selection from some student work, from an assignment given, from a note received—and then writing about the selection and reviewing other pieces already included. Over time, patterns emerge, but that takes a while. Some faculty eventually share their portfolios with a trusted colleague who can help them see the patterns presented. Start working on yours as soon as possible and let it grow into a dynamic document that serves you in your quest to keep your edge.

Focusing on the Differences You Are Making

When one of the authors of this book had finished her student teaching, the father of a student wrote her a letter about what a difference she had made to his son. When she told her own father about it, he (a minister) told her that she needed to put the letter, and all the other letters like it that she would get, into a "warm fuzzy" file. He told her that he had started one when he was a new pastor and that on "cold prickly" days, when it seemed that no one was happy with what he was doing, he would get out the warm fuzzy file to read through and to remind himself that he was making a difference and that people did appreciate it.

Start a warm fuzzy file—today. Make a label for a folder and gather up any notes, letters, student evaluations, or whatever else fits, and put it all in there. If you have never kept anything like that or if you are a new professor and have not received any of these treasures yet, at least you now have a folder ready for when you do. Do not *ever* throw these sorts of mementos away because, unfortunately, there will be cold prickly days and you will want to read through your warm fuzzy file and be reminded of the difference you are making.

In addition to thinking about the difference you are making to individual students, you can also think much more globally about the impact of your teaching. Are you helping to create scientists? Writers? Thinkers? Problem solvers? Are you helping to create better teachers, better statisticians, better doctors, better policymakers, better journalists? You *are* making a difference in what and how you teach. Remind yourself of the potential ramifications of what you do since the lives you touch through your teaching are never the same. Because you change brains—chemically and physically—through your instruction, students are literally not the same when they leave your classroom, lab, or field site as they were when they arrived. That is both an awesome responsibility and a jolt of reality.

You will need reminders of this responsibility and reality on a regular basis—in some years more than in others and at some institutions more than at others. The cold prickly truth is that excellent teachers are not always universally adored, most notably not by their "colleagues." Sadly, some people still think they are living in a "zero-sum" world, that is, a world in which the pie is only so big—if you get more of the pie, they think, then I get less. These are the professors who, when they hear students sing your praises, will denigrate you in a covert (or not so covert) way. These are the professors who, when you have won a teaching award, will pointedly not congratulate you. These are the professors who, upon seeing that you are teaching a class for other professors about sound instructional techniques, will say that you have to focus on your teaching because you lack the ability to do the "real" work of the professorate. It is on these days that you need both your warm fuzzy file and your focus on the real difference that you are making. There are few professions that allow you to have the impact that teaching does. Channel your attention on this impact on a daily basis. It helps keep you going in the positive direction that you desire and know is right.

Taking Care of Yourself

Teaching is a physically, emotionally, intellectually, and sometimes even spiritually demanding profession. You will spend a great deal of your time around people—people who expect you to be a certain way. They need you as colleague, teacher, fellow researcher, co-author, speaker, committee member, administrator, adviser, and . . . well, you get the idea. All of these interactions take energy, and if you do not keep your energy supply replenished, then you will have none to pour into your profession (or into your personal life). So practice moderation in all things that make up your professional life (Boice, 2000) and balance in your daily lifestyle.

For many professors, solitude helps to replenish the supply. You will have to make an active decision to find solitude, and you will have to make the appropriate space. The public's perception that college professors teach a few hours each week and then wile away the other hours discussing ideas under giant elm trees, reading through dusty volumes in ivy-covered libraries, and/or looking at cells under a microscope is so far off from reality that it is difficult even to write this sentence. Today's college professor teaches in a classroom anywhere from three to fifteen hours each week; spends hours and hours preparing for the classroom time; advises students on some very weighty issues; serves on untold numbers of committees around campus and perhaps in the community as well; conducts research in a laboratory, in the library, on the Internet, in the field; answers e-mail and returns phone calls for minutes that turn into hours each day; writes for publication and for presentation at state, national, and international conferences—and more. Nearly all of these commitments happen in the company of others or involve interactions with others. Finding time alone is essential for re-fueling your energy reserves.

Throughout this book, we have written from the perspective that, in today's world, professors are being held increasingly accountable for their work and for the results of that work, that is, the learning of students. Some readers may feel guilty about taking time for themselves, whether in solitude or for other renewing endeavors, and may worry that they are not supposed to be doing so in this age of accountability. Our perspective is that you must take this time to keep yourself refreshed so that you can do your job better. You cannot teach effectively, and so students cannot benefit from your instruction, if you have become so surly or so drained of energy that you are operating far below your potential. Keep this in mind.

In today's society, the term *role model* is often heard. Many professors disdain that term when it is applied to them. Yet, just as many public servants have become elevated to the status of role model, regardless of their desire or willingness to hold that position, professors will increasingly be viewed as people to emulate. The idea may cause you some discomfort, but it is a significant part of your accountability function. Although it may feel like a burden at times, it is most of all a privilege you have been accorded. A guiding question is, "What kind of people do you want your students to grow up to be?" Once you answer that for yourself, you will realize what to model for them.

A Hindu proverb states, "There is nothing noble in being superior to some other person. The true nobility is in being superior to your previous self." In this age of accountability, we challenge you to be superior to your previous self. You, your students, your institution, your community, and an increasingly global society will be better served.

Summary of Key Points

- The academy has changed, is changing, and will continue to change—you must change to thrive and, in many cases, to survive.
- Develop a following among students by being an excellent teacher—word of mouth spreads quickly among students and colleagues.
- Network on campus and within the community to grow your following.
- Make a special effort to help those who have been marginalized in higher education become more successful.
- Avail yourself of the resources of your institution's faculty development initiative.
- Find a colleague with whom you can work closely on your teaching and consider developing a mentoring relationship.
- If you get a mentor, become one for a newer professor or an adjunct instructor.
- Renew yourself at professional conferences, and take part in special sessions devoted to instruction.
- Study your own teaching so that you can increase your talents, as well as to help others be more successful.
- Read outside your discipline area about effective teaching and learning practices.
- Work continually on developing your technology skills.
- Leverage the free resources provided by publishers of your textbooks and other vendors.
- Maintain a teaching portfolio—not only for official reasons but for the reflection opportunities it will provide.
- Keep the passion, the desire, and the quest for excellent teaching alive—the strength of your enthusiasm will inspire others.
- Because the strength of this enthusiasm will inspire others, invest time in yourself.
- Stay focused on the difference you are making in the lives of the students.

Through the Professors' Eyes

KIM: As I look back on the academic year with the help of my mentor, I can now see that it was very good for me. My students were very good and understanding of my newness to this culture. I learned so much and still have so much more to learn, but I am very willing. I do need to work more on my English skills, and I will follow the advice of my mentor to resist the temptation to socialize too much with those on campus from my country. I need to talk more with native English speakers and practice the nuances of the language. I understand proper English very well—it is the slang that my students use that is so confusing. That fact prevents me from being as effective in class discussions as I would like to be. My written work, which I work on very much, is okay. I registered for an oral communication class for non-native English speakers at the local community college. At the first class meeting, there was a reporter from the local newspaper who interviewed me, and the interview appeared in his article. The university provost saw it and invited Dr. Zheng and me to a meeting next week to discuss formalizing a mentoring program for other international professors—what an honor! That should help me gain what my department colleague calls exposure. My spouse and I also decided that we needed to join some groups outside of our immediate neighborhood, because our community is predominately Asian people, and we speak our native language around the community. We joined a book club at the local bookstore and a local historical group that studies the history of the community. That should help us not only with our English skills but also with the local culture. I really like my job and look forward to next year. My spouse and I are hoping to save enough money to build a house and have our parents live with us.

DALE: While eating dinner in a local restaurant the other night, I ran into a former student—the first Hispanic student I ever had. He has a great position with one of the big corporations, and he looked very poised and prosperous. After exchanging pleasantries, he kind of teared up and told me that I made a big difference in his life. Old hard-hearted Dale got a lump in his throat! I never thought much about my role as a mentor making a difference in students' lives. I always thought my research would have an impact, but maybe it's time for me to think about my influence as an educator as well. I must admit that some of the ideas that I tried this year, especially the instructional technology and alternative assessment contracts, worked better than I thought they would. Maybe if I change some of the ways I teach, I could influence more students to major in my specialty. The students who worked with me on my research really got excited about what they were learning, and that contact fostered a human connection that I had never experienced before. I realized that just like Orwin Luke turned me on to this research, and stood by me when I didn't really deserve it, I must accept that kind of role in students' lives more often. Maybe it's time for me to change some of my ways.

PAT: Although I am really looking forward to retirement, I am always seeking ways to improve what I do. I love working with my students and my young colleagues. They are so enthusiastic and they help me rejuvenate and stay current in my field. Because of them, I continue to go to conferences and make presentations, particularly to introduce them to the really exciting aspects of academic life. I like to write and have co-authored numerous articles and books with my students. I plan to be more proactive in the next few years at encouraging even more diverse students to write with me. It is great fun! I enjoy watching my students develop into strong professionals who can stand on their own—that is very satisfying for a teacher. My career has been a great part of my life's journey, one that can continue to be rich as I explore new options. I know the new professors and students will do just fine.

Tips for Thriving

It is essential that you regularly sharpen your teaching edge because it will become dull almost without your noticing it. Your students will notice, however, and eventually so will you. The edge becomes especially difficult to sharpen if you ever lose the passion, the momentum, and the currency within your teaching.

Set aside time each term to take stock of where you are, using some of the ideas from this chapter. This is not intended as a homily—we mean right now! Get your calendar out and mark out a time each semester (for as far out as your calendar goes) in which you will focus on your teaching—whether for one day or longer. Keep it blocked just for that purpose. You will never regret taking the time to do so.

Contact your dissertation adviser or some other favorite professor today. Call or write that person, and express your appreciation for what he or she did for you in the pursuit of your academic career. Ask for perspective, insight, and advice. Share stories. Make a connection. Be reminded of how much you gained from this person, thereby reminding yourself of how much those in your sphere of influence gain from you.

SUGGESTED READINGS

Baiocco, S., and J. DeWaters. (1998). *Successful College Teaching*. Boston: Allyn & Bacon.

Boice, R. (2000). *Advice for New Faculty Members*. Boston: Allyn & Bacon.

Rodriguez, S. (2002). *Giants among Us: First-Generation College Students Who Lead Activist Lives*. Nashville: Vanderbilt University Press.

Zachary, L. (2000). *The Mentor's Guide*. San Francisco: Jossey-Bass.

APPENDIX 14.1

Model Mentoring Agreement

Realizing that an ongoing mentoring relationship between veteran and associate instructors can provide benefits to each party, as well as to Westminster College overall, Chris Smith, Assistant Professor, and Tony Barkwell, Associate Instructor, enter into the agreement below to enable Mr. Barkwell to:

1. Plan and launch his course consistent with accepted practices.
2. Develop, debug, and analyze results of course examinations.
3. Retain students within his course, and recruit students to future courses.

During the Fall 200— semester, Dr. Smith agrees to:

1. Meet with Mr. Barkwell on alternate Friday afternoons for approximately one hour, to review Mr. Barkwell's experiences and provide other information as needed.
2. Speak with Mr. Barkwell as needed by telephone, at 462-9999, between 1:00 and 4:00 p.m. any weekday afternoon.
3. Allow Mr. Barkwell, upon a day's notification, to visit regular class meetings of any evening course being taught by Dr. Smith.
4. Unless agreed otherwise by Mr. Barkwell in advance, treat all communications with Mr. Barkwell as confidential.

Mr. Barkwell agrees to:

1. Accept Dr. Smith's coaching as nondirective, realizing that academic freedom and other professional practices require his acceptance of ultimate responsibility for all decisions discussed with Dr. Smith.
2. Serve as a guest speaker, on a mutually agreeable topic, for a segment of one of Dr. Smith's class meetings, and review that activity immediately afterward.
3. Submit small developmental activities, such as creating several test questions, no later than the prescribed deadline set by Dr. Smith.

4. Serve as a substitute instructor for the Wednesday, October 1, meeting of Dr. Smith's class (5:30 p.m., room 118, Gore Business Building).
5. Unless agreed otherwise by Dr. Smith in advance, treat all communications with Dr. Smith as confidential.

It is agreed—that this arrangement will remain in effect throughout the 200— academic year only—any extension will need to be negotiated in May 200—. Either party may terminate the agreement, without reason, at any point, by e-mailing the other party and cc-ing Dr. X. Brands, at xbrands@wcslc.edu.

_____   _____

Dr. Chris Smith   Mr. Tony Barkwell

_____   _____

Date   Date

REFERENCES

Ailes, R. (1995). *You Are the Message: Getting What You Want by Being Who You Are.* New York: Currency-Doubleday.

The American Heritage Dictionary of the English Language, 4th ed. (2000). Boston: Houghton Mifflin.

Angelo, T. A., and K. P. Cross. (1993). *Classroom Assessment Techniques: A Handbook for College Teachers*, 2nd ed. San Francisco: Jossey-Bass.

Astin, A. W., L. J. Vogelgesang, E. K. Ikeda, and J. A. Yee. (2000). "How Service Learning Affects Students," Higher Education Research Institute, Los Angeles: UCLA Graduate School of Education & Information Studies.

Ausubel, D. P., J. D. Novak, and H. Hanesian. (1978). *Educational Psychology*, 2nd ed. Austin, TX: Holt, Rinehart & Winston.

Baiocco, S., and J. DeWaters. (1998). *Successful College Teaching.* Boston: Allyn & Bacon.

Banta, T. W., and V. M. H. Borden. (1994). "Performance Indicators for Accountability and Improvement." In V. M. H. Borden and T. W. Banta, eds., *Using Performance Indicators to Guide Strategic Decision Making.* New Directions for Institutional Research, no. 82. San Francisco: Jossey-Bass.

Benvennto, M. (1999). "In an Age of Interactive Learning, Some Students Want the Same Old Song and Dance." *Chronicle of Higher Education* 45, no. 39 (June 4), p. B9.

Berk, R. (1998). *Professors Are from Mars, Students Are from Snickers.* Madison, WI: Mendota Press.

Berne, E. (1964). *The Games People Play.* New York: Ballantine.

Birnbaum, R. (2000). *Management Fads in Higher Education.* San Francisco: Jossey-Bass.

Bligh, D. A. (2000). *What's the Use of Lectures?* San Francisco: Jossey-Bass.

Bloom, B. S., ed. (1956). *Taxonomy of Learning Objectives: Cognitive Domain.* New York: David McKay.

Blythe, H. (1998). *It Works for Me.* Stillwater, OK: New Forums Press.

Boice, R. (2000). *Advice for New Faculty Members.* Boston: Allyn & Bacon.

Borrego, A. (2001). "A Wave of Consolidation Hits For-Profit Higher Education." *Chronicle of Higher Education* 47, no. 48 (August 10), pp. A42–A43.

Bowen, R. (2001). "The New Battle between Political and Academic Cultures." *Chronicle of Higher Education* 47, no. 41 (June 22), pp. B14–B15.

Boyle, R., and R. Dunn. (1998). "Teaching Law Students through Individual Learning Styles." *Albany Law Review* 62, no.1, pp. 213–255.

Bridges, J., writer and director, (1973). *The Paper Chase* [film]. Beverly Hills, CA: Twentieth Century Fox.

Brinko, K. T., and R. J. Menges, eds. (1997). *Practically Speaking: A Sourcebook for Instructional Consultants in Higher Education.* Stillwater, OK: New Forums Press.

Brookfield, S. (1995). *Becoming a Critically Reflective Teacher.* San Francisco: Jossey-Bass.

Brookhart, S. M. (1999). *The Art and Science of Classroom Assessment: The Missing Part of the Pedagogy.* ASHE-ERIC Higher Education Report 27, no. 1. Washington, DC: The George Washington University, Graduate School of Education and Human Development.

Brown, D. (2001). "Faculty Practice: The Power of E-Mail." *Syllabus* 14, no. 12 (July), p. 26.

Burd, S. (2002). "Colleges Catch a Glimpse of Bush Policy on Higher Education, and Aren't Pleased." *Chronicle of Higher Education* 48, no. 26 (March 8), p. A25.

Burke, J. C. (1998). "Performance Funding Indicators: Concerns, Values, and Models for State Colleges and Universities." In J. C. Burke and A. M. Serban, eds., *Performance Funding for Public Higher Education: Fad or Trend?* New Directions for Institutional Research, no. 97. San Francisco: Jossey-Bass.

Buscaglia, L. (1990). *Living, Loving and Learning.* New York: Fawcett Books.

Carducci, B. (1994). In E. Bender, M. Dunn, B. Kendall, C. Larson, and P. Wilkes, eds., *Quick Hits: Successful Strategies by Award Winning Teachers.* Bloomington, IN: Indiana University Press, p. 9.

Carlson, S. (2001). "A Web Site of Reviews of Instructors Faces Challenges." *Chronicle of Higher Education* 47, no. 29 (March 30), p. A46.

Carnegie, D. (1962). *The Quick and Easy Way to Effective Speaking.* New York: Pocket Books.

Centra, J. (1993). *Reflective Faculty Evaluation.* San Francisco: Jossey-Bass.

Chism, N. V. N. (1999). *Peer Review of Teaching: A Sourcebook.* Bolton, MA: Anker.

Chronicle of Higher Education. (2001). Almanac Issue 48, no. 1 (August 31).

Colberg, J., P. Desbery, and K. Trimble. (1996). *The Case for Education: Contemporary Approaches for Using Case Methods.* Boston: Allyn & Bacon.

Covey, S. (1989). *The 7 Habits of Highly Effective People.* New York: Simon and Schuster.

Cox, A. M. (2001). "The Changed Classroom, Post-September 11." *Chronicle of Higher Education* 48, no. 9 (October 26), pp. A16–A18.

Cranton, P. (1989). *Planning Instruction for Adult Learners.* Toronto, Canada: Wall and Emerson.

Danielson, C. (1996). *Performance Assessment: A Collection of Tasks.* Princeton, NJ: Eye on Education.

Danielson, C., and L. Abristyn. (1997). *An Introduction to Using Portfolios in the Classroom.* Alexandria, VA: Association for Supervision and Curriculum Development.

Darling-Hammond, L., and B. Falk. (1995). *Authentic Assessment in Action.* New York: Teachers College Press.

Davidson, C. I., and S. A. Ambrose. (1994). *The New Professor's Handbook.* Bolton, MA: Anker.

Davis, B. G. (2001). *Tools for Teaching.* San Francisco: Jossey-Bass.

Dewey, J. (1916). *Democracy and Education.* New York: Macmillan.

Diamond, R. (1998). *Designing and Assessing Courses and Curricula: A Practical Guide.* San Francisco: Jossey-Bass

D'Souza, D. (2001). "Rich Men, Poor Men, Businessmen, and Scholars." *Chronicle of Higher Education* 47, no. 47 (August 3), pp. B14–B15.

Duffy, D. K., and J. W. Jones. (1995). *Teaching within the Rhythms of the Semester.* San Francisco: Jossey-Bass.

Dunn, R,. and K. Dunn. (1999). *The Complete Guide to the Learning Styles Inservice System.* Boston: Allyn & Bacon.

Dunn, R., and S. Griggs, eds. (2000). *Practical Approaches to Using Learning Styles in Higher Education.* Westport, CT: Bergin and Garvey.

Eaton, J. (1999). "Advancing Quality through Additional Attention to Results." *CHEA Chronicle,* www.chea.org/Chronicle/vol1/no11/index.cfm.

Eaton, J. (2001). "Regional Accreditation Reform." *Change* 33, no. 2, pp. 38–45.

Eble, K. (1994). *The Craft of Teaching.* San Francisco: Jossey-Bass.

Ehrenberg, R. G. (2000). "Private College Trustees Must Control Costs." *Chronicle of Higher Education* 47, no. 5 (September 29), p. B14.

Ericksen, S. C. (1984). *The Essence of Good Teaching.* San Francisco: Jossey-Bass.

Ewell, P. T., and D. P. Jones. (1994). "Pointing the Way: Indicators as Policy Tools in Higher Education. In S. S. Ruppert, ed., *Charting Higher Education Accountability: A Sourcebook on State-Level Performance Indicators.* Denver: Education Commission of the States.

Fallons, W. (1999). *Dictionary of Hindustani Proverbs.* Ottawa, Canada: Laurier.

Fallows, S., and K. Ahmet. (1999). *Inspiring Students: Case Studies in Motivating the Learner.* London: Kogan Page.

Felder, R. (1998). "How Students Learn, How Teachers Teach, and What Goes Wrong with the Process." Tomorrow's Professor Listserv, Message 51, Stanford University Learning Laboratory, http://sll.stanford.edu/projects/tomprof/newtomprof/postings/51.html.

Felder, R. M., and L. K. Silverman. (1988). "Learning and Teaching Styles in Engineering Education," *Journal of Engineering Education* 78, no. 7, p. 674.

Feldman, K. A. (1998). "Identifying Exemplary Teachers and Teaching: Evidence from Student Ratings." In K. A. Feldman and M. B. Paulsen, eds., *Teaching and Learning in the College Classroom*, 2nd ed., Needham Heights, MA: Simon and Schuster, pp. 391–414.

Feldman, K. A. (1987). "Research Productivity and Scholarly Accomplishment of College Teachers as Related to their Instructional Effectiveness. *Research in Higher Education* 26, no. 3 (May), pp. 227–298.

Fink, L. D. (1995). "Evaluating Your Own Teaching." In P. Seldin, ed. *Improving College Teaching*, Bolton, MA: Anker, pp. 191–204.

Fisch, L. (1996). *The Chalk Dust Collection: Thoughts and Reflections on Teaching in Colleges and Universities*. Stillwater, OK: New Forums Press.

Gardner, H. (1999). *Intelligence Reframed: Multiple Intelligences for the 21st Century*. New York: Basic Books.

Gedda, G. (2002). "Powell Says Recruit More Minorities." *Associated Press Newswire* (May 17). http://wire.ap.org/APnews/center_story.html@FRONTID=ELECTIONS&STORYID=APIS7JI.

Gibbs, G. (1998). "Teaching Large Classes: Strategies for Improving Student Learning." Tomorrow's Professor Listserv, Message 21, Stanford University Learning Laboratory, http://sll.stanford.edu/projects/tomprof/newtomprof/postings/21.html.

Goetsch, D., and S. Davis. (1999). *Quality Management: Introduction to Quality Management for Production, Processing, and Services*, 3rd ed. Upper Saddle River, NJ: Prentice Hall.

Golding, J. (2001). "Teaching the Large Lecture Class." In D. Royse, ed., *Teaching Tips for College and University Instructors: A Practical Guide*. Boston: Allyn & Bacon, pp. 95–120.

Goleman, D. (1995). *Emotional Intelligence*. New York: Bantam.

Gose, B. (1997). "Efforts to Curb Grade Inflation Get an F from Many Critics." *Chronicle of Higher Education* 43, no. 46 (July 25), pp. A19–A20.

Grabe, M., and C. Grabe. (2001). *Integrating Technology for Meaningful Learning*, 3rd ed. Boston: Houghton Mifflin.

Gregorc, A. (1986). *Adults Guide to Style*. Columbia, CT: Gregorc Associates.

Grunert, J. (1997). *The Course Syllabus: A Learning-Centered Approach*. Bolton, MA: Anker.

Hake, R. (1998). "Interactive-Engagement versus Traditional Methods: A Six-Thousand-Student Survey of Mechanics Test Data for Introductory Physics Courses," *American Journal of Physics* 66, pp. 64–74. http://web.mit.edu/tll/published/new_research.htm

Hannon, K. (2001). "Using E-Mail to Communicate with Students." *ASEE Prism: Exploring the Future of Engineering Education* 10, no. 6 (February), pp. 34–35.

Harris, R. (1997). "Evaluating Internet Research Sources." Virtual Salt, www.virtualsalt.com/evalu8it.htm.

Harris, R. (2001). *The Plagiarism Handbook: Strategies for Preventing, Detecting, and Dealing with Plagiarism*. Los Angeles: Pyrczak Publications.

Hativa, N. (2000). *Teaching for Effective Learning in Higher Education*. Dordrecht, Netherlands: Kluwer Academic Press.

Haugen, L. (2000). "Writing a Teaching Philosophy Statement." Tomorrow's Professor Listserv, Message 193, Stanford University Learning Laboratory, http://sll.stanford.edu/projects/tomprof/newtomprof/postings/193.html.

Hibbard, K. M., and the Educators of Connecticut's Pomperaug Regional School District 15. (1996). *A Teacher's Guide to Performance-Based Learning and Assessment*. Alexandria, VA: ASCD.

Hilt, D. (2001). "What Students Can Teach Professors: Reading between the Lines of Evaluations." *Chronicle of Higher Education* 47, no. 27 (March 16), p. B24.

Hoey, J. (2001). "Institutional Effectiveness: A Back-to-Basics Approach." Presentation to the Commission on Colleges, Southern Association of Colleges and Schools, New Orleans (December 9).

Howard, R. (2001). "Forget about Policing Plagiarism. Just Teach." *Chronicle of Higher Education*, 48, no. 12 (November 16), p. B24.

Howe, N., and W. Strauss. (2000). *Millennials Rising: The Next Great Generation.* New York: Vintage.

Huba, M. E., and J. Freed. (2000). *Learner-Centered Assessment on College Campuses.* Boston: Allyn & Bacon.

James, M., and D. Jongeward. (1996). *Born to Win.* Cambridge, MA: Perseus Books.

Johnson, D. W., R. T. Johnson, and K. A. Smith. (1991). *Cooperative Learning: Increasing College Faculty Instructional Productivity.* ASHE-ERIC Higher Education Report, no. 4. Washington, DC: The George Washington University, Graduate School of Education and Human Development.

Johnson, S. (1999). *Who Moved My Cheese?* New York: Putnam.

Jones, K. (1991). *Icebreakers.* San Diego, CA: Pfeiffer & Associates.

The Jossey-Bass Reader on Technology and Learning. (2000). San Francisco: Jossey-Bass.

Katz, R. N., et al. (1999). *Dancing with the Devil: Information Technology and the New Competition in Higher Education.* San Francisco: Jossey-Bass.

Kearsley, G. (2000). *Online Education: Learning and Teaching in Cyberspace.* Belmont, CA: Wadsworth.

Kelly, C. (1997). "David Kolb: The Theory of Experiential Learning and ESL." *Internet TESL Journal* 3, no. 9.

Kolb, D. (1983). *Experiential Learning.* Upper Saddle River, NJ: Prentice Hall.

Kuhn, T. (1996). *The Structure of Scientific Revolutions,* 3rd ed. Chicago: The University of Chicago Press.

Lao Tzu. (1994). *Tao Te Ching.* Translated by D. C. Lau. New York: Knopf. (From 6th century B.C.)

Light, R. J. (2001). *Making the Most of College: Students Speak Their Minds.* Cambridge, MA: Harvard University Press.

Lovett, C. (2001). "State Government and Colleges: A Clash of Cultures." *Chronicle of Higher Education* 47, no. 34 (April 27), p. B20.

Lovitts, B., and C. Nelson. (2000). "The Hidden Crisis in Graduate Education: Attrition from Ph.D. Programs." *Academe* 86, no. 6 (November/December), pp. 44–50.

Lunde, J. P. (2000). "101 Things You Can Do the First Three Weeks of Class." Tomorrow's Professor Listserv, Message 168, Stanford University Learning Lab, http://sll.stanford.edu/projects/tomprof/newtomprof/postings/168.html.

Lyons, R., M. Kysilka, and G. Pawlas. (1999). *The Adjunct Professor's Guide to Success: Surviving and Thriving in the College Classroom.* Boston: Allyn & Bacon.

Macmillan, J. (1997). *Classroom Assessment: Principles and Practice for Effective Instruction.* Boston: Allyn & Bacon.

"Making Quality Work." (2001). *University Business* 4, no. 6 (July/August), pp. 44–50, 78, 80, 85.

Marincovich, M. (1999). "Using Student Feedback to Improve Teaching." In P. Seldin, ed., *Changing Practices in Evaluating Teaching.* Bolton, MA: Anker.

Massy, W. (in press). *Quality and Cost Containment: Rebuilding the University's Core Competency.* Bolton, MA: Anker.

Matthews, R. S. (1996). "Collaborative Learning: Creating Knowledge with Students." In R. J. Menges and M. Weimer, eds., *Teaching on Solid Ground: Using Scholarship to Improve Practice.* San Francisco: Jossey-Bass, pp. 101–124.

McCabe, D., and P. Drinan. (1999). "Toward a Culture of Academic Integrity." *Chronicle of Higher Education* 46, no. 7 (October 15), p. A19.

McKeachie, W. (2001). *Teaching Tips: Strategies, Research, and Theory for College and University Teachers,* 11th ed. Boston: Houghton Mifflin.

Meister, J. (2001). "The Brave New World of Corporate Education." *Chronicle of Higher Education* 47, no. 22 (February 9), p. B24.

Middendorf, J., and A. Kalish. (1996). "The 'Change-Up' in Lectures." *National Teaching and Learning Forum* 5, p. 1+.

Millis, B. J., and P. G. Cottell, Jr. (1998). *Cooperative Learning for Higher Education Faculty*. Phoenix: Oryx Press.

Moulds, R. (1997). "An Interactive Annotations Assignment." *The Teaching Professor* 11, no. 4 (April), p. 6.

Moxley, D., A. Najor-Durack, and C. Dumbrigue. (2001). *Keeping Students in Higher Education*. London: Kogan Page.

Murray, J. P. (1997). *Successful Faculty Development and Evaluation: The Complete Teaching Portfolio*. ASHE-ERIC Higher Education Report, no. 8. Washington, DC: The George Washington University, Graduate School of Education and Human Development.

National Center for Educational Statistics. (2001). www.nces.ed.gov/pubs2000/projections/chapter2.html.

Novak, G., E. Patterson, A. Gavrin, and W. Christian. (1999). *Just-in-Time Teaching: Blending Active Learning with Web Technology*. Upper Saddle River, NJ: Prentice Hall.

Ohmann, R. (2000). "Historical Reflections on Accountability." *Academe* 86, no. 1 (January/February), pp. 24–29.

Olsen, F. (2001). "Getting Ready for a New Generation of Course-Management Systems." *Chronicle of Higher Education* 48, no. 17 (December 21), pp. A25–A27.

Palmer, P. (1998). *The Courage to Teach*. San Francisco: Jossey-Bass.

Panitz, T. (2001). "Yes Virginia There Is a Big Difference between Cooperative and Collaborative Learning." Tomorrow's Professor Listserv, Message 237, Stanford University Learning Laboratory, message 237. http://sll.stanford.edu/projects.tomprof/newtomprof/postings/237.hml.

Popham, W. J. (1999). *Classroom Assessment: What Teachers Need to Know*, 2nd ed. Boston: Allyn & Bacon.

Ratey, J. J. (2001). *A User's Guide to the Brain*. New York: Pantheon Books.

Ravitz, J., Y. Wong, and H. Becker. (1999). *Teaching, Learning and Technology National Survey*. www.crito.uci.edu/tlc.

Reis, R. M. (1997). *Tomorrow's Professor: Preparing for Academic Careers in Science and Engineering*. New York: IEEE Press.

Reisberg, L. (2000). "Are Students Really Learning?" *Chronicle of Higher Education*, 47 no. 16 (November 17), pp. A67–A70.

Restak, R. (2001). *The Secret Life of the Brain*. Washington, DC: Joseph Henry Press.

Rhem, J. (1998). "Problem-Based Learning: An Introduction," National Teaching and Learning Forum (December), 8, 1, http://www.ntlf.com/html/pi/9812/pbl_1.htm.

Rodriguez, S. (2002). *Giants among Us: First-Generation College Students Who Lead Activist Lives*. Nashville: Vanderbilt University Press.

Royse, D., ed. (2001). *Teaching Tips for College and University Professors*. Boston: Allyn & Bacon.

Ruben, B. (2001). "We Need Excellence beyond the Classroom." *Chronicle of Higher Education* 47, no. 44 (July 13), pp. B15–B16.

Ruppert, S. S. (1995). "Roots and Realities of State-Level Performance Indicator Systems." In G. H. Gaithers, ed., *Accessing Performance in an Age of Accountability: Case Studies*. New Directions for Higher Education, 91. San Francisco: Jossey-Bass.

Sanders, W. B. (2001). *Creating Learning-Centered Courses for the World Wide Web*. Boston: Allyn & Bacon.

Schmidt, P. (2002). "Most States Tie Aid to Performance, Despite Little Proof That It Works." *Chronicle of Higher Education* 48, no. 24 (February 22), pp. A20–A21.

Schmidt, P. (2001). "State Higher-Education Leaders Want to See Improvements in Job Training." *Chronicle of Higher Education*, online daily news (August 1).

Scriven, M. (1995). *Student Ratings Offer Useful Input to Teacher Evaluations*. ERIC/AE Digest, ED398240. Washington, DC: ERIC Clearinghouse of Assessment and Evaluation.

Seldin, P. (1999). *Changing Practices in Evaluating Teaching: A Practical Guide to Improved Faculty Performance and Promotion/Tenure Decisions*, Bolton, MA: Anker.

Selingo, J. (2001). "Pennsylvania Rewards Fast Graduation, but Public Colleges Cry Foul." *Chronicle of Higher Education*, online daily news, http://www.chronicle.com/daily/2001/08/2001080301n.htm.

Senge, P. (1990). *The Fifth Discipline*. New York: Doubleday.

Silberman, M. (1996). *Active Learning: 101 Strategies to Teach Any Subject*. Boston: Allyn & Bacon.

Slaughter, S. (2001). "Professional Values and the Allure of the Market." *Academe* 87, no. 5 (September/October), pp. 22–27.

Sousa, D. A. (2001). *How the Brain Learns: A Classroom Teacher's Guide* Thousand Oaks, CA: Corwin.

Spence, L. (2001). "The Case against Teaching." *Change* 33, no. 6 (November/ December), pp. 10–19.

Stage, F. K., P. A. Muller, J. Kinzie, and A. Simmons. (1998). *Creating Learning Centered Classrooms: What Does Learning Theory Have to Say?* ASHE-ERIC Higher Education Report 26, no. 4. Washington, DC: The George Washington University, Graduate School of Education and Human Development.

Stark, J., and L. Lattuca. (1997). *Shaping the College Curriculum*. Boston: Allyn & Bacon.

Stewart, I., and V. Joines. (1987). *T A Today: A New Introduction to Transactional Analysis*. Kingston-on-Soar, UK: Lifespace.

Tapscott, D. (1998). *Growing Up Digital: The Rise of the Net Generation*. New York: McGraw-Hill.

U.S. Department of Education, National Center for Education Statistics, 1999–2000 National Postsecondary Student Aid Study (NPSAS: 2000).

U.S. News and World Report, America's Best Colleges, (2002).

Vargas, J. (2001). "Improving Teaching Performance." In D. Royse, ed., *Teaching Tips for College and University Instructors*, Boston: Allyn & Bacon, pp. 254–280.

Waller, C., R. Coble, J. Scharer, and S. Giamportone. (2000). *Governance and Coordination of Public Higher Education in All 50 States*. Raleigh, NC: North Carolina Center for Public Policy Research.

Wallerstein, J. S., J. M. Lewis, and S. Blakeslee. (2000). *The Unexpected Legacy of Divorce: A 25 Year Landmark Study*. New York: Hyperion.

Walvoord, B. E. and V. J. Anderson. (1998). *Effective Grading: A Tool for Learning and Assessment*. San Francisco: Jossey-Bass.

Wankat, P. (2002). *The Effective, Efficient Professor.* Boston: Allyn & Bacon.

Weimer, M. (1990). "What to Do When Somebody Criticizes Your Teaching." In M. Weimer and R. A. Neff, eds., *Teaching College: Collected Readings for the New Instructor,* Madison, WI: Magna, pp. 143–144.

Wellman, J. (2000). "Accreditors Have to See Past Learning Outcomes." *Chronicle of Higher Education* 47, no. 4 (September 22), p. B20.

Wellman, J. (2001). "Assessing State Accountability Systems." *Change* 33, no.2, pp. 46–52.

Wiggins, G. P. (1993). *Exploring the Purpose and Limits of Teaching*. San Francisco: Jossey-Bass.

Wilson, R. (2001). "Ohio State 'Taxes' Departments to Make a Select Few Top-Notch." *Chronicle of Higher Education* 47, no. 38 (June 1), pp. A8–A9.

Wright, W. A., P. T. Knight, and N. Pomerleau. (1999). "Portfolio People: Teaching and Learning Dossiers and Innovation in Higher Education." *Innovative Higher Education* 24, pp. 89–103.

Yamane, D. (1996). "Collaboration and Its Discontents: Steps toward Overcoming Barriers to Successful Group Projects." *Teaching Sociology* 24 (October), pp. 378–383.

Zachary, L. (2000). *The Mentor's Guide*. San Francisco: Jossey-Bass.

http://www.nces.ed.gov/pubs2000/projections/chapter2.html
http://www.cpsr.org/cpsr/privacy/ssn/ferpa.buckley.html

INDEX